Oscar T. Shuck

California Anthology

Striking Thoughts on Many Themes

Oscar T. Shuck

California Anthology
Striking Thoughts on Many Themes

ISBN/EAN: 9783743329195

Manufactured in Europe, USA, Canada, Australia, Japa

Cover: Foto ©Thomas Meinert / pixelio.de

Manufactured and distributed by brebook publishing software (www.brebook.com)

Oscar T. Shuck

California Anthology

California Anthology:

OR

Striking Thoughts on Many Themes,

CAREFULLY SELECTED FROM

CALIFORNIA WRITERS AND SPEAKERS,

—BY—

OSCAR T. SHUCK,

COMPILER OF THE "CALIFORNIA SCRAP BOOK" AND EDITOR OF
"REPRESENTATIVE MEN OF THE PACIFIC."

SAN FRANCISCO:
FROM THE PRESS OF BARRY & BAIRD, 419 SACRAMENTO ST.
A. J. LEARY, PUBLISHER, 402 AND 404 SANSOME ST.
1880.

I VENTURE TO INSCRIBE

THIS VOLUME

--TO A--

DISTINGUISHED CITIZEN OF CALIFORNIA,

A CONSPICUOUS PILLAR, AND A FORMER
GOVERNOR, OF THE STATE,

WHOSE PERMISSION, ON ACCOUNT OF HIS ABSENCE IN EUROPE, I HAVE
NOT BEEN ABLE TO SOLICIT,

THE HON. LELAND STANFORD,

NOTED ALIKE FOR THE HEALTHFULNESS OF HIS PUBLIC SPIRIT
AND THE PURITY OF HIS PRIVATE LIFE.

THE EDITOR.

Names of Writers and Speakers Quoted in this Volume.

ANDERSON, REV. T. H. B.
BAKER, GEN. E. D.
BALDWIN, JOSEPH G.
BANCROFT, HUBERT H.
BARNES, GEN. W. H. L.
BARSTOW, GEORGE
BARTLETT, W. C.
BAUSMAN, WILLIAM
BELL, SAMUEL B.
BENNETT, NATHANIEL
BONTE, REV. J. H. C.
BOOTH, NEWTON
BIERCE, A. G.
BRIGGS, REV. M. C.
BROWNE, J. ROSS
BUNKER, WM. M.
BURNETT, PETER H.
CASSERLY, EUGENE
CLARKE, CHAS. RUSSELL
COLLINS, GEN. JOHN A
COOLBRITH, INA D.
COOPER, SARAH B.
CRADDOCK, CHAS. F.
CRITTENDEN, R. D.
CURTIS, N. GREENE
DALL, W. H.
DAVIDSON, PROF. GEORGE
DEERING, F. P.
DWINELLE, JOHN W.
EWER, REV. F. C.
FELTON, JOHN B.
FIELD, JUDGE STEPHEN J.
FINNEY, SELDEN J.
FISHER, PHILIP M·
FITCH, THOMAS

FOOTE, GEN. L. H.
FREELON, T. W.
FREMONT. GEN. J. C.
GEORGE, HENRY
GOODMAN, JOSEPH T.
GORDON, GEORGE
GRAY, DR. HENRY M.
GUARD, REV. THOMAS
HALLIDIE, A. S.
HAMILTON, REV. L.
HARMON, J. B.
HARTE, F. BRET
HAYES, WILLIAM
HIGHTON, HENRY E.
HOWARD, J. G.
HURLBUT, G. C.
IJAMS, REV. W. E.
KELLOGG, PROF. MARTIN
KENDALL, W. A.
KEWEN, COL. E. J. C.
KING, THOMAS STARR
LATHAM, MILTON S.
LE CONTE, PROF. JOHN
LE CONTE, PROF. JOSEPH
MARSHALL, E. C.
MCDONALD, DR. R. H.
MCDOUGALL, GEN. JAS. A.
MCKINSTRY, JUDGE. E. W.
MONTGOMERY, ZACHARY
MOORE, GEORGE R.
NEALE, MRS. JAMES
O'CONNELL, DANIEL
PIXLEY, F. M.
PLATT, REV. WILLIAM H.
PRATT, JUDGE L. E.

NAMES OF WRITERS AND SPEAKERS.

Pratt, Judge O. C.
Proffatt, John
Randolph, Edmund
Redding, B. B.
Reid, Henry H.
Rhodes, W. H.
Robinson, Tod
Royce, Josiah
Sargent, A. A.
Scott, Rev. Dr. W. A.
Shafter, Jas. McM.
Shattuck, Judge D. O.
Shinn, Charles H.
Shorb, Dr. J. C.
Shurtleff, Dr. G. A.
Sill, E. R.
Skidmore, Miss H. M.
Soule, Frank
Speer, Rev. William
Stanford, Leland
Stanly, Edward

Stebbins, Rev. H.
Stoddard, Chas. Warren
Stone, Rev. Dr. A. L.
Stout, Dr. A. B.
Stuart, Hector A.
Sullivan, Francis J.
Sumner, Chas. A.
Swift, John F.
Tilford, Frank
Tompkins, Edward
Tuthill, Dr. Franklin
Upham, M. J.
Waite, E. G.
Warwick, J. H.
Wattson, John V.
Wheeler, Judge E. D.
Winans, Joseph W.
Winchell, Judge E. C.
Williams, Samuel
Wilson, Samuel M.

GENERAL DIVISIONS.

Part.		Page.
I.	Science and Art,	9
II.	Literature and Education,	49
III.	The Conduct of Life,	83
IV.	Religion and the Future Life,	131
V.	The Farm and Garden,	157
VI.	Society and the State,	181
VII.	Fraternal Societies,	261
VIII.	Distinguished Men,	299
IX.	Californiana,	361
X.	Miscellany,	391

I.

SCIENCE AND ART.

PART I.

SCIENCE AND ART.

1. OH, SCIENCE! Thou thought-clad leader of the company of pure and great souls that toil for their race and love their kind; measurer of the depths of earth and the recesses of heaven; apostle of civilization, handmaid of religion, teacher of human equality and human right, perpetual witness for the divine wisdom—be ever, as now, the great minister of peace! Let thy starry brow and benign front still gleam in the van of progress, brighter than the sword of the conqueror, and welcome as the light of heaven.—*Gen. E. D. Baker.*

2. SCIENCE DESTROYS NOT, BUT FULFILLS.—The end and mission of science is not only to discover *new truth*, but also, and even more distinctively, to give *new and more rational form to old truth*—to transfigure the old into the more glorious form of the new. Science is come *not to destroy*, but, aided by a rational philosophy, *to fulfill* all the noblest aspirations, the most glorious hopes of our race. Sometimes, indeed, the change which she brings about may be like a metamorphosis—the useless shell is burst and cast off and a more beautiful and less gross form appears, but still

it is always a process of evolution—of derivation. We never shall reach a rational philosophy until we recognize this fundamental truth. The *new* must include the *old*, the old must incorporate and assimilate the new, and each must modify and be modified by the other. Progress in all things—in geology, in society, in philosophy—is by *evolution and growth.—Prof. Joseph LeConte.*

3. SCIENCE THE STUDENT OF NATURE.—The writings of the metaphysicians, from the earliest dawn of scientific inquiry, have done much to retard the progress of the physical sciences, which were classified by them as belonging to an inferior sphere of intellectual pursuits; and it is not the least merit of the mathematicians of the last and present centuries to have pricked that bubble, and by the immense discoveries to which the calculus has given rise, to have shown the superiority and practical utility of their method. The true philosophy of nature must have nature for its basis, and apply to it the scientific discipline. It consists in applying the reasoning faculties of the mind to the rational conception of cause and effect in the infinite variety of natural phonomena. Whenever philosophy leaves nature as the object of its inquiries, when the mind of the philosopher attempts to contemplate *itself* as an object, independent of the natural phenomena which are connected with and reflected from it, he sets himself an impossible task, and begins to reason in a circle. The conception of the grandeur, order, harmony, and *unity* of nature, whether it acts on an infinitely great, or an infinitely small scale, is the true end of all human phi-

losophy, as the knowledge of the laws of nature is the true means of increasing the happiness and power of the human race.—*Milton S. Latham.*

4. A PROGRESS STEADY AND SERENE.—Amid the cyclical movement of society, the rise and fall of nations and civilizations, the flux and reflux of opinions, the revolutions of all kinds, which agitate, like a seething cauldron, the popular mind, science alone—because it is the simplest and purest embodiment of the human intellect, unaffected by the passions which mingle with all other pursuits—science alone, among all human works, moves steadily onward and upward, ever increasing in grandeur and beauty. Like a magnificent temple, grandly and steadily it rises, under the busy hands of thousands of eager workers, the greatest monument of human genius.—*Prof. Jos. LeConte.*

5. SCIENTIFIC METHODS.—Scientific methods bear the same relation to *intellectual* progress which machines, instruments, tools, do to *material* progress. The civilized man is not superior to the savage in physical strength. The wonderful mechanical results achieved by civilized man are possible only by the use of *mechanical contrivances.* So, also, the scientists differ from the unscientific not by any superior intellectual power. The astounding intellectual results achieved by science have been attained wholly by the use of *intellectual contrivances,* called methods. As in the lower sphere of material progress, the greatest benefactors of our race are the inventors or perfecters of new mechanical contrivances or machines; so in the

higher sphere of intellectual progress the greatest benefactors of our race are the inventors or perfecters of new intellectual contrivances, or methods.—*Prof. Jos. LeConte.*

6. PROCLAIMING TRUTH, SCIENCE ENRICHES FANCY. The most casual observation is sufficient to convince every reflective mind that in the present century we feel the necessity of reconciling the worlds of reason and imagination. This reconciliation cannot be effected in a moment; it must be the result of repeated and prolonged efforts. In this work of establishing harmony between these two great faculties of the soul it is evident that science is destined to play a very important part. Whenever old and deep-rooted errors are exploded by the increase of knowledge, a feeling of insecurity arises in the ill-instructed multitude. The half-educated pretender gladly embraces the opportunity to promulgate his narrow-minded views; doubt, scepticism and infidelity, with regard to all intellectual questions, take the place of security, faith and mental repose. Hence arises that strange dread, possessed by so many, of the results of science; a dread which threatens to destroy that world which their faith and feeling for the beautiful had created. They are thus consigned to a state of vacuity and nothingness, which would indeed be lamentable and fearful, were it unavoidable. The triumphant conquests of science which give us the purest pleasure are, for such unhappy beings, no less than the dangerous approaches of a desolating foe. The source of the evil must be sought in the ignorance of the true principles of science and in

the weakness of man's faith in the eternal and indestructible nature of truth. When the former ideas of the physical universe are broken up, there is a period of insecurity and mistrust, in which even the more thoughtful of men feel a vague apprehension that the enlargement of the empire of reality must necessarily contract the domains in which the creative powers of fancy delight to rove. It seems to me that such a view is based upon a misconception of the subject. For it is evident that each step that we make in the more intimate knowledge of science, leads us to the threshold of new labyrinths. The circle of illumination is enlarged; but the shadowy, half-transparent, vapor-veiled circumference, by which it is perpetually bordered, incessantly recedes before the eyes of the enquirer, constituting a fairy-land where imagination revels and lends a definite outline to the ever unfolding manifestations of ideal creation. Thus it is, that every accession to the sciences enriches the fields of fancy by bringing new mysteries within their sphere, and opening to them higher and more soul-elevating sources of enjoyment.—*Prof. John LeConte.*

7. TRUTH THE GUIDING STAR OF SCIENCE.—So far as my observation goes,—so far as my intercourse with men of scientific pursuits teaches me, Science is the embodiment and personification of peace. Its very existence is the issue of calm experiment, persistent investigation, and deliberate thought. It seeks no bubble reputation at the cannon's mouth; no ephemeral glory in the fierce conflict of politics. It is born, bred and nurtured in the serene quietness of Nature.

The devotees of Science are warriors only in another sense,—they dare be true, earnest and brave in the pursuit of true knowledge; and firm, steadfast, and unyielding in maintaining that which is demonstrated.

Men of original research in Science are in the fullest sense of the word Discoverers, forced to traverse the great ocean of illogical thought and imperfect observation; and when they reach the shores of Investigation, it is an essential part of their undertaking to burn their ships of early prejudice, of traditional superstitions, and of inconsequent learning.

Their guiding star in all research, in all deduction, is Truth,—and Truth for Truth's sake alone. The struggle for mastery over the errors of the earlier education is intense, and can only be fully understood by those who have conquered. And yet as new relations in Nature are unfolded, the observer soon finds the scales of defective teachings falling from his mental vision, and he is impelled by the very truthfulness of his work to urge his labors, and to gather into consecutive order the fruits of his discoveries.

And it must be gratifying to every teacher of youth, and of older age—I mean teachers in the broadest terms which the word will admit—the preacher, the artist, the professor, the actor—to know how the moral sense of truth is enlarged, intensified, and attuned by the very effort of investigation and deduction. I can fancy no other occupation except that of the mathematician, that will, in its workings alone, bear comparison with original research in thus developing one of the highest attributes of our present condition. And the spread of this taste for examination is to me the most hopeful sign in an age when charlatans in many professions are endeavoring to cut loose the moorings of public and private morals.

The history of the Inductive Sciences abounds in examples and lessons bearing pertinently upon the position and relations of discovery with society at large; and it would appear pedantic even to mention the early observers in astronomy and physics; investigators whose advances were notedly marked by the long and persistent opposition which they encountered. The "warfare" was decidedly one-sided; the aggressors were assuredly not the investigators; nevertheless, the attacks of prejudice, of scholastic dogmatism, of unreasoning credulity, were powerless to stay the march of deduced Truth.

Almost in our own time we have had presented to us several remarkable fields of investigation that were held and entrenched by the blindest faith, and nothing but the unwavering labor of the investigator has drawn light and truth from them.

With the opening of the present century there dawned a new era in Palæontology; a few clear minds had caught its whisperings, and it has emerged a science. The previous investigators had indeed been in advance of their times, but the modes of independent thought had not then been fully developed; and moreover, their conclusions were warped and trammelled by the same causes that had so long repressed the acceptance of the new cosmogony. But the clear truths of discovery accumulated, and of necessity the earlier education was pushed aside whenever and wherever it stood in conflict with the deductions of the bolder thinking. System now guides investigation, and method has constructed coherent and more comprehensive theories. To-day there is admitted no "sports of nature" on the palæontological record, but order, succession, and inevitable law. The stratigraphical record of the earth is now read as certainly, if not so easily, as the hieroglyphics of Egypt, or the cuneiform inscriptions of Assyria.

It seemed almost seeking and courting the condemnation of the so-called "learned professions" when the Archæologist first propounded the proofs of man's early existence on the face of the earth; and yet the searchers after truth have brought such evidences of his presence here, even before the last glacial period, that only the "doubting Thomases" can fail to see the import and weight of their investigations. Very much more remains to be done before the "mint stamp" is placed upon any given archæological theory ; but the stream of evidence gathers volume and momentum, and will yet carry the law with it.

And in the "new chemistry" is it not remarkable what great strides have been taken, and what broader horizons have been opened before us, in the investigations and illustrations of "the Molecular Theory?" The old atom of our student days still claims and still holds a qualified existence, but the wonderful microcosm of the "molecule" has immensely enlarged the views of the physicist, and enabled him to almost penetrate the arcana of ultimate matter. The mathematician sees in it the opportunity for the legitimate application of his analysis, and we may rest assured, from the present progress in the examination, that he will ultimately master the problem. And curiously enough, in this branch of science, the modern investigator has trodden upon the domain of the metaphysician, and shown that the infinite divisibility of matter is a phantasm of the brain of the closet philosopher; for the atom and the molecule have their sizes determinable. By direct experiment, also, the chemist has placed three distinct bodies of the same volume in the space occupied by one of them; and again confounded the "inner consciousness" of the metaphysical dreamer.

In the rich field of Zoology and Biology, we have found, and we may reasonably expect to find, more of the highest developments in the law of evolution, for the very essence and integrity of the law, in one of its more important phases, is ever-present within our means of investigation. It is comparatively young among the modern sciences, and yet its deductions point unerringly to the same pole in the heavens of true knowledge.

For these sciences, and for all the others, the specialist must be peculiarly gifted for research; his education develops as he advances; and his deductions are founded only upon the sequence and coherence of observed facts. All the streams of knowledge will flow into the same great channel and homologate. We may not imagine that channel banks-full until our race reaches a higher development; we may not hear the announcement of the grand formula of evolution, but we experience the lively satisfaction of the ancient geometer, and know that we are on the right line of research and deduction towards it. And yet in our hopefulness and trustfulness of the very evolution of law in the cosmos, we feel that at any day may arise the man and the brain to grasp and announce the intimate relations of all matter and of all forces.

These views are not confined to the scientist; you know that, in one shape or another, they are permeating the earth. The war-cries of dogmatism, of imperfect education, of unquestioning faith, may be raised against them, but the world "still moves."

The discovery of America was an epoch of restless inquiry, and opened a fresh field for growth and cultivation of free thought and free deductions; the activity of the last century has wonderfully accelerated their exposition; and to-day our children are starting where we are leaving off.

To every teacher of youth, to every adviser of maturer age and thought, the newer education must come in direct conflict with part of their earlier and more contracted education; and they must abandon the dicta of mere "schools" and teach these higher laws of science, or be dragged at the wheels of irresistible mental and moral progress.—*Prof. Geo. Davidson.*

8. SCIENCE KNOWS NOT PREJUDICE OR PASSION.—It is the felicity of the scientific man, that the truth he seeks is cosmopolitan. It knows not state or nation, tribe or race, but is world-truth and world-law. The distinguished representatives of that truth have a clear at-

mosphere, and if their moral nature is strong enough to sustain itself in those rarified heights, they lead a life of singular dignity and freedom, their minds dashed with no color of prejudice or passion—seeking what is. To know what is in the world of things, is the vocation of the man of science. His reputation is the reputation of truth, strong and still as the sun; and his name is the property of mankind.—*Rev. Horatio Stebbins.*

9. THE EVOLUTION OF SCIENCE AND ART.—This age is one of science, as contra-distinguished from the ages of poetry, the arts, conquest and superstition.

The Greeks, who are our masters, and the masters of all the succeeding ages in all that relates to sculpture, poetry, taste, refinement of thought and feeling, rhetoric, logic, eloquence and ideal philosophy, were yet children in the natural sciences, though they were far from being deficient in certain branches of mathematics and were accurate observers of men and things.

There is not a principle in abstract logic which was not as well understood by Aristotle as it now is by the most eminent in Europe or America, and no abstract principle of moral philosophy which the Greeks did not elaborate, refine, and adorn with the elegance and grace of their language, and their peculiar adoration of the sublime and beautiful.

But their artistic taste, and the ideality of their conceptions, rendered them far more apt to speculate on the natural sciences and to establish beautiful theories, than to go through the painful process of methodical investigation, aided by actual experiments.

They were most accurate observers of nature, as far as the latter is revealed to the senses, and they possessed a wonderful combination of thought, and reasoning to draw conclusions and to build up systems; but where their senses erred they necessarily arrived at wrong conclusions; and they had no means of following nature into her dark chambers of inquisition, putting questions to her, compelling answers and racking the truth from her by means of philosophical apparatus. They had no telescope, no microscope, no physical instruments or chemical laboratories of any importance, and the mechanical arts were not sufficiently advanced to furnish either.

The heroes of the Iliad knew neither iron nor steel; they fought their battles with arms made of copper, and the accomplished Aspasia, though decked with gems of art which our modern cameo cutters would vainly imitate, knew neither gauze, silk, nor muslin.

Considering the limited means of observation and construction possessed by the Greeks, they achieved wonders in the correct classification of phenomena and their accurate description of them, and in the acuteness of the process of reasoning brought to bear upon them.

But they had not data enough to reason from, though they had in many instances a presentiment of truth amounting almost to intuition. And to their everlasting honor be it spoken, they sought truth, merely for the sake of truth, on account of its divine essence and ennobling character.

There was no stimulus given to inventors and discoverers in the shape of patents and privileges for the accumulation of large fortunes; and the answer given by Archimedes to his pupil who wished to devote himself to the divine science of mathematics, because its application had saved the state, furnishes a powerful contrast to the sordid motives which but too often govern our modern votaries of science.

"Science was divine," replied Archimedes, "before it served the state, and he who only worships her on account of the uses to which she may be put, desecrates her shrine." Yet even Archimedes, with his knowledge of geometry, mechanics and hydraulics, would now be scarcely able to pass an examination for admission into the Polytechnic School of Paris, or rank with an undergraduate of the Military Academy of West Point.

The Romans, at the period of their Greek conquest, were a semi-barbarous people, but naturally possessed of great aptitudes. They soon perceived and imitated the superior civilization and refinement of the Greeks, and as Pliny expressed it in one of his letters, "were in turn subdued and conquered by the vanquished."

But the Romans never equaled the Greeks in the fine arts; neither did they materially add to Greek science.

They were essentially a military people, who looked upon themselves as the masters of the world, and upon the rest of mankind as tributary to their greatness. To carry out this view required not only great valor (*virtus* it was called) and great generalship, but also fixed principles of policy in regard to their neighbors and the peoples subjected to their rule. The Romans cultivated statesmanship, and felt at an early period the necessity of law. The relations of property called for the exercise of legislative wisdom, and led to the enactment of codes which have become models of legal reasoning to all subsequent legislators.

The code of Justinian is still in force in many countries in Europe, and Roman law, as an introduction to the study of all other law, is required in most European Universities. No nation has elaborated the spirit or science of law more fully than the Romans, and if the legislators of England and France have found it expedient to vary from it in one or the other respect, it was done simply with a view of meeting the altered state of society, and the new relations of property arising from new modes of acquisition. Leibnitz, the great mathematician and logician, compared the study of the Roman law to a course of mathematics, so vigorous did he find its process of reasoning, its logical deductions, and its demonstrative justice. Our common law derived from England is undoubtedly better adapted to the wants of a free and simple hearted people, for the common law is a school of freedom, a bulwark against tyranny ; but no law has, like the Roman, so entirely met the requirements of abstract justice.

Greeks and Romans then were our masters. Greek philosophy and art, and Roman law and statesmanship, have assisted in shaping our present civilization. But Greek philosophy had to be stripped of its poetical dress, and to Roman law had to be added the chapter on *inalienable human rights and the duties of nations toward each other,* to prepare the further development of the intellectual and moral faculties of man. The

Romans had no idea of international law; no suspicion that a conquered nation had any rights at all, or that Rome had any obligation to a foreign nation, except those which were dictated by her own interests. Her conduct toward neutral powers and toward the conquered, were alike the result of policy.

Some of the Greek philosophers—among others, Socrates, in his dialogues—had much higher conceptions of the mutual duties and obligations of men and peoples; but they never succeeded in having their views adopted, as a principle of action, either state or individual. In this respect our civilization and learning are far in advance of the ancients, and far more in harmony with the general laws of nature. We have evidently advanced in knowledge, though we may remain far behind the Greeks, not only in performance, but also in the appreciation of the fine arts. We have no reason to regret this deterioration in one respect, and advance in another; for, in spite of the fostering care bestowed by legislation on science and art, there is a certain antagonism between them distinctly marked in the history of each nation.

The inspirations of the artist consist in an intuitive perception of truth, and in an undefined, but nevertheless entire appreciation of the harmony of all created things. Imagination must of course elaborate each individual conception of the artist; but it must always be in harmony with nature, or, to use a more familiar phrase, it must be "true to nature." The process of science is the reverse. Here nothing is intuition; all is either analysis or synthetic reasoning from cause to effect. Both processes are gradual, and necessarily exclude the influence of the imagination. In the artist, union of design is the first essential pre-requisite; in science, union is the result of many truths combined into one after a long process of reasoning. The exclusion of the imagination from scientific pursuits precludes artistic conception and *vice versa*.

The arts have preceded science all over the world, as poetry was written before prose. Men *felt* truth before they were conscious of it, as a child learns to speak before it studies grammar, or as a mind may be logical without having paid much attention to categories. Science consists in conscious truth,—in truth demonstrated. It is this latter perception of truth which gives man power over matter, which teaches him his moral and physical status in the universe, and brings him in contact with the infinite. Greek and Roman art flourished without rigorous perceptions of scientfiic truths, and painting and statuary reached the highest perfection of art in the fifteenth and sixteenth centuries, amidst grotesque superstitions, which, notwithstanding the great discoveries of that period, in more than one respect checked the progress of scientific pursuits.

The first impulse to the logical pursuit of science was given by Bacon. Not that he established any particular theory or hypothesis of his own, but because he *upset* all those which had hitherto been established, and which had prevented all real scientific progress. He is the founder of experimental philosophy; that is, the knowledge of nature arising from certain proofs furnished by nature herself when subjected to certain tests. Philosophers had ever after to deal in facts, not in theories; and when these facts were not obvious to the senses, they had to be illustrated by actual experiments.

Experience, not ingenious conjecture, was henceforth to guide the explorer of nature and her laws. The metamorphosis wrought by this change of system in the mode of reasoning on natural subjects, changed Astrology into Astronomy, Alchemy into Chemistry, and the search after the Philosopher's Stone into Mineralogy and Geology. It has added many new branches to science, branches for which even the names were wanting in former ages, and which have since led the way to the most important inventions, changed the form and aspect of the civilized world. And it has also shown to us that all natural sciences are intimately connected with each other; that there is, in fact, but one great science—that of nature—and that all the sciences men have cultivated from time to time, in different ages, are but so many fractional parts of that universal unit.—*Milton S. Latham.*

10. THE MASTERBUILDERS IN THE TEMPLE OF SCIENCE.—In the noble army of Science—that army so compactly organized for the conquest of darkness and the extension of the empire of light—there are many valiant fighters, but there can be but few leaders. In the construction of the great temple of science—that eternal temple made without hands—the only temple ever erected by man worthy to be dedicated to the

great Author of Nature—there are many busy, eager, joyous workmen, but there can be but few *master-builders.*

As we look back over the history of science, we see, at long intervals, certain men who seem to tower far above their fellows. In what consists their greatness? They are men who have introduced *great ideas* or *new methods* into science—ideas which extend the domain of human thought, or methods which increase our power over nature, facilitate the progress of discovery, and thus open the way to the conquest of new fields. Such men were Copernicus, and Galileo, and Kepler, and Newton, and Herschel, in astronomy; such were Linnaeus, and Buffon, and Cuvier and Agassiz, in organic science.—*Prof. Joseph LeConte.*

11. EVOLUTION AND MATERIALISM.—It is believed by many that science starves all our noblest faculties, quenches all our most glorious aspirations, and buries all our heavenly hopes in the cold earth of a vulgar materialism.

Now, it is indeed true, that there has been in these modern times a strong tendency, a current of thought, in the direction of materialism. It is true, too, that this tendency is strongest in the domain of science, and among sciences, strongest of all, in biology and geology; but I believe it is true, also, that this is only a passing phase of thought, an ephemeral fashion of philosophy. As a sympathizer with the age in which I live, still more as a scientist, and most of all as a biologist and geologist, I have felt the full force of this tendency.

In this stream of tendency I have stood, during all my active life, just where the current ran swiftest, and confess to you that I have been sometimes almost swept off my feet. But it is the duty of every independent thinker not to yield blindly to the spirit of the age, but to exercise his own unprejudiced reason; not to *float* and *drift*, but to *stand*.

I wish frankly to acknowledge that I am myself an evolutionist. I may not agree with most that evolution advances always *cum æquo pede*. On the contrary, I believe that there have been periods of slow and periods of rapid, almost paroxysmal, evolution. I may not agree with most that we already have in *Darwinism*, the final form, and in *survival of the fittest*, the prime factor of evolution. On the contrary, I believe that the most important factors of evolution are still unknown—that there are more and greater factors in evolution than are dreamed of in the Darwinian philosophy. Nevertheless, evolution is a grand fact, involving alike every department of nature; and more especially evolution of the organic kingdom and the origin of species by derivation, must be regarded as an established truth of science. But remember, evolution is *one* thing and materialism *another* and quite a different thing. The one is a sure *result of science;* the other a doubtful *inference of philosophy*. Let no one who is led step by step through the paths of evolution, from the mineral to the organic, from the organic to the animate, and from the animate to the rational, until he lands logically, as he supposes, into blank and universal materialism; let no such one, I say, imagine for a moment that he has been walking all the way in the domain of science. He has stepped across the boundary of science into the domain of philosophy. Yet the step seems so easy, so natural, so inevitable, that most do not distinguish between the teachings of science and the inference of philosophy, and thus the whole is unjustly accredited to science.—*Prof. Jos. LeConte.*

12. Evolution the Grandest Idea of Modern Science.—Evolution is certainly the grandest idea of modern science, embracing alike every department of nature. The law of evolution is as universal as the law of gravitation. The one is the universal law of time, as the other is of space. In its widest and truest sense, evolution constitutes the subject matter of at least one-half of all science.

Now, in this wide sense, there can be no doubt of the evolution of the organic kingdom. There may be, and in fact there is, much difference of opinion as to the *causes* or *factors* of evolution—there may be, and in fact there is, much difference of opinion as to the *rate* of evolution, whether always uniform or often more or less paroxysmal; but of the *fact* of progressive movement of the whole organic kingdom to higher and higher conditions, and that the laws of the progressive movement are similar to those which determine the movement in all evolution, there is no longer any doubt. These formal laws of continuous movement—*e. g.*, the law of differentiation, the law of progress, etc.—these are the really grand things about the evolution theory, and for these we are indebted to Agassiz. Yes, Agassiz, although he, to his latest utterances, contested modern views, was himself the great founder and apostle of evolution. All the laws of the evolution of the organic kingdom, as now recognized, were announced by him. His whole life and strength were devoted to enforcing and illustrating these laws, although he denied the existence of any discoverable *cause* except the Great First Cause. To him the organic kingdom seemed a great *work of art*, wrought out through inconceivable time to higher and more perfect conditions, according to a plan predetermined in the mind of God; and he was undoubtedly right. Darwin, on the other hand, attempted to discover the *secondary causes* by means of which this marvellous result was attained. To him the organic kingdom, as a whole, was a great and complex *organism* developing under the operation of *resident forces;* and he also, as I conceive, was right. Agassiz announced all *formal laws* of the universe of *time* as Kepler did those of the universe of space; he was the legislator of the dark abyss behind us, as Kepler was of the overarching abyss above us.—*Prof. Jos. LeConte.*

13. Evolution not Ungodly.—There are three corresponding views in regard to the origin of the individual,—of you, of me, of each of us. The first is that of the little innocent, who thinks God made him as he (the little innocent) makes *dirt-pies*; the second is that of the little hoodlum, who says, " I wasn't made at all, I growed;" the third is the usual adult belief— that we are made by a process of evolution. Do you

not observe, then, that in the matter of the origin of species, many good theologians and pietists are in the position of the little innocent? They think that species were made *without natural process.* On the other hand, most evolutionists are in the position of the little hoodlum; for they think that species, *because they* "*growed,*" *weren't made at all.* But there is a higher and more rational philosophy than either, which holds that the ideas of *making* and of *growing* are not inconsistent with each other—that evolution does not and cannot destroy the conception of, or the belief in, an intelligent Creator and Author of the Cosmos. This view combines and reconciles the two preceding antagonistic views, and is therefore more comprehensive, more rational, and more true. But let us not fail to do justice—let us not overlook the fact that the most important and noblest truths are overlooked only by the hoodlum and materialist. Of the two sides of the shield, the little innocent and the pietist sees, at least, the whiter and more beautiful.—*Prof. Jos. LeConte.*

14. SCIENCE AND ART OMNIPOTENT.—Science and Art flourish best in a Republican soil. Their achievements are of no hot house growth. Where the human mind is left free to grapple with Nature, the contest is unequal. The intrepid Franklin grasped the motive power of the Universe. Morse, the artist-philosopher, tamed and subdued it into obedience, and endowed it with thought and speech. Swift as the flash of God's eye, and in mysterious silence, the thought of one hemisphere is uttered in the other. The events of

to-day are matters of history to-morrow. Space is annihilated, and time is no more. The intensity and activity of our existence are truly appalling. Omnipotence, a grand and fearful attribute of Deity, has been usurped by man. The elements are subjected to his will, and perform the most menial services. The winds and waves are set at defiance, and commerce and humanity rejoice at the achievements of steam. Labor, the great element of Democracy, has been elevated to a Science, and its light illuminates the workshops of the world. The hand of invention strikes the shackle from toiling millions.—*John V. Wattson.*

15. GREAT IDEAS IN SCIENCE.—Let me illustrate the effect of the introduction of great ideas into science. I will select one example from astronomy, and one from geology.

Before the time of Copernicus and Galileo, this, our earth, was *all of space* for us. Sun, moon, and stars were but little satellites revolving about us at inconsiderable distances. Astronomy then was but the *geometry* of the heavens, the geometry of the curious lines traced by these wandering fires on the concave of heaven. But with the first glance through the telescope, the phases of Venus and the satellites of Jupiter revealed the existence of other worlds beside our own. In that moment the fundamental idea of modern astronomy, the idea of infinite space filled with worlds like our own, was fully born in the mind of Galileo. In that moment the intellectual vision of man was infinitely extended.

Again, before the time of Buffon and Cuvier, this, our human epoch, the history of our race, was *all of time* for us. Shells and other remains of marine animals had, indeed, been found far in the interior of the continents, and high up the slopes of mountains, and there had been much speculation as to their origin. Some may have thought by means of these to extend the limits of our epoch, but none dreamed of other epochs. Some may have thought they were discovering new coast islands along the shores, but none dreamed that these were the evidences of new worlds in the infinite abyss of time. It was reserved for Buffon and Cuvier first to recognize the entire difference between fossil and living species. In that moment was born the fundamental idea of geology, the idea of infinite time containing many successive epochs, or time-worlds like our own. In that moment the intellectual horizon of man was again infinitely extended.

These two are the grandest moments in the history of science; yea, in the intellectual history of our race. The one opened the gates of infinite space, and showed us many space worlds; the other opened up the gates of infinite time, and showed us as many successive creations or time-worlds.

We see, then, the intellectual impulse communicated by a great new idea.—*Prof. Jos. LeConte.*

16. O, SCIENCE! high-priest of truth, interpreter of nature, explorer of the infinite! unto whom it is given to walk upon the waters of the deep, to tread the ocean's bed, to pass through furnaces of fire, to kiss

the burning lips of the crater, to play with the thunderbolts of heaven, and to cleave thy bright way among the everlasting stars! We greet thee as the sovereign genius of a wide and widening realm. Pursue thy glorious march of conquest, multiply thy triumphs and enlarge thy dominion, giving to humanity thy garnered fruits, and ever leading us to higher planes of knowledge. So may we keep in harmony with God's will.—*Oscar T. Shuck.*

17. CHEMISTRY, youngest daughter of the Sciences, born amidst flame, and cradled in billows of fire!—*W. H. Rhodes.*

18. THE GREAT SCIENTIFIC EXPLORER.—In the darkness of the night, from his vessel's prow, Columbus saw waving lights in front of him, which the dawn of morn showed him to come from regions new and undiscovered, but which had been so near him in the night, that he had scented the perfume of the trees and flowers. And so I doubt not the eager searcher for truth, the Columbus of Science, has often seen in the darkness of this life, glimmering lights from the other world—lights which the morning of immortality has revealed to him as coming from regions which had been so near to him in the night of life, that even then a little more light, a little more range of organs, would have discovered them. It has often seemed to me that the great scientific man, after death, must have started to find how near he was, when in this world, to the discovery of the whole secret of being. Often I have imagined such a one saying to

himself: "Why, this great truth was hidden in facts long familiar to me in my studies on earth. This great mechanism, every spring of which I now comprehend, simple as is all the mechanism of God, needed but one more generalization; one more syllogism; one more bold effort of the reason, and I had found it out, even with the dull organs of mortality.—*John B. Felton.*

19. The winds of heaven trample down the pines,
    Or creep in lazy tides along the lea;
Leap the wild waters from the smitten rock,
    Or crawl with childish babble to the sea;
But why the tempests out of heaven blow,
    Or what the purpose of the seaward flow,
No man hath known, and none shall ever know.

Why seek to know? To follow Nature up
    Against the current to her source, why care?
Vain is the toil; he's wisest still who knows
    All science is but formulated prayer—
Prayer for the warm winds and the quickening rain,
    Prayer for sharp sickle and for laboring wain,
To gather from the planted past the grain.—
                                 A. G. Bierce.

20. NO ANTAGONISM BETWEEN SCIENCE AND RELIGION.—I am ready to say and boldly maintain that there is not, and cannot be, any real antagonism or controversy between true science and true religion. All truth is of God, and is a unit. Science and religion are twin sisters from the throne of the Eternal Lawgiver. There is no real controversy between them—

no strife but as to which branch of knowledge can do most for mankind. Properly interpreted, they come from the same glorious hand and tend to the same result—the happiness of mankind and the glory of the Creator. I honor science, and heartily bid God-speed to every honest investigator of the laws of the universe. As a theologian, I have never had the slightest fear concerning the advance of true science. Our natural philosophers cannot travel so far, but they will find the Creator has been there before them; and as they climb through space and journey among planets and systems unnumbered, they will all find that the ladder by which they have ascended to the very outposts of the universe was built for them by the hand of an all-wise Lawgiver, possessed of supreme intelligence, will, and power.—*Rev. Dr. W. A. Scott.*

21. ESSENTIALLY there is no conflict between religion and science, and never can be. Their boundaries are undefined, as the boundaries between the known and the unknown, the apprehended and the comprehended, always will be.—*Rev. Horatio Stebbins.*

22. Fine art has an ideal which it seeks to *embody*. Morphology also has an ideal (the archetype) which it seeks to *discover*. The ideal of art is that *toward which all* nature ceaselessly *strives*,—the ideal of science, that *from* which all nature is ceaselessly *unfolded*. Both must ever remain ideals at an infinite distance from us. We must forever approach, but can never attain them. For the ideal of science is to be found only in the

eternal thoughts of God the Father—the ideal of art only in the person of God the Son. Religion, more perfect, and far more practical than either, strives, through the influence of the third person, the Holy Spirit, to embody the same ideal, not in human thought nor in human works of art, but in human life and human character.—*Prof. Joseph LeConte.*

23. DRAWING.—Drawing, or the art of design, is often pointed at as a superfluous study. It is only another mode of writing; it is the shorthand of idiographic teaching; while the hands are young and the fingers pliant they are the most easily trained to precision; the picture teaches at a glance that which it would cost pages of verbal description to explain. The books of science of the present day teem with illustratrations, and therein it is that the youth of this age far outstrip those of former years in the rapidity of their education. He who learns to-day will teach to-morrow, and to him should be given every facility with which to stamp his thought on paper. Let the machinist, the engineer, the shipbuilder, the architect, the mechanic, the engraver, all answer what can they do without their drawings and their plans?—*Dr. A. B. Stout.*

24. THE HOME OF ART.—The home of art is where Nature stimulates the sensual and spiritual-intellectual. Art flourished under Grecian skies. Inspired by the spirit of beauty that dwelt where the chiefest joys of earth, sea, and sky were blended, the Parthenon arose upon the brow of the Acropolis in the transparent air of Attica, classic groves were adorned

with marble men, and chastest temples solemnized with statues of gods. As art has flourished in a zone where the charms of Nature invite man to their enjoyment, and away from anxious cares for self-preservation, so to the stimulation of a generous climate and its attendant advantages for æsthetic culture, we are to look for the founding of the great schools of art upon our continent. Where else are they to appear but on the Pacific shores of the Great Republic ?—*E. G. Waite.*

25. ART IN CALIFORNIA.—The little that has been done in California in Art is rather a sign of better things to come. Art must not only have inspiration, but it needs wealth and the society of a ripe community for its best estate. It is possible to paint for immortality in a garret; but a great deal of work done there has gone to the lumber-room. Not only must there be the fostering spirit of wealth and letters, but Art also needs a picturesque world without—the grand estate of mountains and valleys, atmospheres, tones, lights, shadows; and if there be a picturesque people, we might look for a new school of Art, and even famous painters. Where a poet can be inspired, there look also for the poetry, which is put on canvas.

In spite of our civilization there is a great deal that is picturesque among the people—the Parsee, Mohammedan, Malay and Mongol, whom one may sometimes meet on the same street—the red shirt of the Italian fisherman, and the lateen sail which sends his boat flying over the water. The very distresses and distrusts of men here have made them picturesque.

Moreover the whole physical aspect of the country is wonderfully picturesque. The palm tree, lifting up its fronded head in the desert, the great fir tree, set against the ineffable azure of the heavens, the vine-clad hills, th serrated mountains, which the frosts have canonized with their scaled and unscaled fountains, and all the gold and purple which touch the hills at eventide—these are the full rich ministries of Nature. It may take Art a thousand years to ripen even here. For how many ages had the long procession of painters come and gone before Raphael and Michael Angelo appeared?

Our young Art school will some day have its treasures; and there will be hung on our walls the portraits of other men, whose culture and influence will be worth more than all the gold of our mountains. Let the artist set up his easel and write his silent poem upon the canvas. Welcome all influences which soften this hard and barren materialism. Before the mountains were unvexed by the miner's drill, the land itself was a poem and a picture. One day the turbid streams will turn to crystal again, and the only miner will be the living glacier sitting on its white throne of judgment, and grinding the very mountains to powder. Fortunate they who can catch this wealth of inspiration. These are the ministers and prophets whose larger and finer interpretation of Nature is part of the treasures of the new commonwealth.—*W. C. Bartlett.*

26. SCULPTURE.—It is said that the ancients have exhausted the domain of sculpture, because they have delineated the human form in its greatest perfection.

They have done this and we concede it. But form is not all. There are also action, passion and sentiment. We claim that we have advanced somewhat in two thousand years, and during that period have attained to a higher and more sentimental civilization. If this claim be true, then we have higher ideas and sentiments to express in painting and sculpture than had our predecessors in art, Zeuxis and Apelles, Phidias and Praxiteles. We may hope to equal them in the expression of physical beauty, and to excel them in moral and sentimental beauty.

Let us, meanwile, be just to the ancients. They have left us so many impure and obscene remains, that many critics have considered them as characteristic specimens of their art. But a careful observation demonstrates that these impure remains are almost always in a style of art imperfect, both in design and execution, and that able artists would not degrade themselves to such subjects. Even at the Renaissance it is remarkable how the greatest modern artists often gave the grossest material interpretations to those mythological fables out of which the ancient Pagan artists constructed the most poetical conceptions. Titian represents Danæ as purchased for the embraces of Jupiter by a shower of golden ducats poured into her lap. The Pagan artist, whose work is preserved at Pompeii, pictures her as an innocent maiden seated upon a green bank in the recesses of a garden, who unveils her bosom to a warm, moist mist, golden with the evening of sunshine, which gently wafts itself over her, and in this form the treacherous and seductive god insinuates himself beneath the folds of her drapery. The modern artist portrays Leda submitting herself to Jove, approaching her under the form of a swan in the grossest and most material modes. The ancient painter depicts a swan fleeing from a vulture, and received by a compassionate virgin into her bosom, and shielded there by her arms and beneath her garments. And we are constantly called upon to wonder how the great artists of the fourteenth century could lend themselves to the most material conceptions.

To say that modern art may not excel ancient art, is to say that we are to make no progress in sentiment and idea. The ancients expressed perfectly all they had to express. The Greek ideal and Roman ideal have survived to us. The Hebrew ideal has not come down to us, for the Jews did not cultivate sculpture or painting; nor the Egyptians, because among them it was reduced to merely conventional and sacerdotal forms. But there is nothing christian nor spiritual in Grecian or Roman art. Could a Greek or Roman artist even conceive such a picture as the Beatrice and Dante of Ary Scheffer? a love so intense, so unsensual, so perfect, so pure? And the Nydia, whom our own Randolph Rogers has consigned to immortality, is not a heathen but christian conception. "Greater love hath no man than this, that he give his life for his friend." In this marble there is the very highest expression of this sentiment; a prophecy not merely of self-sacrifice to the Glaucus, whom Nydia loves with all the love of woman, but also of sacrifice to Ione, whom he loves, the very rival of the devoted victim.

Does all the poetry of antiquity mount to the conception of such a devotion as this? Does all the art of antiquity excel its realization in the living marble?

In his beautiful romance of Zanoni, Bulwer represents a sage who had won from nature the secret of immortal life upon earth, as apostrophizing the simple herbs which men unconsciously crushed beneath the tread of their feet, but in whose juices were concealed potential agencies which contain life and death, strength and paralysis, vigor and disease, wakefulness and sleep, hope and despair, madness and reason, tears and laughter. But it seems to me that the great magician, the sculptor, has a vastly larger power than this. He breathes the breath of genius upon the dead marble, and it instinctively starts into perpetual life, in every possible form of action or repose, and beaming with every conceivable expression of passion or sentiment. And so with prophetic vision we can see the highest expression of the highest sentiment of the future perfected civilization going down to immortality with our own Nydia; with the gladiator forever dying, yet never dead; with the perpetual agony of the Laocöön; with Niobe lamenting to all future generations the slaughter of her children; and with Apollo, eternally triumphing with the majesty and beauty of a youthful god.—*John W. Dwinelle.*

27. ANCIENT ARCHITECTURE.—In the morning of time, and long before civilization had visited the world, before the races of men had emerged from their tribal relations, the sounds of the Masons' labor were heard.

With such implements as the forest, the spoils of the chase and the quarry afforded, they performed their allotted tasks. Then began the earliest attempts at monumental architecture. They consisted of mounds of earth, solitary upright stones, tables of rock, and circles of the same material, often enclosing vast areas dotted with similar objects. These rude monuments, erected at a time and by peoples over whose history rests the pall of everlasting silence, are found in every land. They stand on the plains and mountains of Europe, amid the deserts of the Orient, and in the shade of the primeval forests of America. They bear no design, and have no device or inscription to explain their origin or purpose. They are the weird and voiceless relics of a remote and unremembered past. We can only conjecture that they were intended to commemorate some important event, and aid in transmitting the tradition of it to future generations. Long after the commencement of historic time such a custom prevailed, for we read in the holy writings that a leader of Israel placed a stone near the sanctuary where the Most High had spoken to his people, and said: "Behold this stone shall be a witness unto us, for it hath heard all the words of the Lord." At last the creative genius of a mortal, whose name or birth-place is unknown, conferred on his race a blessing like to that of the fabled Prometheus when he brought to earth a spark from the celestial fires. With an inspiration almost divine he discovered a mode of transmuting the dull ores of earth into lustrous metals, and fashioned them into the manifold tools and implements of labor.

The light that shone from the first forge of the prehistoric age was the grandest illumination this world has ever witnessed. We can imagine that the bright-eyed spirits of art, science, and of myriad industries beheld its rays from their starry home, and amid the heavenly symphonies of shining orbs winged their flight to a planet which now wooed their embraces. With the iron-age architecture assumed the exactness of a science while it retained all the graces of art. In the Valley of the Nile we find the earliest achievements of architectural genius; efforts which in grandeur and massiveness are unrivaled, and which may endure till Time shall be no more. In a narrow strip of inhabitable land extending from the river to the rocks and deserts, Temples, Tombs, Pyramids and Obelisks rise in sublime vastness, the wonder and glory of the world, and the admiration of the ages. What mechanical agencies were employed in their construction, or what tools were used in tracing the inscriptions which are carved on their walls, are mysteries which the researches of science have failed to solve. The great pyramid of Ghizeh, far higher than any edifice which modern art has builded and dwarfing by comparison the most spacious cathedral of Europe, carries the imagination beyond the period of authentic history into the twilight of tradition. When our continent was peopled by nations that have vanished like shadows from the earth; before the Israelites had escaped from thraldom and placed the oracles of God near the waters of Siloa; ages before civilization had dawned on the banks of the Tiber or the shores of Greece, this pyramid and other tombs and temples of the Nile had witnessed the silent march of the centuries as they sped onward to the eternity of the past. Hundreds of generations of men have toiled and passed away—empires have arisen, flourished and died—creeds, systems, and dynasties have disappeared, leaving no trace on the sands of time; mountains have been upheaved by volcanic fires of the globe, islands have emerged from the depths of ocean and sunk beneath its waves, flaming worlds have shone in the firmament and wandered from their orbits into night and chaos; and yet, amid all changes and revolutions, these monuments have stood in their imperishable and unchangeable majesty on the confines of the mighty desert.

On reflection we can readily trace to their proper cause the peculiar characteristics of the works of Egyptian masonry. The vast and shadeless deserts, the Nile with its turbid waters flowing from mysterious and unexplored sources to the sea, the sea itself—all surrounding, unfathomable and unknown—were types of the illimitable and eternal Egyptian architecture that received from the influence of such scenes, form and expression. It was an inevitable result. Hence arose the structures whose massive strength and gloomy vastness have defied the power of man and the elements to mar or destroy.

At a much later period, and in the Isles of Greece we behold architectural efforts, in style and design as divergent from the sombre monuments in the Valley of the Nile as the versatile genius of the Greek differed from the gloomy mind of the oriental builder. The happy temperament and brilliant fancy of the former revelled in the adoration of the beautiful. He delighted in every form of art and every manifestation of nature that pleased the senses or charmed the imagination. He peopled the rivers, groves, and mountains of his native land with beings of more than mortal loveliness. He heard the glad voices of his joyous deities in the rush of the waves, the rustle of the leaves, the murmur of the winds, the music of the waterfall, and embodied his poetic conceptions in sculpture, architecture, and verse that lives when the works of his plastic hand are in mouldering ruin. The Grecian temples in their freedom, lightness, grace and variety, reflected alike the ideal character of the religion of the time, and the intellect of the people. The glory of Greece has departed. The same sun that gilded the gardens of Attica, and the plains of Marathon, shines now on the ruined walls and desecrated shrines of her temples. Land of philosophy, song, poesy and eloquence, whose immortal spirit illumes and instructs a world, how art thou fallen, and yet how lovely in thy desolation! Roman, Goth, Moslem and Frank have ravaged thy fields and robbed thee of thy treasures of art, but happily none can tear from thy brow the amaranthine wreath of fame, or pale the glorious memories of the past.

> "No earth of thine is lost in common mould,
> But one vast realm of wonder spreads around,
> And all the muses' tales seem truly told."

Rome, in the style of her temples, imitated, with very slight differences, Grecian architecture. Her architects essayed at one time to improve on the beautiful original, and gave to the world the Tuscan and Composite orders. Vain attempt to rival in marble the magnificent conceptions of Greece! The Doric, Ionic and Corinthian pillars, with their graceful shafts, capitals and exquisite mouldings, upheld and adorned the temples of gods throughout the empire. To Rome, however, the civilized world is indebted for the introduction of the Arch. The Greeks and the Egyptians were either neglectful or ignorant of its uses and principle. The Romans employed it not only to embellish and improve their cities, but carried it into distant provinces, and by its aid constructed bridges across wide and rapid streams for the passage of their victorious legions. In their forums with splendid architectural porticos, in their theatres and amphitheatres which could seat armies, in their mighty aqueducts through which the waters of rivers were conducted to their cities, the genius of the Roman people asserted its superiority, and left models for the nations of the present day to admire and imitate.

With the fall of the Roman Empire in the west there arose another order of architecture. It indicated a new era in the world's history. In the fourth and fifth centuries the Goths and other races poured from their northern homes upon the doomed provinces of Rome. No human power availed against their resistless march. From the shores of the German ocean their camp-fires extended to the walls of the Imperial City. Among these warlike nations what is known as the Order of Gothic Architecture had its origin. It was introduced by them into the north of Italy in the fourth century, and remained unchanged until the Crusaders at a later period engrafted upon it the designs of buildings which they had viewed with delight in the Mohammedan and Saracenic lands of the East. In the tall spires, pointed arches and delicate traceries of the Gothic architecture, we see the influence of fancies that had been moulded by the lights and shadows of the forest—by the overarching branches of the grand old trees, the caves with their sparry columns, and by the mountains with their dark gorges and beetling crags.

The Greeks dedicated their temples to the protecting deities of a city or state and displayed in their adornment a poetic character and speculative tendency. The Gothic races on the contrary designed their religious edifices for the worship of a personal, ever-present God by the individual man. This idea predominates in the plan of every cathedral of the medieval ages, and is perhaps to-day the distinguishing trait which renders the Gothic architecture for devotional purposes more suitable than any model from antiquity.—*Frank Tilford.*

II.

LITERATURE AND EDUCATION.

PART II.

LITERATURE AND EDUCATION.

28. EDUCATION AIMS TO PERFECT MAN'S NATURE.—Education includes all the influences that are, or can be, brought to bear upon the individual, to form his constitution, actions, thoughts, and feelings; soil, climate, parentage, laws, manners, customs, home, society, literature, and whatever else helps to build up the man into the perfection of his nature, or hinders the attainment of that perfection.—*Rev. Horatio Stebbins.*

29. A RIDDLE.—A science in itself, it is the parent of all sciences, and though most studied, yet least understood. In what form, and by what agencies, and under what control, it ought to be administered, is a still unsettled problem. Constituting a state question of vital interest to all the foremost nations, it has only led into conflicting and distractive theories, while the enigma it presents still waits solution. No Œdipus can read the riddle of this modern sphinx.—*Joseph W. Winans.*

30. BUT ONE OF SEVERAL ELEMENTS.—The necessity for the education of all the people must be con-

ceded, but the power of education is often over-estimated by our writers. It is but one of several patent elements, all of which are necessary to liberty and security. The capacity to know, and the will to perform, are two very different things. Education will create the first, but cannot always confer the second. The history of mankind would seem to sustain this statement.—*Peter H. Burnett.*

31. THE PROFESSIONAL TEACHER.—I have the highest respect for a teacher who devotes his life to teaching as a profession. Educated at great expense, always studying to keep up with all discoveries in science and advances in literature, he debars himself from all opportunities for fortune that may disclose themselves in the avenues for wealth in the profitable world, that he may be poorly paid and have the consolation of knowing that some portion of mankind has made progress, and that the world will be the better because he has lived in it. Without men and women who will make this sacrifice, society would soon revert to its original barbarous condition. Civilization is a perpetual struggle. After two thousand years of Christian teaching we can see daily that the cloak of civilization is but a thin garment, easily discarded and scantily covering the original savage. The teacher, clergyman, and the Christian missionary should be the most honored by society. They accept small pay and make lifelong sacrifices that the race may advance in knowledge and virtue.—*B. B. Redding.*

32. THE NECESSITY FOR COMPETENT TEACHERS.—
To bring a school of one or two hundred boys and girls, quick living minds, bright possibilities, into contact, day after day, with a sluggish, stupid, empty mind, the refuse of some college class, rejected with disdain by one of the other professions, is something worse than absurd and ridiculous; it is no less an atrocity than that Mezentian punishment committed by the terrible ingenuity of Heathenism, when "it tied the healthy man to the loathsome corpse, and left the living and the dead to corrupt together." No, my friends, if there be any place under the sun from which stupid men and women should be inexorably banished, more than from any other, it is the teacher's desk. Better, by far, that they be set to work to make clumsy chairs and leaky boots and shoes, than to mar and ruin God's marvellous handiwork in a boy or girl. For the sake of the rising generation, for the sake of future developments in science and art, for the honor of the country, for a credit to ourselves, for the sake of the world, give to your schools nothing but a high and suitable order of mind.—*Rev. F. C. Ewer.*

33. EDUCATION AS A MORAL FORCE.—Education is not exclusively a literary, scientific, and æsthetic power, but it is besides, a potent moral force. It renders him who, by his birth, was but an agency of evil, by his intelligence an instrument of good. Although there may be instances where the vices of humanity have been expanded into greater vigor, and rendered more destructive by the aid of knowledge, yet these are but exceptional. It is a sarcasm, rather than an argument, which urges that the innate evil is only intensified by education into educated evil, and thus rendered more capable of mischief; for the very discipline of mental culture, the habitudes it forms, the ideas it creates, the lessons it imparts, whether from nature, by scientific exploration, or from literature by the lofty sentiments of the poets, philosophers, historians and moralists of every age—all tend to stimulate the moral sense. Thus grappling with man's mental, intellectual, and moral nature, education brings them from their lethargy into complete development. It is the fulcrum Archimedes needed to accomplish the *Kosmon Kineso.* It is the philosopher's stone which transmutes man's baser metal into gold. It is the chisel of Thorwalsden which forces out from the rough marble block a sculptured form of symmetry and beauty. The ugly duck, in the pathetic Apologue of Andersen, though persecuted by the flock, was a true swan from the beginning, and only grew from its original deformity into the natural comeliness of all its tribe. In seeming, merely, did it constitute the meaner bird. But education is not limited unto development. It recreates that which it beautifies. It turns the ugly duck into a swan, by an absolute reversal of its nature. —*Joseph W. Winans.*

84. INTELLECTUAL HONESTY.—What do we mean by intellectual development and the emancipation, or freedom of thought? There is reason to believe that there is a good deal of vague idea and loose talk, and

perhaps some cant about these things. It is quite natural that there should be. New ideas are, to some minds, a little too bracing at first, and bring on the exhilaration of surprise, and a man is excited at finding the lost key of the universe. I met such an one the other day. He had got everything, but a nutshell to put it in. But let us forgive something to that pleasant confidence that in a moment of undue familiarity would lift the veil from the face of nature. The cant that is sometimes heard is not altogether discreditable, for cant is almost always about that which is good, and only indicates a lack of intellectual and moral fibre.

By intellectual development, we do not surely mean that any new faculty has been added to the mind; neither do we mean that any accession has been made to the fundamental and essential principles of human nature. By intellectual development, I understand *the gradual growth of improved methods of the mind in its inquiries after the truth of things and events in the material and in the human world.* It is a better logic, it is a better observation of facts, a finer perception of analogies, a more subtle detection of difference, a long-minded staying power of generalization, and a firmer grasp of the law of cause and effect. The illustration of this is found in the fact that the reasons that satisfied the mind of an early age do not satisfy the mind of a later age, even when those reasons come to the same result. Socrates, in the Phædo, draws persuasions for a belief in immortality, from the succession of day and night. That would hardly satisfy the mind of to-day; the truth requires a better method in the mind. Intellectual development has been attended by a reconstruction of the methods on which science depends, and Bacon, on the empirical side, and Descartes, on the intellectual side, are its great historic exponents. It is no spread-eagle glory, but a patient, subtle process of intellectual power. There are laws of thought; and reasoned truth, that knows no fortuitous luck, and no blind gropings of chance or passion, is the only worthy achievement of the mind. Intellectual development is not merely an individual endowment, but a common-sense of truth and right reason in the common mind. It is the increase of the idea of order, law, cause, and consequence in the mind of an age.

Freedom of thought has no existence, except when based on intellectual development, such as this. On any other grounds, free thought is in the intellectual world what free love is in the sensual world. Without this recitude of the intellect, thinking itself is a vagary, and truth is a caprice of self-will. To be intellectually honest, is the last accomplishment of a mind that moves without passion or prejudice in the happy rhythm of truth, simply seeking to know what is. Intellectual honesty is much more rare than moral honesty.—*Rev. Horatio Stebbins.*

35. THE PURSUIT OF KNOWLEDGE.—The pursuit of knowledge may be likened to the ascent of a mountain. With slow and painful steps we climb its rugged side. Thorns and brambles block the way and lacerate the flesh. Through the rank undergrowth no vista is disclosed, no prospect opens. Dense thickets close

each avenue of sight. From the thick atmosphere there comes a sense of stifling to the panting breast. Repeated pauses are enforced, to obviate exhaustion. As we mount higher, casual gleams appear of the expanding landscape far below, then flit away. New difficulties thwart our progress while we rise, until the jaded spirit seems about to faint. But when the summit is attained, how utterly all consciousness of past endurance sinks beneath the gorgeous vision which there bursts upon our gaze: "All is forgot in that blithe jubilee." So it is with the course of learning. Constrained into a hateful discipline, the mind shrinks from that dry detail of rules and problems, lines and angles, rudiments and grammars, which, from the outset, guides the student on his upward path. They seem to him a miscellaneous array of things incongruous, without vitality or application, to be forced into memory by long and painful effort, for no seeming good. To them there is no landscape, no vistaed revelation of utility or beauty,—nothing but a close, stifling mental atmosphere that chokes the spirit. Yet when the student's life mounts higher up; when these abstractions merge in bright and living truths; when physics ultimate in those experimental facts which throw new light on science; when grammar opens up the rich resources of the Greek and Latin tongues, with all the modern classics—throwing open to the scholar's reach the grand ideas born in every age, the burning thoughts and glowing words of sophists, statesmen, orators and poets; when mathematics guide him to an undiscovered star; then is the mountain summit scaled, and knowledge vindicates its power in the insufferable glory there revealed.—*Joseph W. Winans.*

36. THE EVOLUTION OF MIND.—Genius alone, unaided by education, can have but a feeble flight. Innate intellect may exalt a self-taught poet; but cannot alone constitute an astronomer. The diamond in the rough may pass forever unheeded, but not until the friction of the wheel of labor and study shall have elicited its latent fire, will its polish reflect its merit.

The development of education should follow the evolution of mind. The course of education is the mirror of nature, and should be achromatic in its reflections of light. The direction of its instruction should be predicated upon the growth of the organic intellect.

The first feeble glimmerings of brain-work in the infant, in its instincts to get nutrition, are progressively fostered by the mother until it learns to feed alone; the first rays of mind which kindle curiosity in the child are brightened by showing it noisy and glittering objects; the parent-puzzling boy, with his "whys" and "wherefores," is satisfied with lettered blocks, pictures and puzzles, until, with growing brain and expanding intelligence, he explores with his eyes the natural world around him, and finally, in manhood, seeks in books aid from his predecessors, aspiring to grasp in his comprehension all the forces in illimitable space. These, then, are the natural epochs in life's education, and such the course to pursue in man's tuition. The education of the past has shot wide of this mark. How vain would be its recapitulation. Search the historic schools of philosophy. Look at the inflictions of religious and political powers.

But "the Now" is another era. The Present, in behalf of the Future, speaks with a loftier voice. With "Truth" inscribed upon her banner, and "Freedom" emblazoned on her escutcheon, Science calmly but surely advances, without arrogance, yet, with a step in her march, accelerated beyond what has ever heretofore been known. Doubtless it was this progress in learning, this aspiration for freedom of thought, this expansive spirit of Science, which gave origin and impetus to the grand fusion of the divided German States into the great unified German Empire; for Germany, however it may be a people's Empire, in Science, is Learning's Republic.—*Dr. A. B. Stout.*

37. THE PEN.—Ah, thou little implement, how much of undeserved reputation hast thou blazoned! How many noble thoughts depicted! How many philosophical reflections embodied! The tomes of history are thy biography! Without thee tradition perishes. The troubadors who despised thee are extinct, and their improvised sonnets forgotten. With thy aid, the epics and heroics of the dead poets still survive to crown their names with immortality! "The pen," said the dramatist, "is mightier than the sword;" and the dramatist has said truly. It is the architect of mind that molds its language into form, and frescoes it with the word-limning of the scholar. It rescues, preserves, transmits, and fixes its subject like the granite base, for

the building of a structure of fame. It stimulates the prosperity of states, and secures the triumph of diplomacy. Heroes depend upon it for their ovations. To literature it is the galleon, with flowing sails—freighted with intellectual treasures. The down-hearted take courage from the fearlessness of its strictures, and tyrants tremble at its power. This is thy eulogy, my companion, and my friend. Plucked though thou be from an ignoble wing, the Damacus steel can make no deeper or surer incision. The sword has no such panegyric. The phrase, "It destroys," is at once its history and its epitaph—and for the record of even this brief sentence, it is indebted to thee. Yes, thou art much greater than the sword; and so let the thesis and the antithesis of thy measurement go together.—*William Bausman.*

38. PHYSICAL AND MENTAL PLEASURES. — The purely animal pleasures are adapted, evidently, by their narrowness of range, to this little span of life—hardly is there variety enough in them to go around the threescore-years-and-ten. Who, as he has sat down to his table, has not felt how monotonous and drear a life of a thousand years would be, with the same dull round of beef, pork, mutton or venison? Who has not sympathized with me, when, long suffering man that I am, my temper gave way at the seventh reception of the saddle of lamb in the same week? "Madame," I exclaimed, "it seems to me that since our bridal we have had nothing but saddle; if this goes on, I shall be like the horse that Motherwell's pathetic verse has immortal-

ized. He went forth in the morning, and in the evening,

> "Home came the saddle,
> But he nevermore."

Who has not congratulated himself on his mortality, as he has taken up his cup, filled with the perpetual water, with its slight modification of wine, spirits, tea and coffee, and the more palatable of these, prohibited by that stern old moralist, the gout, who stands like a country schoolmaster, ready to mark the slightest deviation from soberness, with his inevitable chalk? Yet, from this limited variety, Heliogabalus must sup, and Lucullus dine; and the culinary genius of a Vatel, who kills himself because a soup is too little seasoned, must compose the dishes by which the sated palate of a Louis Fifteenth is stimulated.

But for the mind—for the intellect—for the investigation of truth—here, variety is boundless. Here, desire finds ever new changing food to gratify it. Here, as bodily faculties fail, and physical pleasures pall, the pleasures of the mind constantly increase in variety and intensity. In the gratification of these desires, we find our minds created for no finite bound of time, but everything is graduated on an eternal scale.—*John B. Felton.*

39. THE REPUBLIC OF LETTERS.—The world had better lose all other arts combined than to forget its A B Cs. Sometimes I have thought of them as of twenty-six soldiers that set out to conquer the world—that A was an archer, and B was a bugler, and C was a corporal,

and D was a drummer, and E was an ensign, and F was a fifer, and G was a gunner, down to Z, who was a zouave; and these twenty-six drill-sergeants have subdued the kingdoms of the earth and air, taken possession of the realms of thought, and founded a republic of which the wise and noble of all time are citizens and contemporaries, where their is neither death nor forgetfulness—the imperial Republic of Letters.

Again I have thought of them as of a telegraphic cable, laid beneath the waters of time, safe from disturbing storm and tempest—so short, the child's primer will contain it; so long, it connects the remotest ages with the present, and will stretch to the last syllable of recorded time.—*Newton Booth.*

40. STYLE.—No two styles are alike. They all differ, and must differ, because souls differ. Style is to the matter as atmosphere is to the landscape. Hang a New Hampshire air over Florence, and is it Florence still? Strip the style of De Quincey of its matter, and it is like taking the sound out of a grove of pines. No one has yet sounded this mystery of a style—how it is that an item penned by one man is common-place, and the same fact stated by another is a rifle-shot or a revelation; how words locked up in a form can contrive to tip a wink; how a paragraph may drip with the honey of love; how a phrase may be full of infinite suggestion; how a page may be as gorgeous as a tropical landscape, or as cool as a December day in New England. The style is the man. There are elements in Hawthorne very repulsive, yet there is something

infinitely attractive in his purest artistic English, of a higher order than Irving's. Whittier's style is like a trumpet sounding through his Quaker soul. There is an advancing melody in all of Longfellow's handiwork, from the sweet sixteen air of his "Songs of Life," to the chapters of "Hiawatha," and his latest poem.— *Thomas Starr King.*

THE PRESS.

41. Observe how the outer bark of the madrono and eucalyptus, with the coming of every summer, bursts, rolls up and falls to the ground, as so much rubbish. That is a sign of expanding life. A great deal of newspaper rubbish to-day is a sign of growth. The outer rind and bark of things fall to the ground by that vital force which is continually developing a larger and nobler life in the community. No man will hereafter go to the head of this profession without fair scholarship, a wide range of observation, a large capacity to deal in a general way with human affairs, and that keen insight which catches the spirit and essence of this ongoing life. Most difficult of all. is a certain power of statement, which no school can teach, and without which the highest plane of the journalist cannot be reached. Your long story will not be heard. The world is waiting for the man of condensation. Tell it in few words. If you can master this eclecticism of thought and statement, I know of no more promising field for a young man to-day than that of journalism; if one cannot, the potato-field, in a season of blight, is quite as promising.

The newspaper has been gradually encroaching on the domain of literature. It has absorbed monthly magazines, or forced publishers to resort to illustrations— to a sort of picture-book literature for grown-up children. It has driven the lumbering quarterlies into smaller fields, and diminished their relative importance. The average citizen craves the news from a journal having the very dew of the morning and of the evening upon it. It must come to him damp and limp, bringing whatever is best at the smallest possible cost. The newspaper is the herald of the new era. Its errand must be swift, its statements compact, and its thought eclectic and comprehensive.

Three thousand years ago, one of the grand old prophets spoke mysteriously of the "living spirit of the wheels." Was it other than the modern newspaper thrown off by the pulsing of the great cylinder press? But observe, that through yonder Golden Gate, which the sun and the stars and the lamps of men glorify day and night, the devil-fish comes sailing up, and is not concerned whether his accursed *tentacula* close around saint or sinner. Is not that the fullest symbol of a public journal conducted by ignorant and unscrupulous men? Rather would you not choose, as a more fitting symbol of the ideal journal, one of the small globules of quicksilver, which you shall find on any of these encircling hills, so powerless to draw to it an atom of filth or rubbish, but ever attracting the smallest particle of incorruptible silver and gold?—*W. C. Bartlett.*

42. The liberty of the press is the highest safeguard to all free government. Ours could not exist without it. It is with us, nay, with all men, like a great, exulting, and abounding river. It is fed by the dews of heaven, which distil their sweetest drops to form it. It gushes from the rill, as it breaks from the deep caverns of the earth. It is fed by a thousand affluents that dash from the mountain top to separate again into a thousand bounteous and irrigating rills around. On its broad bosom it bears a thousand barks. There genius spreads its purpling sail. There poetry dips its silver oar. There art, invention, discovery, science, morality, religion, may safely and securely float. It wanders through every land. It is a genial, cordial source of thought and inspiration wherever it touches, whatever it surrounds. Upon its borders there grows every flower of grace and every fruit of truth. I do not deny that that river sometimes oversteps its bounds. I do not deny that that river sometimes becomes a dangerous torrent, and destroys towns and cities upon its banks; but I say that without it, civilization, humanity, government, all that makes society itself, would disappear, and the world would return to its ancient barbarism. If that were to be possible, or thought possible for a moment, the fine conception of the great poet would be realized. Civilization itself would roll the wheel of its car backward for two thousand years. If that were so, it would be true that

> "As one by one, in dread Medea's train,
> Star after star fades off th' etherial train,

> Thus at her fell approach and secret might,
> Art after art goes out, and all is night.
> Philosophy, that leaned on heaven before,
> Sinks to her second cause, and is no more.
> Religion, blushing, veils her sacred fires,
> And, unawares, morality expires."
>
> *—Gen. E. D. Baker.*

43. A free press is the great economic illuminator of politics, art, religion, society, morals. It is at once the tribunal of taste and the articulator of thought. It is the handmaid of enterprise, the fortress of order, the mailed, invincible right arm of freedom. Like commerce, it gives health and vigor to the life of nations; like commerce, its sceptre stretches from the shining temples of the Orient to the swimming forests of the Thames. Its shrouds stiffen and its white sheets fill with the winged gales of progress. Beating foaming paths through conquered waters; dashing on steeds of fire along iron ways; harnessing the elements to its chariot; reading the mysteries of the magnet; making a courier of the lightning, and guides of the sun and stars, it courses its way in majesty, in power and in glory, over a boundless sea of possibilities, and its dominion broadens with every swell of the tide. Its many-colored fabric is meshed and fashioned in the beneficent loom of cumulative emprise, and its shifting shuttle marks the pace of the world's advance.

—Thomas Fitch.

BOOKS.

44. The distance of a star, the age of a planet, the flow of history, the stories of biography, the vast spaces of fiction, the richest music—such knowledge and such society may be ours through only a hundred books, with a cultivated taste; such an altar may be erected in our memories, and such stately worshipers may face it as Mrs. Browning describes in her "Vision of the Poets." The title to such a treasure is a taste for literature—reading with rigid selection and exclusion—reading for an end.—*Thomas Starr King.*

---

45. There are books of fact, books of life, and books of art. The first include the sciences; the second embrace history, biography, and all the inquiries into the substance of truth, as regards man's proper conduct and destiny; the third comprehend verse and prose, not discussing abstract truth, but poetry, the drama, and the world of fiction. A very few books of the first class suffice to start us. But it is a shame that we know so little of what constitute the glory and shadow of the world we live in—geology, which opens the cellar department, and astronomy, which interprets the dome of our habitation. The leisure evenings of a single winter, devoted to the Connections of Mrs. Somerville, to Lyell's geology, Mitchell's stump speech concerning astronomy, Nicoll, Buckland and Gardner would so stretch the mind that one could not go to business in the morning, nor look out at night a moment at the sky, without feeling what grand preparation had been made for his living. A traveler assures us that in a certain part of Liberia the people can see the satellites of Jupiter. The great heads of the Celestial chapters that hint the immensity of the Zodiac should always be in memory's sight: and half a dozen fascinating books tell it all—books to be read not as water is poured out on the sand, but as it is fed to the roots of a tree. The deepest facts of thirty centuries may all be sounded in the leisure of a winter, so, at least, that a twilight intelligence concerning them shall illuminate the memory. The distance of a star, the age of a planet, the flow of history, the stores of biography, the vast spaces of fiction, the richest music,—such knowledge and such society may be ours through only a hundred books.—*Thomas Starr King.*

46. All healthy souls love the society of trees; and the mold which feeds them is a better fertilizer of thought than the mold of many books. You see the marks of fires which have swept along these mountain sides; here and there the trunk of a redwood has been streaked by a tongue of flame, but the tree wears its crown of eternal green. It is only the dry sticks and rubbish which are burned up, to make more room for the giants, while many noxious reptiles have been driven back to their holes. Possibly the wood-ticks number some millions less, but very little that is worth saving is consumed.

We shall need a regenerating fire some day, to do for books what is done for forests. May it be a hot one when it comes. Let no dry sticks nor vermin escape. Ninety in every hundred books which have got into our libraries within the last half century will fail to enlighten the world until there is one good, honest conflagration. Something might be gained from the ashes of these barren books; therefore, pile on the rubbish, and use the poker freely. Let not the fire go out until some cords of doggerel, concocted in the name of poetry, have been added thereto. The giants will survive the flames; but punk-wood, moths, and wood-ticks will all be gone.—*W. C. Bartlett.*

47. Guard against desultory reading. Yellow-backed literature, poorly-edited newspapers, and bad books, are the curse of this age. A pyramid of such trash is only fit to be burned for a light to read a good author by. Read but few books, and learn them well, and affectionate caressing will take the place of formal visits. We have too many books; some of them are a curse to the student, and contemptible to the critic. Select a few of the best writers of ancient and modern times, and read them well, and your mind will be the best disciplined. Under the wear and tear of life, men usually forget much that they have read, because their memories are confused by irregular exercises; while on the other hand, organized and disciplined memories cling tenaciously to their stock of knowledge. When old age begins to assail the mind, legions of acquirements stretch themselves along the battlements of memory, and dispute every inch of its advance; and if there is a moment in man's eventful life when he is

grand, it is when the treasures of the mind are seen resisting, with unrelenting vigor, the encroachments of decay, as the pulses cease in the dead body. It is told of Rumford that he proposed a scheme to the Elector of Bavaria, by which he might economize in feeding his soldiers. His plan was small rations, and thorough mastication, holding that a crumb, well masticated, was better than a pone untoothed; so, a page, digested, is better than a book devoured.—*Rev. T. H. B. Anderson.*

48. There are friendships, regal and rare, begotten of communion with authors. Books smile, salute and fraternize; they are courteous, urbane, affable, friendly or fascinating, as the case may be. Their companionship is no myth or figure of speech. Their friendships have emancipated many a soul from the thraldom of chill and bitter loneliness. So viewed, how sacred is the mission of every printed page! Shall it carry health and healing, courage and sustenance, light and melody, hope and aspiration, or shall fever, or apathy and gloom distil and drop from its noxious sentiments and fancies? Happy they who, with voice or pen, lubricate the jarring wheels of life by kindly interchange of generous word or helpful message! Who, casting aside, with generous gesture, all selfish considerations, awaken by the concords of their own nature, music in the hearts of others, until even the prodigal in his exile shall catch the far-off melody of the home song, and turn repentant footsteps thither.

—*Sarah B. Cooper.*

49. Literature may not create character, but it may influence it. Genius, a gift often connected with erratic fire, is ever hungry for intellectual food; but because it has in some cases floated down to depravity, is no argument against indulging the mental appetite. Libraries open up to us the delicate organization of the brain, the wonderful formation of the eye, and their perfect connection, the strange meaning of the hand, the scratches upon the rocks, the marvellous beauties of the flower, the mysteries of the ocean, the land, the clouds, the air, and the starry wonders of the heavens.—*Thomas Starr King.*

50. The supreme privilege and advantage that society to-day enjoys over society five hundred years ago, is privilege of reading printed literature. Our education is conducted now by the first masters. At college we may have had third-rate professors, but for a dollar or two we have at our homes for professors, Faraday to teach us chemistry, Goodrich to instruct us in Greek, Owen to read us anatomy, Schlegel to explain the philosophy of literature, and Macaulay and Guizot to read lectures on the laws and heroes of the last eighteen hundred years. Books are our university, spirits are our teachers. All other helps to our cultivation are feeble in comparison. To hundreds of thousands of people the sky contains less of celestial phenomena than an ordinary treatise on astronomy. Thousands of men might skirt and tramp the whole region of the Alps and Andes, with eyes open too, and still know less of mountains than one learns on quietly reading the fourth vol-

ume of Ruskin's "Modern Painters." Though they roamed with the Wandering Jew, and heard him by the month detail the course of human events, they would know, when the last session ended, less than on reading Montesqueu's "Compend of Laws." The evenings of a single week in reading Agassiz' "Essay on Classification," would discover, to a man of average brain, more knowledge of natural history than if, two by two, all the animals of the globe were to parade before him, and when that pageantry had vanished, he were led into a museum where every species of the myriads that compose the crust of the globe were labelled and displayed.

Plato disparaged books in comparison with conversation. They, said he, stand like paintings—in just one form and attitude—and to all questioning return one and the self-same answer. Now, it is by the grace of printing that we know this saying of Plato. True, to know a *man* is greater than to know the greatest book, yet no talk with Milton would have evoked a "Paradise Lost," or a "Comus" from his lips. Had you called on Newton, you might possibly have heard him fret— surely you would have heard him talk no chapter of queries as to Optics. If you had called on Shakespeare, he might have treated you to as much sack as you could stagger under, but in the interview he would not take you up to the region of his "Cassio" and "Imogene," or down into the depths of his feelings. Call on Thackery at London, and he might entertain you with his grievances at the hands of the member of his club who sketched his broken nose rather too distinctly, but he would not sketch you a Major Pendennis. Dickens, on your call, would be too busy with domestic troubles to unveil that tropical sea of fancy, out of which the Agnes of "David Copperfield" sprung, like a new Aphrodite, from the foam. It would be pleasant to see truly reported an hour's free conversation with Thomas DeQuincey, but for six bits, one may purchase his "Suspiria de Profundis," and sink into the music of the prose, the most rich and masterly since Hooker. You often may have thought what a privilege it had been to live in the time of Jesus; to hear the sermon on the Mount fall from his lips, to be present when he unsealed the eyes of Bartimeus, to be on the mount of transfiguration with him.

Have you considered that by virtue of two hundred duodecimo pages, we all know more of him than any dweller in Canaan, any Gallilean, any citizen of Jerusalem could have known? Did they who saw but fragments of his life, see more than we, whose scope embraces all of it, from the birth in Bethlehem to the ascent from Olives? Was the privilege of the woman of Samaria, who heard him but briefly, and misunderstood most of what she heard, greater, or was your privilege greater—you who hear what he said at the well, who stand within ear-shot of the talk with Nicodemus at night—who hear all the parables, the promises, and see him blessing little children? Let every one who has a taste for books and music thank God that he was not born earlier. Books *and* music! Books *are* music. What was *knowing* Beethoven compared with *hearing* the Andante of the Fifth Symphony?

If the organ should grow conscious, and could play of itself, what music would it chatter, beside the flood of harmonies that pour out from it at some vesper-time when the player to its keys hints the thoughts that some master has set down in books! It is the chatter of genius that we get from their conversation—the earnest, noble, stirring thoughts we find when we sit down alone to their books.

Books constitute not an Empire, but a Republic of Letters. Every steam engine looks to me like a snorting democrat. "Take a good stare at me, I'm one of the b'hoys," he seems to say. He seeks to know north and south, the east and west. He chafes and frets to be running on an excursion past Great Salt Lake, making Brigham Young fain to stop his ears at the screeching, with the great U. S. Mail on board, and the old flag gleaming through the clouds that issue from the smoke-pipe, with no star lacking. Genius may be miserly, and hoard its wealth, but the steam cylinder press screams: "In any nook or corner of the land, is there a desirable thing, let me know, and you will get it cheap at your door to-morrow. It will give you public documents, fish out forgotten knowledge, rummage private correspondence, ransack creation." The man of genius may be mean, and wall himself in from the world, but the palace of truth that he rears in his seclusion is as free to the world as St. Peter's is to the poorest believer in Rome. The ticket of the Alphabet admits you and me.

When we come to talk more practically about books, we see the necessity of selection. In the Imperial

Library at Paris (the largest in the world) there are eight hundred thousand volumes, and one hundred thousand MSS. "Art is long, and time is fleeting." The reader who had begun in the reign of King David to read them, if stopped only on Sundays, to rest his eyes and go to church, would be now about checking the the last volume. [Spoken A. D. 1861. EDITOR.] Set side by side single copies of all the books that have been printed, and they would reach from the vineyards of Los Angeles to the snowy beard of Mount Shasta. No man lives, no German professor, the juices of whose body are a decoction in equal parts of tobacco-juice and beer, can in all his life-time read through half the volumes of our San Francisco Mercantile Library. A hundred volumes might be selected which, if read with care, during their leisure hours, would make men of average brains better informed than are any, except those who are supereminent in knowledge—not the sort of specific knowledge which the great German grammarian in Latin craved, who, in his old age, remarked that if he were to live life over again, he would devote himself entirely to the dative case.—*Thomas Starr King.*

NOVELS.

51. A nation's literature is an index to its civilization. The cultivation of the study of letters and a high standard of literary work are consequent upon the refinement of a people. But may not literature bear to its country some more important relation than that

of a result? May it not be a great element of national growth? I believe that literature is more than a mere accompaniment of culture, that it is a prime factor in advancing culture, that it is a proximate cause of civilization, that it may be made a mighty motor in redeeming from sluggishness and immorality the populace when taught to read.

For a clear understanding of the idea I desire to illustrate, consider civilization to mean the moral and social status of a people, and literature to be their learning and their fancy preserved in writing. It is the part that the latter may take in raising the moral and social condition of our country, that we are to regard. The department of literature that is most popular, and, therefore, is most influential for good or for ill, that most earnestly requires the watchfulness of those who admire purity of character among us, is the department devoted to fiction. Of the various writings of the fictitious school, the novel may be most easily turned to civilizing humanity, or to pandering to its most degraded tastes. The novel reflects the experiences, the aims, the heroism of mankind; it holds up for sympathy, emulation or contempt, acts and emotions. All the manifold springs of human conduct find a source in the novel. With the novel the power lies of spreading abroad a sense of honor and of creating respect for true dignity of manhood. It should be life reproduced, not a mere representation of the phases of existence, but an impressive guide to the grand purpose of living.

Romances are more numerous and of a better order in Great Britain than in America. Some authors believe that the supremacy of the English, in this respect, is due to their systematized life. One writer, of observant mind, has assigned as a reason, to which he attached much importance, that in England almost the only readers of this style of literature, are found among those who have little to do, the nobility and the wealthy classes; that their leisure makes them exacting, and their exactions must be heeded to insure the author's success. If this fact has a tendency to perfect the novel, it is entirely independent of the subject matter, upon the treatment of which its lasting merit and power for usefulness must depend.

The subject matter is the life portrayed. What are the distinctive marks of life in this republic, drawn by lapse of time? The cardinal principle of a democracy is original equality. We all start equals. It is curious, but true, that we claim equality with those only who have risen above us. The endeavor to justify our pretentions, is one of the causes of the restlessness peculiar to us. I do not say that envy and jealousy actuate us in seeking to better ourselves. I prefer to think that it is the possibility of improvement made manifest by the achievements of others, that impels us onward. But whatever may be the inner motive, the outward fact still remains. Democratic life is essentially nervous, active, a chapter of successes and reverses. It is with the details of this life our novelist must deal. Do they not present to him a more inviting prospect than the regulated order of an aristocratic existence?

Yet this is the life of which DeTocqueville has said that "nothing conceivable is so petty, so insipid, so crowded with paltry interests, in a word, so anti-poetic." Anti-poetic let it be; earnestness, not poetry, is the essential of a novel. But petty, insipid, or crowded with paltry interests, never. Here the individual lives, here man stands an architect of fame, with his doubts, with his passions, in the presence of rare prosperities, or inconceivable wretchedness. These things are real, they are to be the theme of the novelist's story. In them each one will find something to touch his sympathy, to make him quiver with hope and exultation, or bow in pity. 'Tis sympathy moulds the most of us, and especially the lowly. To that the novelist's creations must appeal that we may be made to glow with the inspiration of manly purpose and with the possibilities born of resolve.

It may be asked why the novel has not made its appearance ere now, if it is so well adapted to our system of living. In struggling to exist we have had no time to look about us and write; and during our literary infancy, the literature of a mother-tongue was in its prime. Moreover, a literature can not be built in a day. The true novel can be drawn only by one of keen observation and wide sympathies. I speak of sympathies, not alone towards one's fellow man, but towards one's fellow people. Until some national feeling has sprung from the formative existence of a people, until national traits are developed, in which we all take pride, we can expect no one to possess that subtle kinship with men at large, requisite to the broad effective purpose of the democratic novel.

Our country has been pushed to conclusive heights,

from which she is gradually settling to that stable condition of society from which alone prosperity can be evolved. The trials of past years have brought us to realize that this is not a grand speculation, but that steady, honest exertion is the only precursor of success. The presence of schools in all quarters familiarizes the popular mind with letters. We have had the fancies of Poe, the natural beauties of Bryant and Longfellow, the sunny mysteries of Hawthorne, and the sturdy purity of Emerson. The time has come in our literary and historic growth for the advent of the novelist. It is for those who feel an interest in perpetuating the romance of life and of meaning, to aid the author in his self-imposed task of writing for the advancement of his race, not with the sole motive of enriching himself. He is but an artist who introduces into his living pictures realistic forms. The age is propitious to the growth of strong men and women, whom the writer must copy. The novel, true to the world it represents, must have much in common with humanity; to be true to itself, it must turn this common bond to the enobling of humanity. The quality of his models and the nature of their thoughts and utterances determine the value of the novelist's gift to his country. It is for the people to furnish him with the originals of those instructive lives which he is to present as an example to his readers. And especially is it the duty of those whose studies bring them in contact with the grandest characters of reality and of fancy, by their private lives and public opinions, to aid in fostering a general spirit of rectitude, that the novelist may be filled with it, and that all may know it and feel its nearness when breathed upon from the pages of the opened volume.

Then can the novel be made to elevate the moral and social status of a people. The companion of man's quiet hours, it will speak to him in his retirement, when he can commune with the thoughts its teachings may inspire. It will address him without the hollow sounding of words to mock the solemnity of what it says. It will have influence with him because it confides in him privately and makes him the unobserved discoverer of his own failings. It will benefit him, because his better nature, despite him, will be moved by all that is beautiful in its passages. In the presence of the true novel, man will grow erect in truth, as the human form, before the figure of the Apollo, unconsciously straightens itself.—*F. P. Deering.*

---

82. The monthly reports of our Mercantile Library show that novels are as ten to one of all other books read in San Francisco. It is useless to quarrel with the fact, as it is absurd to quarrel with any primal passion of our being. It is folly to cast a slight on novels, as a class. They constitute no *class*, but a mighty branch of literature. The English and the German novels differ as much as a leopard and a hippopotamus. We are wont to speak of English books, pervaded with the Byronic spirit, as the "Satanic" in literature; but as Milton's fiend could find no bottom to the abyss, so from far deeper gulfs than any English novel ever opened, we see arising in the worst French fictions the

presiding demon of all cancerous corruptions, issuing with appropriate odor, as if from Swedenborg's excrementitious hell.

Bow with me to the genius of woman in modern times, as I call the roll of the choicer works of English fiction. Such creativeness as is displayed in the production of Charlotte Bronte and the author of "Adam Bede," has never been known since Shakespeare. A library of novels is like a gallery of pictures. One man saunters through it to see what the pictures are about; another sits down before the master-pieces to see what the artist was about; the first sees the paint, the second the paintings. It were well if every person, after reading a novel, were compelled to write out or to think out the axis of the whole. Suppose some reading circle should, at each session, agree to settle on one point, as to show which of all Scott's works exhibits the greater power; why Charles Reade, who is so brilliant in description, so graphic and unapproachable in dialogue, can't sketch a character but he must degrade both it and himself; why the close of Bulwer's "What Will He Do with It?" is such an unmitigated piece of snobbery that we feel inclined to pitch book and author to some place where types are never set up more; why Mrs. Stowe's "Dred," the first volume of which is far the grandest she ever wrote, in the second volume runs so swiftly to weakness and failure; why the drawing of Rochester stands out more surprisingly on the tenth reading than on the first; why the author of "Adam Bede" is the most eminent of living novelists; why each character on her page stands out like a star against the blue sky in a clear, cool night; why the "Mill on the Floss," though still an able and more bitter book, is inferior to "Adam Bede." I have often thought that perhaps the pulpit could do no better service than to discourse faithfully, once a quarter, on the health or disease of the novel that all the ladies in the parish are just reading. It is often remarked that when his eyes are shut, man cannot, except by the odor, distinguish between beef and mutton, elk and pork. It is no reason why he should not with his eyes open.—*Thomas Starr King.*

EDUCATION A SUPREME DUTY.

58. Minds there are, even in this generation, which outvalue, even according to the most material standard, all the rest of the world besides. The mind of Ericsson was a fortification to the whole coast of our country in time of war—of more worth than walls of earth and stone, on which millions have been spent. The active brain of Field set itself to work, and Europe and America became joined together by an imperishable band, like gigantic Siamese twins. The mind of Garibaldi is Italy's hope of liberty. The mind of Bismarck contains Germany, centralized and united; and the traveller, whether he visits the cities or plains of Europe, or ascends the Alps, still finds himself surrounned and enveloped by the intellect of Napoleon—dead half a century ago.

Minds there have been of so much service to the generation in which they have lived, that all the united efforts of the millions of their contemporaries were valueless beside a single reflection or a single thought of theirs; and minds like these may be in the neglected children around you. Is it sound mercantile sense to waste a product so rich and so accessible? To use a California figure of speech, every child has in his intellect a mine of pay-ore; every one of these mines will richly pay the working, and sometimes it will happen to you to strike a pocket of intellect that will enrich your whole generation. When such a mind is lost, for want of cultivation, who can tell how far the advance of the world is retarded? Who can say to what point of progress the world would not have attained, had it had the benefit of the well developed powers of those minds which, for want of education, have been utterly lost? How grand, how swelling might have been the song of the mute, inglorious Milton! How vast the discoveries of some Newton, who has lived his ignoble life with as little reflection as the clod he worked! Who can tell but that minds have lived which, if educated, would have told us the secret of the birth of the sun and stars, would trace life to its source, would have opened new worlds to our gaze, and brought old ones nearer together. I tremble as I think how near the world was to losing altogether, for want of education, those glorious creations of Shakespeare. The accident that gave him to us makes us thrill, as it shows us how many stately ships of intellect, which have left their native haven freighted to the water's edge with the cargo for which mankind is famishing, have gone down in the darkness and the night. And if you wish that future generations should know and bless your name, link it to that of our great University, from whose loins shall spring the manly, stalwart minds, of which you will be the fathers. Aye, this is true fame—fame that lives.—*John B. Felton.*

III.

THE CONDUCT OF LIFE.

PART III.

THE CONDUCT OF LIFE.

54. DUTY.—God demands greatness of us all, and not goodness merely. There is not a person so humble or so feebly gifted that the call is not to him or to her. If we have few qualities that can influence, and but a narrow sphere to fill, still we have ourselves to develop and ourselves to rule.—*Thomas Starr King.*

55. OUT of the confusion and chaos of every unfinished, toilsome life, an Eden may arise; light may break forth. It is a vigilant regard for little things that begets happiness.—*Sarah B. Cooper.*

56. BE PROMPT in your attention to professional calls, even if they be not urgent, and be punctual in the fulfilment of your appointments. He who delays until evening that which he can and should do in the morning, carries a burden on his mind all day for nothing. It is prompt performance which enables some persons to accomplish so much more than others.
—*Dr. G. A. Shurtleff.*

57. Life should bear good fruits. — Let me hope, for myself and us all, that when we have filled out our allotted space in this world; when we are attended by weeping friends, for the purpose of removing us to our last resting place, that it shall not be said of us that we have lived without purpose, but that we have gathered friends in the days of our manhood; that we have left fruits to bloom when we have departed.
—*Gen E. D. Baker.*

58. The seasons when men are used as pipes through which to blow the Divine breath of Inspiration are short and soon pass away. Extraordinary success always brings extraordinary trials in its brilliant train, which must be met with becoming fortitude.
—*Thomas Starr King.*

59. In mirth, men are sincere; in sobriety, hypocritical. It is behind the mask of gravity that the fantastic tricks which turn and overturn society are performed. Joy is more dificult to counterfeit than sorrow. We may cloud the sun with smoked glass, but we cannot dissipate the clouds with any telescope of human invention.—*Hubert H. Bancroft.*

60. A premium on heels involves a discount on heads, while a fair valuation of each argues a healthy condition.—*Sarah B Cooper.*

61. We must be not merely tolerant, but liberal; and must advance by the law, not of antagonism, but of sympathy. I do not care to acknowledge as my friend the man who is so narrow as to see nothing good outside of his own little clique, or party, or faith, or race. I honor the cosmopolitan soul.—*Rev. W. E. Ijams.*

62. EACH MAN is a divinely chartered corporation, to trade with all nature, to enrich himself by commerce with all that he can reach by any of his arts; and the moment that this commerce ceases, he begins to die, though he may continue to exist until all of his stored stock is exhausted.—*Thos. Starr King.*

63. THE JUSTICE of heaven is sure and unerring. Success may for a season gild a wicked career, and throw around it a false and illusive lustre, yet, just as certain as night follows the day, retribution waits on crime. This lesson is repeated in the pages of universal history, is inscribed on the tombs of dead nations, and written in the experience of all living men.
—*Frank Tilford.*

64. A DANDY lives not by the clock or almanac, but from one neck-tie to another; a fashionable woman lives from one wrinkle to another; the politician from one Presidential election to another; the epicure from one turtle to another; the philosopher from the perception of one principle to the dawning of another; the philanthropist from one act of charity to another.—*Thos. Starr King.*

65. ON MANY a tomb-stone, where it is written, "Here lies so-and-so, aged seventy years," the true inscription would read, "In memory of a soul who, in

seventy years, lived about five minutes, and that was when he first found himself in love."—*Thos. Starr King.*

66. THE POPULAR notion that a ghost is a soul unclothed with a body, is fallacious; your genuine ghost is a body not vitalized by a soul—a mere machine for converting potatoes and meat into the straps and cords of humanity. The soulless rich man is mere bank paper that adversity tears to shreds. The soulless office-holder is a bladder, which at the expiration of his term of office, is pricked, collapses, and tumbles out of sight. But the dandy is entitled to stand in the first rank of ghosts—he is a whiskered essence, an organized perfume.—*Thomas Starr King.*

67. IF MEN, like balloons, could be allowed to cut loose from their bodies, and soar to their actual planes of culture and refinement, we should see some slinking into the alleys, some rising into the brilliant sphere of truth, some to the rosy realms of beauty, and some, the selected band, into the serene light of charity. It would be Dante's dream again, the series of circles narrowing down to the base of the pit, and circling with broader sweeps as it rose to the joys of Paradise.—*Thomas Starr King.*

68. NOBLE LIVES.—Life is a channel of intellectual power. Living is a fine art. Great lives mean more than the noblest orations. There are facts in Fenelon's life that are as rich and eloquent as any passages in Shakespeare. Washington was not felt as a literary power; his words do not kindle us; but his

faith, decision, fortitude did, and continue to. His soul lived a literature more terrible to despotism than ever was penned. We speak of Cordelia as one of Shakespeare's noblest creations, and Jennie Deans as one of Scott's richest productions. Is it any less to be a Jennie Deans or a Cordelia than to write her? Is the echo more musical than the notes that create it, or the mirror's reflection more perfect than the face that is mirrored? If lives could take outward shape, we would learn better to appreciate their nobleness.—*Thos. Starr King.*

69. LET YOUR THOUGHTS GROW. To have beautiful thoughts and suppress them, is like destroying the seed of a beautiful flower. How can you have beautiful flowers unless you cultivate and cherish them? First preparing the soil best adapted to their growth, and selecting those seeds and plants you wish to cultivate, you are well repaid in beholding them spring up to greet you with beauty and fragrance. How pleasant to see homes decorated with those beautiful teachers of love and purity. We can cultivate beautiful thoughts by expressing such as come to us, freely, without stint, without thinking how they will please. When you have a train of beautiful thoughts, be free to speak them. It may incline other minds to new ideas which may draw forth the language of harmony. How many beautiful ideas have been suppressed, for fear of what the world might say—thoughts that flow like living waters from the soul.—*M. J. Upham.*

70. MARRIAGE.—As we advance in life the cordage of kindred breaks away. Aged parents drop in the tomb. We know that sisterly fondness, once so earnest, has diverged into a new channel. A husband and offspring have become the reservoirs of her affections. The stern cares of life have long ago solidified a brother's heart. It is true we form occasional and strong frienships with the outer world. They are rarely more, however, than companionable and mental affinites. They ruffle a little the heart's surface, while the emotional depths are undisturbed. There is no union and interblending of soul. In intercourse with his fellows, the most communicative man reserves a host of sensations and delicate sensibilities. They are the soft murmurings and dulcet warblings from the better and purer portions of our nature. He feels it profanation to breathe them into the ear of his dearest male friend. A mother could sympathize with them. But since she is dead they have sunk back upon the heart. They will lie there forever, unless a loved and confiding wife attract them forth by the magnetism of a tender and unsullied soul. This unfettered intercommunion of feeling is the joy and rivet of the marriage tie. If falsehood or concealment intervene on either side, a calamitous future will inevitably ensue.
—*James G. Howard.*

71. THE TREE of Love should have generous opportunity to strike root, and gather strength and tenacity, before the scion of marriage be grafted into it; for, though shoot and stock become thereafter one tree, yet

the graft determines the kind of fruit it shall bear. Before marriage, Love's Inquisition should be keen-eyed, keen-eared, almost relentless, in ferreting out the subtle faults and weaknesses of the enthroned ideal; but, after leaving the bridal altar, all inquisitorial robes should be thrown aside at once and forever, and upon the threshold of every new day should be inscribed the gentle suggestion:

> Be to each fault a little blind;
> Be to each failing wondrous kind.

—*Sarah B. Cooper.*

72. OH, CHARITY! friend of the fatherless, comforter of the afflicted! On thy starry brow is stamped the sign-manual of the Omnipotent; on thy cheek is the smile of heaven; in thy hand is the balsam of life. Child of Christianity! in the quivering light that gleams in thy glowing features are seen the emblems of Peace, Joy and Hope! Thy softening and refining influence is divinely sweeter on the great ocean of life, as it ebbs and flows and beats upon the shores of time, than silvery notes of music, which, rippling o'er the moonlight waves, ravish the delighted soul of man. What pleasant memories dost thou not bring with thee! What delicate flowers dost thou not plant in our hearts! What poems, filled with jeweled thoughts, dost thou not whisper in our ears! The pencil that would paint thy beauties should be tipped with the hues of heaven!—*Francis J. Sullivan.*

73. THERE IS no such thing as infallible affection. From the apples of discord is expressed the vinegar of

hate; while from the sweet grapes of kindness is distilled the wine of perpetual bliss.—*Sarah B. Cooper.*

74. HE WHO composes a poem that has no burning thought in it, is not so original as he who constructs an original mouse-trap. The one, is a mere artisan in words, the other an original thinker in wire and wood.
—*Thomas Starr King.*

75. THERE ARE two classes of men not to be intimidated. They are the saints who believe in the "Love of God," and the savants who believe in the "Reign of Law." These two ideas are profoundly tanquilizing.
—*Rev. W. E. Ijams.*

76. DISCIPLINE.—

Upon the patient earth
A thousand tempests beat,
To call to life the flowers
That make her glad and sweet.

So, o'er the human heart
The countless griefs that roll
But wake immortal joy
To bloom within the soul.
—*Ina D. Coolbrith.*

77. "THE BRAVE DAYS OF OLD."—Ah! talk not to me of living then and now. We plume ourselves, poor fools, and say that more of life is given us in the short space we run it through, than was vouchsafed our ancestors a century or two ago in thrice the time. Puffed up by our mechanical contrivances which we call science, our parcelling out of earth and ores which we call wealth, our libertinism which we call liberty; casting ourselves adrift from our faith, calling in question the wisdom and goodness of our Maker, throwing off all law but the law of lust, all affection save avarice and epicurism, we plunge headlong into some pandemonium, or cast ourselves under some soul-crushing juggernaut of progress, and call it life, and boast one year of such demoniacal existence to be worth ten, aye a hundred, of the old-time sort.—*Hubert H. Bancroft.*

78. GREATNESS.—Our tests of the kinds of greatness are apt to be defective. The world rates that highest which upheaves, demolishes and ruins. If at night some constellation should suddenly begin to shoot out Bengal lights, flooding the heavens with pyrotechnics, the world would look up and admire the power of the Deity; or if some filibustering comet should kindle the azure with flame, men would say, "Now, at last, we see the finger of God," who never have noticed the imperial bounty of the sun, and never have admired its unerring punctuality. Happily the center of our solar system has no French ambition for display. If the sober sun would, it could spill over sheets of flame from its full caldron that would wrap in fire the fifty globes that it is now content to robe with verdure and paint in flowers. It is a magnificent symbol of character.—*Thos. Starr King.*

79. THE HUMAN TEMPLE.—In physiology, and in the history of diseases, you have the image or sym-

bol of every spiritual distemper. Whoever deals with the body of man, deals with the highest production of the Divine Architect. The Almighty published more wisdom in the humblest man that walks the earth than in the solar system. Man is the crown of matter. Whoever lives has stepped into a body provided for him, with no less evidences of divine skill than were displayed when He harnessed the forces of the universe. Every pain that afflicts the body has its symbol in the sins that infest the soul; and in the rhetoric of diseases you can describe every trouble of the body or of the State; there is no single bad element of the body but can be represented by analogy of the body's sicknesses; no noble grace of body, purity of blood, elasticity of heart, or bounding pulse, but has its analogue in the soul. Does not God, by these crossing lines, write that Godliness and health are inseparably connected?

—*Thos. Starr King.*

80. MORALITY ESSENTIAL TO SUCCESS.—A pure, irreproachable moral character is essential to success. It is the impregnable fortress in all the battles of life. It affords a sense of security in every difficulty, and inspires a feeling of courage, self-appreciation and reliance, when one's progress is assailed by the viler elements of human nature. To how many distinguished personages, to how many public fiduciaries, to how many great financial and business institutions might I point, that, for want of a proper moral ground-work and solidity, have fallen in the very hour of apparent triumph! No hereditary prestige, no admitted social

elevation, no wealth which silver and gold represent, no literary accomplishments, no scientifiic attainments, no endowment of genius, no learning and skill, nor all these combined, can secure the greatest possible professional success without an integrity of character which shall command public confidence and become a recognized, steadfast quality of the individual. The distinctions of public and professional life only serve to make moral defects, if they exist, more conspicuous, as the polish of the lapidary on precious stones selected for display, reveals the unsightly flaws which obscurity had concealed.—*Dr. G. A. Shurtleff.*

81. THE INFLUENCE OF EXAMPLE.—The will within us is the ultimate fact of consciousness; yet how little have the best of us, in acquirements, in position, even in character, that may be credited entirely to ourselves! How much to the influences that have moulded us! Who is there, wise, learned, discreet, or strong, who might not, were he to trace the inner history of his life, turn like the stoic Emperor to give thanks to the gods, that by this one and that one, and here and there, good examples have been set him, noble thoughts have reached him, and happy influences have touched to bless him? Who is there that with his eyes about him has reached the meridian of life, who has not sometimes echoed the thought of the pious Englishman as the criminal passed to the gallows: "But for the grace of God, there go I."—*Henry George.*

82. ALL DOES NOT FADE.—The few legends of

the deluge, of God's providence, and a few facts in the writings of the Babylonian historian relating to the kingdom of the Supreme, have adhered to the keel of history, while the waves of time have submerged almost all beside. The acts of many great warriors, the philosophic speculations of sages, the big scrolls that recorded them, have all perished. What a lesson for us all! Earthly grandeur and wisdom are mean and rotten things. But acts of love to God and beneficence to our race are glorious and eternal. The tear of tenderness in a child's eye glitters in the sight of angels in heaven, though the most brilliant words and deeds of the great appear at that distance opaque and valueless. The secret sigh of a penitent heart is heard by those that surround the majestic throne of the Almighty, though the huzzas of the multitude, and the explosions of the field of victory only shake the dull atmosphere above us, and soon die away to be heard no more.

—*Rev. William Speer.*

83. CONFLICT ETERNAL. — You enter a great factory. You are dazed and deafened by the din and clangor of the whirling machinery, by the buzz of the spindles, the clatter of the loom, the hiss of the belting, the grinding of the shafts, the churning of the engine. The noise is disagreeable, but it must be tolerated. The noise is the audible expression, the articulate speech of work. Stop the noise and you stop the work. And in this seething sea of sounds—this delirium of noisy tumult, this dizzy maze of flashing wheels and flying shuttles—there is perfect order. The

engineer, with hand on the throttle of the engine, sends the pulsing life through every vein and fibre of the vast organism. Every cog and wheel and shaft and spindle becomes animate. A mass of raw material is caught up in the eddy of this maelstrom of mechanism, and comes out the perfected fabric.

So in human society, the tumult and agitation, the strife and warfare, are but the clatter of the machinery, the grinding of the mills of God. Stop the racket in the world's great work-shop, and you stop its work. Close the valve of the engine of human progress, and the silence of death comes over the world. And so the conflict will go on—must go on and on forever. As long as there is growth there will be agitation. As long as there is development there will be friction. While seasons roll, the sun shines and the stars glitter, there will be the clash of warring forces. While man toils, suffers and aspires, some vexed question will distract human counsels, some knotty problem will perplex the soul of the student. When all the questions have been settled, when all the problems have been solved, when the world's great debating school has closed its doors forever, this round earth on which we strut our brief, unquiet existence, will have been remanded to the limbo of dead planets.

I cannot think even of heaven as a place of eternal, unvarying rest—a place where saints in glory fold their hands in immortal listlessness; where cherubim and seraphim, angels and archangels pass endless æons of ennuied existence, divorced from care and work. I prefer to think of it as a place of ceaseless but blissful activity, where every faculty of mind and soul finds range for expansion and incentive to growth; where ransomed spirits shall compete for angelic honors, and press forward toward the shining summits of the celestial Zion.—*Samuel Williams.*

84. THE SUSPICIOUS MAN.—There is not in the world a being more unfit to live in it, to perform the ordinary business of life, to be successful in his undertakings, than the man who has become suspicious and distrustful, who attributes bad motives to acts, and who has lost confidence in his kind. He may have arrived at his conclusions from a bitter experience; he may have been often cheated and deceived; where he had a right to look for gratitude he may have encountered the cold look or averted eye; but he has made the mistake of taking the exception for the rule. He has reasoned to himself: " Because I have been deceived, man is deceitful; because I have had kindness met with ingratitude, man is ungrateful." What is there for such a man to do but to hang himself, like Timon? He is but one; he can not be ubiquitous; he cannot always wake and watch. How can such a man perform large enterprises, where trust in many men is necessary? How can he be a General, where he must rely upon the highest qualities in thousands? How can he be a statesman, when he has no faith that the laws he frames have any goodness in human nature to address themselves to? How can he perform the slightest task, when he stands on the outside of the great army of mankind, ready to run at the first sign of approach?

Man is so constituted that even the intellect of Napoleon can only work through the brains and arms of others. What a feeble creature Napoleon would have been if he had not had implicit reliance on man! Instead of such a man drawing strength and inspiration from others, their strength would be to him a constant menace; their enthusiasm would be hypocrisy; their faces, lighted into radiance at his approach, would be the mask to hide the malicious, envious and deceitful heart. And what is the condition of him who has failed to gain the sympathy of his fellow-men! How his own sympathies wither and fade, deprived of the sunlight that beams from other human hearts! What fruit or flower grows on the barren waste of his intellect? The voice of the heart becomes mute when it speaks to ears that are deaf.—*John B. Felton.*

85. MEN OF THOUGHT AND MEN OF ACTION.—The man of action is as necessary to the man of thought, as woman is, as a wife, to man; and either one of them is a dead failure without the other. The man of action takes up the living thoughts that have been born from the brain of the thinker, and turns them into useful things. Whence all our commerce, whence all our practical science? First the great thinker, then the practical man. I admire the heroism of the men of action. I admire the bravery of the men who will take a system of thought and put it into life, and make it redound to the glory of man. We have glorious heroes in commerce, in agriculture, and in all the practical affairs of life, and not one is less glorious than the

other. The man of action and the man of thought stand as twin-brothers—I would say as man and wife. Whence the vitality, the astonishing vitality of this country? Why is it that in the old lands people are so sluggish? It is because the men of action and the men of thought are kept apart, and hence there are no children, and the man of action providing no seed, runs to seed, and the man of thought piles up thought that has to wait probably hundreds of years for some man of action to get hold of it. Here the University and the primary school stand hand in hand; and it will be to our glory, showing us that in the future the man of thought and the man of action will strike hands; and the very fact that on festive occasions we recognize this relationship, is proof that in future we are to have a magnificent race—the thinker appreciating the man of action, and the latter in return appreciating the thinker.—*Rev. J. H. C. Bonte.*

86. TRUTH.—Make all the deductions which you will, and see how much there is left in the nature of man to sympathize with and to love. There is truth—lying and deceit are but the exceptions—and the basest man yields to a temptation and swerves from his own innate desire when he lies. The great protection which the law gives to property and life is based on the general devotion to truth in men. In the oath administered to the witness, when on the story he tells hangs a human life, the law, with an experience taught it by ages of reflection on human nature, appeals, and appeals with safety, to two great attributes common to all

men—reverence and truth. Relying on man's love to God and his devotion to truth, the juryman renders his verdict and the judge pronounces sentence. Every commercial principle and every rule of business take for granted and assume the existence of original high moral qualities in man. The credit system, the promissory note, the trust in a man's word, the relation of servant to master, of principal to his agent, all have lying at their base the principle that when no eye is on him, when temptation to do wrong holds out impunity, when interest conflicts with duty, man's nature is worthy of trust. Analyze every custom of society, and you will find that it implies and assumes that human nature is good, true, kind, benevolent, full of reverence and love. The desire to please, love of your kind, benevolence, charity, all lie at the base of the evening party, the social dinner, the elaborate toilet, the courteous salutation, the curtsy and bow.—*John B. Felton.*

HOME.

87. Never is there a home like the home of our youth; never such sunshine as that which makes shadows for us to play in; never such air as that which swells our little breasts and gives our happy hearts free expression; never such water as the laughing, dancing streamlet in which we wade through silvery bubblings over glittering pebbles; never such music as the robin's roundelay and the swallow's twittering that wakes us in the morning; the tinkling of the cow-bells; the rustling of the vines over the window; the chirrup of the cricket; and the striking of the old house-clock, that tells our task is done. The home of our childhood, once abandoned, is forever lost. It may have been a hut, standing on the ugliest patch of ground the earth affords, yet so wrapt round the heart is it, so charged with youthful imagery is every stick and stone of it, that the gilded castle, built in after life, with all the rare and costly furnishings that art and ingenuity can afford, is but an empty barn beside it.—*Hubert H. Bancroft.*

88. EVERY MAN should own his home, if he can. That philosophy which tells a man to drift on over the ocean of this uncertain life without a home of his own, is wrong. The man who does not own his home is like a ship out on the open sea, at the hazards of the storm. The man who owns his home is like a ship that has arrived in port and moored in a safe harbor. One man should no more be content to live in another man's house, if he can build one of his own, than one bird should annually take the risk of hatching in another bird's nest; and for my own part, I would rather be able to own a cottage than to hire a palace. I often see men eager to effect an insurance upon their lives, and this is well—it is right. But the man who owns his home has effected an insurance upon his happiness and the happiness of his family—which is as much to him, if his mind be right, as his own, and constitutes his own. I have seen the homes of the people in foreign lands; I have heard them talk of their condition and lot in life, and this is the main theme of thought with mankind

everywhere. As I listened to them I discovered how it is that the Switzer, in his hut in the Alps, where the limit of vegetation is reached and the winter storm howls and rages around him, is happier than the Italian tenant on the beautiful plains of Lombardy, amidst the bloom and fragrance of perpetual summer. It is the consciousness of the ownership of a home which, no matter how the storm rages, nobody can take from him, and which he can make happy in spite of the storm. I would say to every man, buy a home if you can, and own it. If a windfall has come to you, buy a home with it. If you have laid up enough by toil, buy a home. If you have made money in stocks, buy a home. Do not let anybody tempt you to put all your winnings back into the pool. Take out enough to buy a home, and buy it. Put the rest back if you will. Gamble on it if you must, but buy the home first. Buy it and sell it not. Then the roses that bloom there are yours. The jessamine and clematis that climb upon the porch belong to you. You have planted them and seen them grow. When you are at work upon them you are working for yourselves and not for others. If children be there, then there are flowers within the house and without.—*George Barstow.*

88. A MAN'S HOUSE should, and to some extent must, express the tendencies of his vital breath. Beasts burrow into the earth for physical shelter. A man, besides shelter, will hint his greatness in the size of his house, his love of floral beauty in his carpets, his sweet memory of the water-courses in his service pipes, his

bounty in his larder and his table. The pictures on his wall, the books on his shelves, his furniture, will have some strong vascular ties to himself, and we ought no more to be able to step out of our own houses into other men's, and feel at home there, than we can step out of our skins into other people's. Like crabs and lobsters, which sweat their shells, our houses should be the true representations of ourselves, and should distinctly show the shape of our tasks and methods of life.—*Thomas Starr King.*

CHILDHOOD.

90. The cost and care of properly feeding, clothing and educating the child, are but the price which nature demands of parents for the incomparable treasure of the child's love, honor and obedience; and just in proportion to the extent to which parents neglect or refuse to pay this price, in precisely the same proportion do they forfeit their right to this inestimable boon.
—*Zachary Montgomery.*

91. SADDEST of all the sights of a great city, such as San Francisco, are the little children of the quarters where poverty hides—saddest and most menacing. Pinched, ragged, and dirty; yet in every little body a human soul; in every little body latent powers that might strengthen and bless society, but that may only awake to curse, perhaps to destroy. Is it not waste and worse? Out of just such human stuff have grown earth's best and noblest; and out of such waste have come the

vermin that have gnawed, and the wolves that have destroyed—they who have shattered the domes of national glory, and in palace walls given the wild dog a lair. Who shall wrap himself up and say, "This is not my affair?"—*Henry George.*

92. WE SHOULD begin laboring in the regions of mind, muscle, or morals, almost simultaneous with being. We prune the tree soon after it lifts its head above the earth's surface. The trunk is straightened, the extra branches taken off, the soil around well stirred; and then we look forward to the time when we can sit down in its deep shade to contemplate the goodness of the great Creator. So in the physical development of the child, care and attention are requisite; wholesome food, warm clothing, fresh air, and a proper amount of exercise. Unless these things are provided, the child will be a dwarf, unable to meet and cope single-handed with the thousand ills that flesh is heir to. The rule will hold good in the domain of mind. The parent must direct the mind of the child into the right channel; give it books to study that refine and elevate. There is a kind of literature extant that is pernicious, more poisonous than the exhalations of a stagnant pool, spreading a blight over the whole being. Books that a few years ago were not seen in parlors, are now sold publicly, and read publicly by public men. Encyclopedist and pamphleteer, philosopher and demagogue, are uniting in giving organic structure and form to unbelief and impiety, elevating them to the dignity of sciences, and reducing blasphemy to a trade. You must begin

with a child before its habits of life and modes of thought are fixed; then, if it goes astray, you have cleared your own skirts. To God it stands or falls.
—*Rev. T. H. B. Anderson.*

93. Asceticism.—Did it ever strike you that the asceticism of the middle ages, which retreated to the cloister, content with water-cresses as a bill of fare, was never very fruitful of high and profound discourse? The philosopher who goes up into the clouds to talk, and prefers gruel to trout before going, makes an epigastric mistake. He has taken in the wrong ballast, and has omitted some good phosphorescent material which might have created a nimbus around his head as he entered the clouds. A mistake in the gastric region leads to errors of the head and heart. I do not know whether there is any ground of hope for a people who have not only invented cast-iron stoves, but have invented "help" in the form of the she-Titans, who have made a wholesome dinner well-nigh impossible. Death on a pale horse is poetical enough; but death in the black stove of many a kitchen is terribly realistic.
—*W. C. Bartlett.*

94. Friendship.—There is no solitude like soul-solitude. Often, to be with the multitude is to be most alone; and sometimes to be most alone is to enjoy the divinest fellowship. Friendship, the most sacred and helpful, do not make contact an absolute condition of communion or ministration. The subtle law of sympathy defies distance; it permits conscious fellowship in the most abject isolation, and evokes the glad and grateful reponse, "Yet, I am not alone."

To make a full and perfect friendship, there must be harmony of taste, feeling, and aspiration; the natures must match each other in every faculty. There is such a thing as kinship in this regard, apart from that tenderer sentiment which we call love. In the selection of its companionships, the soul is dominated by laws all its own. In every perfect friendship there is honest comradeship of spirit—a kind of duality in unity. The surest guarantees for the perpetuity and advantage of such friendships are education, culture, character and moral worth.

Friendship of the noblest type is love refined of its dross, clarified and etherialized ; it is unselfish, constant, self-forgetting. In its devotion it disdains itself, and in calamity it is inflexible as adamant.—*Sarah B. Cooper.*

95. SYMPATHY.—It was my happiness once to know one of the most gifted of his race, and to be admitted to his intimate society. He had been, in his earlier life and in matured manhood, a lawyer; but the glory of our great countryman, Washington Allston, turned him aside from the studies of his youth, and in his later life he gave himself up to Art. The noise and bustle of the court, and the angry contention of men jostling each other in their struggle for antagonistic interests, had disgusted him with his fellow-men, and so he betook himself to a beautiful solitary crag'

overlooking the ocean. I saw him there. He showed me his paintings. He made me see and feel his beautiful conceptions. I expressed my gratification. "Sir," said he, "I perceive that you do not understand painting, but your voice is full of sympathy. Often the farmers come to see me, and they say, as they look upon my historical paintings, on which I have labored night and day, waking and sleeping and in dreams, to infuse life and beauty of ideal expression and grace, 'why don't you paint portraits?' Paint portraits! Why, the idea makes me shudder. But then it comes to me in my solitude, clothed in a human voice, and that a kind one." "Yes," he continued, "this solitary life is a chimera. We must see in living faces that we have the sympathy of our fellow-men. Our ears must drink in their voices. Mine thirst to hear them."

Sympathy! Why, it is when all men sympathize with us that we are conscious of high powers, that courage and hope nerve our arms. It is in the crowd, amid the roaring of cannons and the crash of wrecks, but with the human voice in his ears, with its answering hurrah, that the sailor cheers, as the waves stifle his utterance, and his dying hands hold above the water the still lighted torch, in a last effort to fire the gun. Put the same sailor alone on the solitary raft, in the dark night, upon the ocean, and the wind, as it hurls the billows over him, bears away but a moan of agony and despair.

The real martyrdom of Marie Antoinette was not when the ax of the guillotine, in mercy, descended. It came when in that long march to death she saw in faces upturned in scorn, in balconies crowded with men and women deriding her agony, in the stern features of the soldiers around, that her kind had excluded her from the pale of sympathy. From a window above her, as she passes on, a mother holds out her child, and the little one stretches forth its arms, as motioning to embrace the dying queen. At that proof that one kind heart, in all that crowd, feels for her, the rigid features relax, the set teeth open, the brow unbends, and the stony eyes fill with tears.

But while a man must have the sympathy of his kind as a necessity of his nature, to gratify a want imperious as hunger, if he wishes to be great, to have a profound respect for himself, to be constantly urged forward to heroic deeds, he must have the close, intimate, particular sympathy of some class or order. He must be united to men by some peculiar bond of a common absorbing interest, by the tie of some cause to which they all consecrate their lives, by the union in a kindred pursuit, to which their minds and hearts are wedded.

In this order must be his life; to it his affections must be given; for each member of it he must cultivate respect, and from it he must receive his distinction and reward. Is he covetous of power? He must first labor to make his order powerful, and then strive to wield himself its united force. Is he anxious for the respect, love, and admiration of his fellow-man? He must find it in the respect, love, and admiration of the members of his own profession, who are capable of appreciating him; and the feeling inspired among his fellows, will extend itself to the world. Nor is there any danger that, thus merged in a class, he will lose his individuality. On the contrary, by contact with others, engaged in the same pursuit, by generous rivalry, by the stimulus which comes from great deeds or discoveries of kindred spirits, his own peculiar power is excited, developed and felt.—*John B. Felton.*

96. WHAT LIFE MAY BE.—To widen the comprehension of what life may be, consider that every mind is a digestive system, every sense an avenue or duct for transmitting nutriment from without to the living spirit. Beauty is as real a thing as a flower. The corn and market stuffs of the Saco valley go into the granaries and cellars of but few people, but there are many men out of New England who carry the slopes and ridges, the rocky tendons and the dome itself of Mount Washington with them wherever they go. They coil their strength around the White Hills as an anaconda coils about a goat; they crush and swallow and digest them, and live on their riotous strength ever. What Creation has poured of its spirit into its deep notches and gorges, they drink in as a bee sips honey from a flower; they sip of it in the honey of art. Look at a great picture. What is its substance? The canvas? the pigments that may be scraped off and weighed in scales? Or is it the suggestion that the painter has made to bloom above his group of colored patches, or the saintly expression that he has laid on with his oils? What nature means is more than what nature physically is. Indeed, we are born to live royally; to feed on sliced stars and strata, and the philosophy of Bacon.—*Thos. Starr King.*

RICHES.

97. I do not know which is the more deplorable, to be without money or to be its slave. Money is the best of servants, but the worst of masters. As a servant it is the "open-sesame" to all the world, the master-key to all energies, the passport to all hearts; as a master it is a very demon, warping the judgment, searing the conscience and fossilizing the affections. Wrapped by their cold silence in an eternal slumber deep as that of Endymion, its victims are lost to the beauties of earth and the glories of heaven. Give me the independence, the command of myself, of my time, my talents, my opportunities, that wealth alone can give, but save me from the gluttony of greed, the fetters of avarice, the blind beastliness and intellectual degradation engendered by an inordinate heaping up of riches.
—*Hubert H. Bancroft.*

98. If an aroma could always attend gold, telling you by what ways it was gained, whether it was inherited or won by enterprise and skill; and, if earned, whether in ways useful or hurtful to the higher interests of society, there would be no danger of a mean worship of money. If a man's silver and gold told the story at once whether he earned it in making sugar or turning it into liquor—in raising wheat or in speculating on it—in weaving honest cloth or in weaving shoddy, in putting soles to shoes for soldiers or sham ones which prove that the makers hadn't any souls at all, money would carry its own judgment with it. In any such system the farmer need not fear to let the aroma of *his* money expend itself far and wide. It would sprinkle the wholesomeness of winds, the perfume of blossoms, the strengthening smell of the soil, the fragrance of noblest uses.—*Thomas Starr King.*

99. Next to being born blind or deaf, or otherwise deformed or diseased, the greatest calamity that can happen one is to be born rich. The greatest calamity because the chances are a hundred to one that beside becoming thereby enervated in body and mind, such a person, when pricked by those adversities which sooner or later befall, will collapse like a blown bladder. To the wealthy of California was given one blessing forever denied their children: they were born poor. They were the makers of their money; and that in itself implies some merit, howsoever unintellectual they were satisfied to remain, or howsoever immoral some of them may have become in the operation. For a passionate pursuit of wealth is in itself debasing; but passionate progress does not long continue. Not less than the unsuccessful, the fortunate in the struggle for wealth die; and the generation following, lacking, peradventure, the money grasping mania, will not exert itself as did its predecessor; and to every five hundred who ride their father's fast horses to the devil, perhaps five turn their attention to ennobling pastimes.

In all the abnormities of moral economy, there is none so productive of evil as this laborless inheriting of the results of labor. Nature nowhere so debases herself. The vine-root and the flower-stalk, workers

with the invisible in life's great laboratory, in the subtle chemistry of their own secret processes, bring from the same soil, each after its kind, painted and perfumed fruits and flowers, which are nature's riches. Wealth is the product of labor applied to natural objects, and to be of benefit to the individual, must grow from his own personal efforts. The productiveness of a community depends upon the knowledge and skill of its members, rather than upon natural advantages.
—*Hubert H. Bancroft.*

100. WHAT IS IT, canst thou tell me, Oh Sidi Ben Hamet, richest of the rich men of Blida! What magic influence is there in money, that it should change the very features of humanity—that it should beget twinkling little eyes without a visible spark of the divine essence in them, and noses that seem made to smell out the flaws of a sinful and erring world, that the owners may run up a debit against their fellow creatures—that it should give to the human countenance, intended by nature to be the mirror of the soul, such a low, groveling and imperturbable character—dry up the warm blood of youth, stifle the noblest emotions implanted in the human breast, and leave but the shell of a man to mock at all that is noble, generous and manly? I hold the doctrine that, as the features of herdsmen become in the course of time like those of the animals with whom they associate, and married couples grow to resemble each other in a long series of years, so bankers and brokers begin after a while to acquire a metallic expression and a jingling tone of voice, as if permeated

with the sheen and essence of precious metals. A gentleman of my acquaintance in the banking business has a habit, when asked for a small loan, of opening his eyes and looking straight at you without the slightest perceptible emotion of sympathy or pity. His eyes, on occasions of this kind, bear a wonderful resemblance to a couple of new ten-cent pieces—they stare at you with a quiet assurance, but give no indication of anything hopeful or pleasant. But what matters it, O, Sidi Ben Hamet, thou richest of the rich men of Blida, that you have plenty of money and I but little? Have you not plenty of trouble too? Do you never get the toothache? Are you exempt from gout? Can you eat more, drink more, or wear more than just enough, without paying the penalty in some shape or other? Do you think your wealth makes you independent? On the contrary don't you feel that it makes you a slave? You have to stay by your coffers and your speculations, or you lose your all.

You know no such thing as freedom. It is only happy-go-lucky vagabonds like us who can claim to be independent. We can travel and see the world; we can skim the cream of it, and leave you thin milk. Having nothing to lose, we have no concern about losing it. A little satisfies us—just to be able to keep moving, seeing, hearing and enjoying; whilst with you, O Sidi! the rust of care is ever gnawing upon your vitals. When you have accumulated millions, what will you do with it? As you brought nothing into this world, so you can take nothing out of it. What a pleasant subject of contemplation it must be for a rich man on his death-bed! A life worn out in toil and trouble to accumulate money; a dozen graceless scamps waiting impatiently for him to die, that they may pounce upon it and spend it gloriously! Well, the Creator has balanced these things very nicely, it must be admitted. Neither you nor I could do it so well, with all our boasted sagacity, O sublime and potent Sidi Ben Hamet!—*J. Ross Browne.*

INTEMPERANCE.

101. IT IS the grand overruling factor in insanity. It is the great Nihilist and Communistic agitator of rational government. The whisky-bottle is the gun used to force the ballot box, and its aim threatens to be fatal to that order which is Heaven's first law.

—*Dr. A. B. Stout.*

102. Intemperance is the great recruiting officer in the employment of ignorance, crime, insanity and suicide. The system of manufacturing drunkards is fostered by by our man-making and man-ruling government with care, energy and efficiency, as though a thoroughly manufactured and confirmed drunkard were worth to society two ordinary sober men. But no sooner is the human reduced to and below the grade of the brute, than the law and courts and executive officers treat him accordingly.—*Gen. John A. Collins.*

103. IN THE brawny chest and muscular arm of Heenan there is *something* to admire, something more

than a mere idea; and the battering of a human face is
not half so disfiguring as the traces of one night's
orgie. Milton has made fiends interesting, and even
murder and war may be woven into readable shape;
but there is no room in Milton's Pandemonium for so
debased a form as the Demon of Alcohol—a form more
sickening than the grizzly terror which guarded the
portal of Hell!—*Thomas Starr King.*

104.—

" DRUNK, your Honor," the officer said;
" Drunk in the street, sir "—She raised her head.
A lingering trace of the olden grace
Still softened the lines of her woe-worn face;
Unkempt and tangled her rich brown hair;
Yet with all the furrows and stains of care—
The years of anguish, and sin, and despair,
The child of the city was passing fair.

The ripe, red mouth with lips compressed,
The rise and fall of the heaving breast,
The taper fingers, so dimpled and small,
Crumple the fringe of the tattered shawl,
As she stands in her place at the officer's call.
She seems good and fair; seems tender and sweet—
This fallen woman, found drunk in the street.

Does the hand that once smoothed the ripple and wave
Of that golden hair, lie still in its grave?
Are the lips that once pressed those red lips to their own,
Dead to the pain of their smothered moan?

Has the voice that chimed with the lisping prayer,
No accent of hope for the lost one there,
Bearing her burden of shame and despair?

Drunk in the street—in the gutter found,
From a passionate longing to crush and drown
The soul of the woman she might have been;
To throw off the weight of a fearful dream,
And awake again in the home hard by—
The wooded mountain that touched the sky,
To pause awhile on the path to school,
And catch in the depths of the limpid pool,
Under the willow shade, green and cool—
A dimpled face and a laughing eye,
And the pleasant words of the passers by.

Ye men with mothers, and sisters and wives,
Have ye no care for these women's lives?
Must they starve for the comfort ye never speak?
Must they ever be sinful and erring and weak—
Tottering onward with weary feet,
Stained in the gutters and drunk in the street?
—*Daniel O'Connell.*

105. THE VICE OF SMOKING.—Of the three methods of using tobacco, that of smoking has insinuated itself most extensively among the youth of this country, and is the most hurtful use that can be made of the weed. Tobacco, employed in this way, being drawn in by the breath, conveys its poisonous influences to every part of the lungs.' There the noxious fluid is absorbed in the minute spongy air cells, and has time

to exert its pernicious influence on the blood—not vitalizing, but vitiating it. The blood imbibes the stimulant narcotic and circulates it through the whole system. It produces, in consequence, a febrile action in persons of delicate habits, where there is tendency to weakness and the tubercular deposit in the lungs. The debility of these organs, consequent on the use of tobacco, must favor these deposits, and thus the seeds of consumption are sown. This practice impairs the taste, lessens the appetite, and weakens the power of the stomach greatly. The prevalence of a craving thirst among smokers can be traced to its action on the lungs, because the nicotine is there, instead of in the stomach. The liquors that are drank do not alleviate the thirst, but rather aggravate it. It is time medical testimony was turned to this point, and the great danger pointed out that threatens to make us a nation of Sybarites and pigmies. The use of tobacco disturbs the regular pulsation of the heart. Tobacco users are thus hourly in danger, and often suddenly fall dead. The habit weakens the mind, enfeebles the memory, paralyzes the will, produces morbid irritability, diseases the imagination, deadens the moral sensibilities, and is continually an assault and battery on the nervous system, the intellect and the soul.—*Dr. R. H. McDonald.*

LABOR.

106. If the world owes you a living, why does it not owe a living to every one? And if to every one, by the sweat of whose brow should that living be made? The world owes no one a living.—*A. S. Hallidie.*

107. RESULTS DIE; agencies are eternal. Merit lies not in possession, but in capability. In measuring a man, the wise ask not what has he, but what can he do? If labor is not better than the reward, then life is a sad failure; for, after a life time of labor, of all that we acquire, we can carry nothing with us out of the world.—*Hubert H. Bancroft.*

108. AS NATURE'S laws are immutable, and work is nature's law, the law of work is immutable. Philosophers talk of success and its conditions. Success has no condition but one, that is work. Honest, well-directed effort is as sure to succeed as the swelling rivulet is sure to find for itself a channel. Let the young man take heart, have patience, and persevere, laboring not as in the presence of a task-master, whom to defraud of time or faithfulness were a gain; but remembering that every good deed is done for himself, and makes him stronger, healthier, wiser, nobler, whether performed in the dark or in the broad light of open day.—*H. H. Bancroft.*

109. MAN'S PRIMAL home was the abode of all loveliness. The heavens were his roof, and never was any so curiously ceiled and painted; the earth was his floor, and never was any so richly inlaid; the shadow of the trees was his retirement, under them were his dining rooms, and never were any so finely hung. The air was balmy and loaded with fragrance; there was no gloomy back-ground to the picture, and a long perspective of coming happiness stretched before him. Here, amid this scene of beauty, aisled above and pillared about, he was to live, to love and *labor*. If our protoparents, with the light of immortality streaming through every avenue of their souls, were called upon to labor, then we may rest assured the great Author of our being intended we should toil with our head, heart and hands.

In the objective world we see a thousand things that prompt us to action. The grass grows; the flowers bloom; the oak expands; the rivers run; and the stars shine forever. In life, the pulsations of the heart never cease; and I have often thought man should draw a lesson of labor from this emblem of our energy. It is the Creator's drum beat, the reveille, arousing mind and muscle to enter upon the march of life.—*Rev. T. H. B. Anderson.*

110. THE HUMAN mind once urged in activity is as nervous as the waters of the ocean. Like those waters, its purity and strength lie in constant motion. If it stagnates, rank smells arise and filthy animalculæ swarm. It becomes an effervescing pool, breeding corruption and mental infusoria. The sole remedy to melancholy with intelligent persons is constant employment of the mind. A big grief will sometimes dash upon the soul as a Switzer avalanche. It racks and tears it with its absorbing magnitude and weight. Divert the mind by employment, and the stupendous grief melts away like that avalanche beneath a vernal sun. When a new fit of melancholy seizes you, betake yourself to

labor and you will endow it with wings. It will fly away. Jefferson and the elder Adams led tumultuous and earnest lives. They were immersed from childhood in most arduous toil. They both died merry old men, because philosophical thought succeeded the throes of political labor. They baptized till their death in the font of continuous toil. The baptism dispelled the impurities of melancholy. Bonaparte, in his latter days, moped and mused in idleness. He died the most wretched of men. He should have written his life and not droned it into the dull ears of others. Benton was found busy when smote by the Great Reaper. Youth and prime struggle for a season of rest. It is the maddest of fallacies. The very struggle ingrains habits that, in pause, will produce misery and death. It is no wonder, in this view of the subject, that an affluent and unavaricious man pursues the game of accumulation until the undertaker bundles his old body into the cemetery. The fiend of melancholy would overtake him in a rustic villa and retirement. His repose and happiness are in labor. Every organ of his body is in fierce labor. Even in dream-land the mind, rudderless, toils away.—*James G. Howard.*

111. MAN, THE individual, is in himself a force, an independent force; and the earth has just so many forces as it numbers living, thinking, acting men; for even in this day of unexampled effort, many exist who do not live; many are sentient who do not think; many concern themselves with manifold affairs who do not act. Beforetime, men were thought for by their rulers,

and thus became mere agents of a despot's will; now, in the general heritage of independence, man has discerned his right, nay, his divine prerogative, of thinking for himself. No longer moping in the thrall of tyranny, or reft of the free franchise of opinion, he has risen into the full stature of his manhood, realized the magnitude of his capacity, and in that knowledge verified the true nobility of labor; of labor in its highest form; the union of the physical and mental, labor of the sinewy arm, labor of the burning brain. He whose vocation is mechanical, is prompted to employ his hours of leisure in the cultivation of the mind; he whose pursuits are mental, to invigorate his frame by frequent action. And thus while mind and body act, react upon each other with reciprocal intensity, man, the lord of creation, though "fallen from his high estate," without a fetter on his tireless wing, is rising higher, higher, in his flight towards the stars.—*Joseph W. Winans.*

112. UNTIL THE horizon of our intelligence uplifts and opens into a clearer Beyond, let the Here and Now chiefly occupy our thoughts.

Here and now, I say, then, it is in work itself, rather than in the accomplished result, that the true benefit of labor lies. We have been wrongly taught; nor is this the only instance wherein our teachers need instructing.

Of all laws that environ us, and they are legion, not one is more palpable than that by the exercise of organs and faculties alone they develop.

In this, science, philosophy, religion, and common sense agree. It is the pivot upon which all progress turns, the central principle alike in universal evolution and in individual development. Organs and organisms improve according to use. The blacksmith does not acquire strength to swing his hammer by running foot races; nor does the logician become proficient in subtle reasoning by counting money or selling bacon. Bind a limb, and it withers; put out one eye, and the other performs the work of two. Mind and muscle alike grow, improve, acquire strength and elasticity, only by exercise. Little is expected of the man who, in youth, was never sent to school, or required to work. So obvious is this that it is hardly worth discussing; and yet this fact proved, all is proved.—*H. H. Bancroft.*

113. BEFORE LABOR in itself ceases to be beneficial, the whole economy of nature must change. The inherent energy of man is significant of his laborious destiny. So nature groans under redundant energy, with here and there convulsive throes. Surrounding us is a universe seeking rest. . This seeking is the normal condition of affairs; for rest only brings a desire for fresh activity. Bodies in motion labor to be quiet; bodies at rest labor to be in motion. So labor is the normal condition of man, both his will and his necessity. If he wills not to labor, necessity drives him to it; if necessity is absent, the spirit of good or the demon of evil stirs him to the accomplishment of he knows not what. Absolute rest once found, and chaos were come again. Activity is nature's rest, God's rest, and man's only rest. What is absolute repose but death?

By work the universe is, and man. Nature hinges on it; by it worlds are whirled and held in place; winds blow, and the fertilizing moisture is lifted from the ocean and dropped upon the hills; by it instinct is, and intellect is made, and soul implanted; by it grass grows, flowers bloom, and the sunbeam enters my window,— else how without work should it have come so far to greet me.

If then to labor is nature's mandate, the reward being no less certain if I obey than the punishment is sure if I fail, what folly for me to look for a miracle in my behalf, and expect to reap the finest fruit of labor, which is improvement, not wealth, never having plowed nor planted!—*H. H. Bancroft.*

CONFLICT AS AN ELEMENT OF PROGRESS.

114. Man is a fighting animal. About the first thing he does on coming into the world is to double up his fists and strike a belligerent attitude. He is never so happy as when harrying his weaker fellow, never so much at home as when in the arena of tumult. His history on earth is a little else than a record of strife and contention, of violence and bloodshed. The first born of the race was a murderer; and his descendents, from that hour to this, have followed war as a business and peace as a pastime. Indeed there seems to be a law of conflict running through all nature. We read there was once a war in Heaven, when Lucifer, son of the morning, organized a revolt against the Lord of Hosts. Everywhere, from the beginning of the world, the strong have preyed upon the weak—the powerful have crowded the feeble to the wall. The struggle for existence, by which the strongest, if not the fittest, survives, is a permanent factor throughout all organic life. Agitation, tumult, the warring of repellant forces, the clashing of alien elements, the ferment of inharmonious constituents, these seem to be the order of nature, the spur and potency of progress. Thus has the world been builded; thus has man advanced from the primitive condition to his present exalted state. Every atom of living matter, from the flower at our feet to the farthest star that glitters in the heavens, obeys this primal law. This law prevails not only in the domain of action, but in the domain of ideas. Every thought that has thrilled the world, and set the pulses of men beating with joyous ecstasy, has met a counter-thought, opposing and warring against it—a counter-current of adverse opinion. Every scheme of progress, every movement towards human advancement, every revolution in the direction of human culture, has been opposed by counter-forces, fought at every step by hostile principles, buffeted by the waves of adverse criticism; and the more vital the principle, the more thorny its path of progress; the more sacred the truth, the more persistent the opposing error. Yet when the battle is ended—when the roar of the conflict is over, it is found that the truth has survived and the error perished.

Conflict is not only a condition but a necessity of

growth. It is the vital impulse that gives to growth its brawn and vigor. There can be no growth that is steady and lasting, no growth of strong and well-knit fiber without the stimulus of resistant forces. It is the fierce baptism of fire that gives to the steel blade its temper, its keen, biting edge, its spotless lustre. The storm that uproots the feebler children of the forest, calls out the latent vigor of the oak. The weak must perish, in order that the strong may have room to grow. The feeble must succumb in the great struggle, else by the fatal inheritance of weakness, life would degenerate, species perish, and the survival of the unfittest ensue. Were the world perpetually at peace, the world would relapse to chaos.

This is the method by which nature works largely, at least in the physical universe. The grim handiwork of conflict is visible, all around us. Look at these majestic hills that bend so grandly, yet so lovingly, over this peaceful scene. What is the story *they* tell? A story of war and tumult, of titanic forces meeting in the shock of elemental battle. Over their now verdant slopes, what fierce floods have swept—around their sunlight summits, what baleful fires have played! The earthquake and the volcano, the lava and the ice flow —the seething hell of internal fires—the remorseless glacier grinding and crashing its way to the sea— upheavals of primeval tufa—convulsions, cataclysms— a wild derlirium of lawless forces struggling for ascendency.

All this time nature knew just what she was about. She worked persistently toward a definite end, to the accomplishment of a definite result. She was preparing the soil, tearing up the old roots, blowing up the old stumps, burning up the old under-brush, destroying the rubbish of an effete and useless past that had served its day and done its work, in order to make room for a higher order of material and sentient existence. She struck the plow share deep into the soil; she sent the axe crashing to the heart of the quivering tree; so that this new garden of the Lord should be so thoroughly tilled that all eyes would delight in its beauty, and all hearts be gladdened by its productiveness. And if the the heavens and the earth shook with the blows of the great husbandman, it was that golden harvests might crown these smiling slopes, that grass might grow and flowers bloom and broad spreading branches of trees give shelter to man and brute.

I have no doubt that during this bit of garden making there was a good deal of unpleasant disturbance. The noise must have been peculiarly exasperating to the original inhabitants. The splinters and rocks must have been flying about in a manner intensely trying to weak nerves. There can be no question that many a rash silurian citizen, that many an incautious plesiosaurus and too curious ichthyosaurus, who crawled out to see what the row was about, got badly hurt. Just as in our day, when there is lively work going on, the fossils who get in the way of the world's workers, come to grief.

So in the moral world. The law of conflict moves through all the tortuous mazes of human history. There is no growth without upturning of the soil.

The ground must be plowed and harrowed before the seed is sown. The wastes of nature must be reclaimed before fruitful harvests can bless the labor of the husbandman. Not only must the soil be prepared, but the refuse must be destroyed. The smoke and smutch may be disagreeable, may fill the air with noisome smells and dim the brightness of the sun, but they must be endured. The wise tiller knows that the more thorough the burning up of the waste matter, the better for the ground and the richer the harvest.

Regarded in this light, the drama of human events is no longer a chaos of incongruous incidents. It acquires unity, harmony, consistency—it moves with an almost rhythmic order. Every act and scene, every episode and incident, has a place and a purpose. What seem disorder, confusion, tumult, strife, are but manifestations of forces moving in the track of Law. They have their places; they perform their part in the economy of nature. They are normal factors in the problem of human development. Instead of being hindrances, they are spurs to progress. Instead of retarding, they assist civilization. Sometimes they appear as symptoms, giving warning of disease, indicating its nature and pointing to its seat. Sometimes they are active manifestations of growth—the riotous coursing of warm, rich blood through a healthful organism. Sometimes they act as checks on too rapid growth, repressing abnormal development—the engineer putting on the brakes to lessen the speed of the train. Sometimes, though rarely, they are merciful agents of destruction —destruction of what is unfit to live, of what should and must perish; the great gardener pulling up the weeds in order that the thrifty plant may grow and the fragrant flower bloom.

It is true, there are periods of apparent decay, periods when the world seemingly not only stops growing, but goes back—the pendulum sweeping a reversing arc toward the black void of barbarism. Sometimes an age, sometimes an era, is offerred up a sacrifice on the altar of progress—is made vicariously to suffer, that other and happier ages may grow and prosper; but even here all is not lost. In the cataclysm of the Dark Ages, when civilization disappeared and the human intellect itself seemed to perish, all was not waste and ruin. Down in the gloom of those sunless centuries forces were silently at work; the seeds of a higher civilization were slowly germinating. If the earth refused the boon of fruit and flower, was it not because the soil, exhausted by the excesses of the past, was taking a rest?

Let it be understood that nothing that is worth saving is wholly lost. Only the dross perishes, the pure gold shines with perennial lustre. From the wrecks of past systems, from the debris of dead powers and principalities, some germ of living truth, some grain of seed to fructify in other soils, is saved. The receding wave leaves some precious spoil on the strand. The Great Builder tears down, that he may build better. He demolishes the old rookeries to make room for regal structures. Ideas are indestructible as matter. A great thought never dies; once it has gone forth to the world, it moves on its shining way forever. It may seem to go out in darkness; it may disappear for ages; but it comes back, like the dove to the ark, with blessings on its wings.—*Samuel Williams.*

115. Lessons of the Hour.—

There are a few sweet lessons that to me
   Have been as fruitful isles, and hights of palm
To sailors shipwrecked on the foodless sea;
   Have been as midnight stars, as winds of balm,
As songs of birds who know the skies are near;
   And these few leaves of hope I cluster here.

First, Courage, for no grief a man may find
   But that some earlier one the same hath borne
With quiet lips, tho' all his friends were blind.
   Thro' earth's laments, and laughters, tears and scorn.
We, who now tread the floor of living days
   Must bear ourselves, nor heed men's blame nor praise.

Next, Labor, Labor—on this pivot move
   The endless forces of the living earth;
Whatever thrills with strong desire and love
   The hearts of men; all deeds of deathless worth
Were wrought by toilers—never man yet bent
   To a great task, and found his life misspent.

Last, Faith, because so often we have found
   A breath of heaven in the fragrant air,
A Love unnamed, a pulse of crystal sound,
   A waking hope when all the days were fair,
A clearer sense of growth from less to more,
   A sound of waves along an unseen shore.

Pause here to question—shall the men to come
   Have faith, and worship with a purer grace,
And stronger than ourselves? The years are dumb,
   And no clear answer falls from any place;
We shape the future—but we hardly know
   With what result, for long doubts trouble so.

Yet we hear voices, and new fervors creep
   Through all the soul from some unknown profound;
A guerdon and a promise from the deep
   Whereof all future is; it is the sound
Of armies in the distance strong and calm,
   Making the darkness melt with their heroic psalm.

It is the voice of men: we helpers here,
   Who shape the coming age as plastic clay,
Know that a mystic light is creeping near.
   The sweet world, furrowed by the flame of day,
Throbs into rosy gold, the night wears fast,
   And better men shall toil when we are past!

Yea! these, the generations yet to be,
   Shall drop their plummets down the wrinkled walls
Of dim abysses—sail the northern sea,—
   Read mystic languages in buried halls;
Or whisper through the lucid breath of stars
   In bright converse with Jupiter and Mars.
                              —*Charles H. Shinn.*

IV.

RELIGION AND THE FUTURE LIFE.

PART IV.

RELIGION AND THE FUTURE LIFE.

116. ALL GENIUS IS FRAGMENTARY. God is at once the perfect artist, the perfect poet, the perfect machinist, dramatist, moralist and sovereign—as deep and perfect in one as in another, and in each and all alike, infinitely accomplished.—*Thos. Starr King.*

117. CHRISTIANITY, by asserting and emphasizing the intrinsic, inherent and immense value of *every soul*, laid the foundation for the doctrine of Equal Rights.
—*Rev. W. E. Ijams.*

118. IT HAS taken even Christians a long time to learn the real glory of their own faith. Each new creed has marked the progress of thought, and the final creed remains to be written. We have, after 1800 years, mastered only the Alphabet of Christianity.
—*Rev. W. E. Ijams.*

119. ALONG ALL the line of ages, we see but one character who ever dared to tell all the truth of a sinning nation, and our ear catches, over the lapse of eighteen centuries, the cry that greeted his reforming voice—a nation's cry of "Crucify him!"—*Edward Tompkins.*

120. People say to me, "but St. Patrick was a Catholic." What is that to me? I only ask, what was his life? I get behind all such narrowness. What did he accomplish for his race? For my part, I look forward to beholding a grand Valhalla of the nations, in which I shall see—yonder, say Massillon; over there, John Bunyan, the Quaker; there, John Wesley; there, Blaise Pascal, a Jansenist priest; by his side, it may be, John Knox; and here, the Unitarian, Thomas Starr King. And yet, withal, I am a true Methodist.
—*Rev. Dr. Thos. Guard.*

121. The belief in God is an inevitable part of our human nature; it is born with us, it is a universal belief; we cannot be brothers without having a common father. However much a man may persuade himself that he believes there is no God, when he is confronted with his own soul, he knows and feels that God exists. If there is no God to whom we owe our common origin, what relation can exist among men?
—*John B. Felton.*

122. Emotional Religion.—Keep out of the society of sickly sentimentalists, and dreamy, morbid enthusiasts. Our friends ought to be people of good common sense, and honest and open moral principles. The religion of "Gush" is not the religion to carry us through any great crisis. Conscience, and not emotion, is what we require.—*Rev. W. E. Ijams.*

123. Decline of Orthodoxy.—The old orthodoxy is virtually dead. You can still find it in books.

It still lives in printed creeds, but it has received so broad an interpretation as to be really a new thing under the sun. Not one minister in a thousand preaches the old creeds as they were preached. The preaching is better than the creed, and let us hope that, by and by, ministers will be honest enough to change their creeds, so that preaching and creed shall be in complete and even liberal harmony.—*Rev. W. E. Ijams.*

124. HOLINESS THE END OF HUMAN LIFE.— If holiness is the beauty and perfection of the Divine Nature, surely it is also the beauty and perfection of human nature. The whole work of man on this earth is to restore or perfect the Divine image in the nature of man—in the reason of man as truth, in the heart of man as love. Now, it is the harmonious combination of all these Divine features that constitutes the beauty of the Divine image, or holiness, in man. Holiness, therefore, is the true end of human life, and every other is false.—*Prof. Jos. LeConte.*

125. FOREKNOWLEDGE OF GOD.—Man, short-sighted and finite, changes or improves his original plan, from time to time, as unforseen contingencies arise. But God, foreseeing and foreknowing the end from the beginning, every possible contingency is included and provided for in the original conception. The whole idea of that infinite work of art which we call nature, is contained in the first strokes of the Great Artist's pencil, and the ceaseless activity of the Deity is employed through infinite time only in the unfolding of the original conception. Can we conceive anything which so nobly

illustrates the all-comprehensive fore-knowledge and the immutability of the Deity?—*Prof. Joseph LeConte.*

126. THE INNER LIFE.—So many of us there are who have no majestic landscapes for the heart—no gardens in the inner life! We live on the flats, in a country which is dry, droughty, barren. We look up to no hights whence shadows fall and streams flow, singing. We have no great hopes. We have no sense of infinite guard and care. We have no sacred and cleansing fears. We have no consciousness of Divine, All-enfolding Love. We may make an outward visit to the Sierras, but there are no Yosemites in the soul.
—*Thos. Starr King.*

127. THE WORDS OF CHRIST.— History, until of late, has been mostly a record of battles, many of which had no effect upon society. But history, truly written, will show that the hinge-epoch of centuries was when no battle-sound was heard on the earth—when in Galilee one was uttering sentiments in a language now nowhere spoken, never deigning to write a line, but entrusting to the air his words. The Cæsar whose servant ordained the crucifixion—all the Cæsars—are dust; but *His words* live yet, the substantial agents of civilization, the pillars of our welfare, the hope of the race.—*Thomas Starr King.*

128. THE CHURCH ESSENTIAL TO THE NATION.— The true life of a nation is moral. The church is set as the spring of that life. To her it is left to promulgate the doctrines from which moral apprehensions arise and moral principles are evolved. She is commissioned to hold aloft true standards, and radiate the light of swift and strong rebuke upon sin in low and high places. While the church lives the nation cannot die. The light of the "city set on a hill" cannot be hidden or obscured from without; it must decline and darken from within. A perversion of religion must both precede and accompany every devastating overflow of depravity.—*Rev. M. C. Briggs.*

IMMORTALITY.

129. The mysteries of the other world are not revealed. The principles of judgment, the tests of acceptance, and of the supreme eminence, are unfolded. Intellect, genius, knowledge, shall be as nothing before humility, sacrifice, charity. But in the uses of charity, the fiery tongue, the furnished mind, the unquailing heart shall have ample opportunities, and ampler than here. Paul goes to an immense service still, as an Apostle; Newton, to reflect from grander heavens a vaster light.—*Thos. Starr King.*

130. THE SOUL is not a shadow; the body is. Genius is not a shadow; it is a substance. Patriotism is not a shadow, it is light. Great purposes, and the spirit that counts death nothing in contrast with honor and the welfare of our country—these are the witnesses that man is not a passing vapor, but an immortal spirit.
—*Thos. Starr King.*

131. THE YEARNING FOR A FUTURE LIFE is natural and deep. It grows with intellectual growth, and perhaps none really feel it more than those who have begun to see how great is the universe, and how infinite are the vistas which every advance in knowledge opens before us—vistas which would require nothing short of eternity to explore. But in the mental atmosphere of our times, to the great majority of men on whom mere creeds have lost their hold, it seems impossible to look on this yearning save as a vain and childish hope, arising from man's egotism, and for which there is not the slightest ground or warrant, but which, on the contrary, seems inconsistent with positive knowledge.

Now, when we come to analyze and trace up the ideas that thus destroy the hope of a future life, we shall find them, I think, to have their source, not in any revelations of physical science, but in certain teachings of political and moral science which have deeply permeated thought in all directions. They have their root in the doctrines that there is a tendency to the production of more human beings than can be provided for; that vice and misery are the result of natural laws; and the means by which advance goes on; and that human progress is by a slow race development. These doctrines, which have been generally accepted as approved truth, do what the extensions of physical science do not do—they reduce the individual to insignificance; they destroy the idea that there can be in the ordering of the universe any regard for his existence, or any recognition of what we call moral qualities. It is difficult to reconcile the idea of human immortality with the idea that nature wastes men by constantly bringing them into being where there is no room for them. It is impossible to reconcile the idea of an intelligent and beneficent Creator with the belief that the wretchedness and degradation, which are the lot of such a large proportion of human kind, result from his enactments; while the idea that man, mentally and physically, is the result of slow modifications perpetuated by heredity, irresistibly suggests the idea that it is the race life, not the individual life, which is the object of human existence. Thus has vanished, with many of us, and is still vanishing with more of us, that belief which in the battles and ills of life, affords the strongest support and deepest consolation.

Population does not tend to outrun subsistence; the waste of human powers and the prodigality of human suffering do not spring from natural laws, but from the ignorance and selfishness of men in refusing to conform to natural laws. Human progress is not by altering the nature of men, but, on the contrary, the nature of men seems, generally speaking, always the same.
—*Henry George.*

132. THE IDEA OF DEVELOPMENT involves the idea of maturity, and this, that of decay; in other words, it involves the idea of cyclical movement; there is no such thing as stability in things material. The universe itself is passing through its cycle of changes which must finally close; the universe itself is enwrapped within the complex coils of a law which must eventually strangle it to death.

Thus the cycle of the individual closes in death, but the race progresses; the cycle of the race closes in death, but the earth abides; the cycle of the earth closes, but the universe remains; finally the cycle of the universe itself must close. The law is absolutely universal among things material. Where, then, shall we look for true, rectilinear, ever-onward progress? Where, but in that world where the soaring spirit of man is freed from the trammels of material laws—the world of immortal spirits.—*Prof. Jos. LeConte.*

133.—

> In thought, in feeling, and in love,
> Things do not perish, though they pass;
> The form is shattered to the eye,
> But only broken is the glass.
>
> Sun, friend, and flower have each become
> A part of my immortal part;
> They are not lost, but evermore
> Shine, live and bloom within my heart.
> —*W. A. Kendall.*

134. INFINITY.—Physical causes have entirely concealed three-sevenths of the moon from our observation. And this must always remain so under existing cosmical arrangements. No conceivable progress in astronomy—no possible improvement in the telescope can remove or abate the difficulty. It is true that it is very seldom that we find the limits of human knowledge so *sharply defined*, as in the case of the physical aspect

of our planetary companion. Nevertheless, nearly similar conditions exist in the intellectual world, where, in the domain of deep research into the mysteries and the primeval creative forces of Nature, there are regions similarly turned away from us and apparently forever unattainable. So likewise, in those systems of double stars, which the astronomer finds scattered through the awful abysses of space; how remote the analogies to our system! What complex reactions must exist between the planets engirdling the double suns and their duplex centres of power and energy! But their features are forever hidden from man; we can never hope to explore those sacred mysteries. It seems to me that no one need regret that there are some enclosed spots, some secluded regions, some quietudes in creation, which will be unexplored and unpenetrated forever. These are the regions in the intellectual world into which faintness, weariness, and broken-heartedness may sometimes flee, and find shelter and repose! Sweet and inviting mysteries—encouraging mysteries—among whose gentle shadows all our holy aspirations, our unnamed yearnings, humbly and tremblingly advance, and find or fashion for themselves images of purity and love—convictions of immortality—vistas of a life to come!—*Prof. Jos. LeConte.*

135. ONE ALL-PERVADING PRINCIPLE.—The Ionic philosophers saw only one all-pervading principle in nature, though personified in the minds of some by one element and in the minds of others by another. Thus, Thales thought it water, Anaxagoras atoms, Anaximenes

air, Heraclitus fire. But whatever it is, science and religion see, feel it, and believe in the same thing, though they call it by different names and numberless sub-names. We feel God in nature and in ourselves as the blind child, feeling with its fingers the lineaments of the face it loves, reads thus the secrets of the heart behind it.—*Hubert H. Bancroft.*

136. FAITH.—Happily, for all things beyond the selfishness of the day, the heart is stronger than the head. No nation has accomplished a high destiny without a belief in something better and higher than itself. Faith is the parent of aspiration. We have a high destiny before us; let us have faith in it; and faith in the Higher Power which beckons us towards its accomplishment.

Years ago, maternal hands led us to the modest church which gently crowns the village green; or by our mother's side we knelt within the dim aisles of the cathedral, which was all lighted up, for us, by the glory of the Madonna and the smile of the infant Jesus. There we heard those sublime words, the crown of the wisdom of Socrates and of the philosophy of Plato, towards which all good men had groped before, and which all good men have followed since: " Do unto others as ye would that they should do unto you." We have been taught the life-giving principles, which are the germ of the religion of the church in all ages —of the religion of England, of the religion of our fathers, the religion of good deeds and noble sacrifices; we have our faith; we will abide by it, and the gates of hell shall not prevail against it.—*T. W. Freelon.*

137. O, Affection, Forgiveness, Faith!—Ye are mighty spirits, ye are powerful angels. And the soul that in its dying moments trusts to thee, cannot be far from the gates of heaven, whatever the past life may have been. However passion or excitement may have led it astray, if at the last and final hour it returns to the lessons of a mother's love, of a father's care—if it learns the great lesson of forgiveness to its enemies—if at the last moment it can utter these words: "Father of light, and life, and love!" these shall be winged angels—troops of blessed spirits—that will bear the fainting, wounded soul to the blessed abodes, and forever guard it against despair. Oh, my friends! those mighty gates, built by the Almighty to guard the entrance to the unseen world, will not open at the battle-axe of the conquerer; they will not roll back if all the artillery of earth were to thunder forth a demand, which, indeed, would be lost in the infinite regions of eternal space! but they will open with thoughts of affection, with forgiveness of injuries, and with prayer.
—*Gen. E. D. Baker.*

---

138. Atheism.—The clinching argument against atheism is not that there is such constant order in the universe, but that so many facts, apparently independent of order, play so beautifully into each other in perfect harmony. Can it be chance that determines the mad but punctual whirling of the universe? Think of a heap of letters dropped from space, sent fluttering through the air, like snow-flakes, and by chance arranging themselves into the scenes, the stirring passages, the solemn climax of the tragedy of Macbeth, so that all the characters should be there! The proposition obliges atheism and probability to look each other in the face. If Macbeth is probable as a result of such a shower of letters, hurled down by chance, then it may be confessed that chance hurled the immense physical alphabet into this grand poem of nature, whose leaves are systems and each word a world.—*Thos. Starr King.*

139. RELIGION NATIVE TO THE HEART.—Religious sentiments are native to the heart of man. They dwell in the heart of the savage, they illuminate the understanding of the sage, they radiate amid the haunts of civilization and refinement. Human nature, after groping for a season in the darkness of its fall, began to trace, amid the aspirations and sublime conceptions of its inner thought, the glimmer of a light divine. Unsatisfied longings, restless strivings after some far-off good, soon taught the soul, through the demonstrations of its inward promptings, that its essence was immortal. What the acute investigations of reason, aided by the deep study of the page of nature, imparted to the contemplations of philosophy, the light of revelation finally made clear. Socrates beheld, and imparted to his acolytes, the sureties of an immortal life and the infinite being of a God. Cicero had bright conceptions of an existence, glorious and unending, in another

world. These minds, and multitudes of others, soared beyond the vain tenets of the day, which frittered away, in a multitude of deified attributes, all just ideas of a God, and their piercing flight ceased not till it penetrated to the lofty realms of truth. In all periods of the world's history, there have been painful spectacles of free opinion, but they have proved exceptions to the spirit of the age. They stand as stands a charred and lightening-blasted oak, among the stalwart giants of the forest. Even in the midst of the dark ages, the spirit of religion still survived. Wherever Romanism was rejected, a Theurgical system took its place, which linked the mind of man to the mysteries of a world unseen, and his spirit to the worship of Divinity.

—*Jos. W. Winans.*

140. MAN'S MISSION.—Franklin, when he interrogated the thunder-cloud, and received in response a shock from the key, an assurance of its relationship to electricity, designed not to change, but to *understand*, the laws that control this element of terror that had been regarded as God's avenging messenger. This knowledge enabled him to construct lightning-rods to protect buildings from its damaging presence. By studying the laws of this ever present but unseen agent, Morse was enabled to subordinate it to the noblest purposes. May not the study of the soul's origin, its capacity and destiny, from a scientific standpoint, reveal to us knowledge that may be applied for our own benefit and to the advancement of our race? There may be laws too occult for our understanding,

but there are none so sacred as to forbid our desire for their comprehension. This immense domain for human exploration, for the present and for the eternal future, demonstrates the grandeur of man's character and mission; and the great minds which occasionally roll up between the centuries and flash their light like meteors in the sky, are an earnest of man's capacities, and the future possibilities of all. Copernicus, Socrates, Plato, Galileo, Newton, Locke, Melancthon, Edwards, La Place, Bowditch, Leverrier and others, are historical monuments, not only for our admiration, but our imitation. It is a glorious as well as a consoling thought, that every person born into this world, is in the possesion of the germs of the undeveloped faculties, which may, at some period in the vast future, transcend in its attainments, these great lights of the world; like an inverted pyramid, spreading outward and upward in its lofty and expansive growth, taking hold on knowledge, that carries it, as it were, into the realms of the infinite. What man has accomplished, it may be possible for all men to acquire. This opens to us the beauty and glory of that life and future into which we all are soon to enter, when to know and to love shall constitutue the two great forces that are to move us onward and upward, into the empire of wisdom and the realms of eternal bliss.—*Gen. John A. Collins.*

141. THE GOLDEN AGE TO COME.—It is a glorious three-fold truth: That over us and over all things there exists a benignant mind; that he presides over all the commotions and revolutions of history; and

that he has an increasing kingdom, which he is evolving out of the very evils of the present, as a lily springs, white and beautiful, out of the quagmire. Christianity invites us to a wide survey. Its visions and vistas are not those of an hour, or a day or a century, but rather those of immeasurable ages. God is in no hurry—He rests not, hastes not. He employed untold ages to complete the solid earth we now inhabit, and he may employ even a longer period to carry to its final stages the grander process of the moral world. The mythology of Greece and Rome placed the Golden Age back in the distant past. Christianity, on the other hand, places the Golden Age forward in a distant future. Their religion was a bright memory, ours a glorious hope.—*Rev. W. E. Ijams.*

142. THE SCEPTIC—ANCIENT AND MODERN.—The ancient skeptic or philosopher, in assailing dogmas and destroying systems, had (at least in his best judgment believed he had) higher ethics and purer systems to offer in their place; while our modern sceptic, in his rage for novelty, affectation of learning, and monstrous lust of destruction, brutally impugns the existing order of things—long established standards of right, our present system of religion and morality, dismantling it of all its holy traditions, ridiculing its struggles, disparaging its triumphs, and consigning to puerility the reverence which centuries have paid it; and when his devilish work is done, when with sacrilegious wantonness he has scattered our sacred treasures to the four winds of heaven, ignored principles which mighty

minds established, and destroyed the chart by which the good men of hundreds of generations have traveled on happy and contented in their journey to God,—I say, when all this work of destruction is complete; when this deadly conspiracy against humanity is fully accomplished; and man's reason, in its hour of grievous unrest, asks the sceptic for something outside of self and its possibilities, upon which it can depend for reference, guidance and instruction; when man's heart, with plaintive prayer, asks for something to love, something to cling to, some source of consolation in this disappointing world, some hope in the bitterness of death, the sceptic's hands are empty, his heart is cold, his voice is silent; having robbed us of our birth-right, in which all these blessings were comprehended, he gives us what he calls a "liberated manhood," what we know to be an incarnate malediction, an existence without an object, adversity without a remedy, a grave without a hope, a death which means annihilation.—*Dr. J. Campbell Shorb.*

143. TRUE RELIGION WELCOMES TRUTH.—The theory that the Bible is an infallible record has wrought incalculable disaster both to science and religion, and is the secret of the alienation between them. Why not, then, admit that a man may be inspired as to spiritual truth, and yet be ignorant as to scientific truth? If religious people would only be reasonable, there would be no more conflict between science and religion. What is religion? Is it not the supreme love of God,

and the unselfish love of my neighbor? Religion, loaded with the traditions of mythology, the errors of Hebrew poesy, or the imperfections growing out of the human element of inspiration, will terminate in the defeat of faith and the triumph of philosophy. Man is naturally a religious being. The instinct of faith in God is a real one. Man is not man without religion. Ministers of the gospel should not be afraid of science. Chemistry should be in alliance with all truth; and we should be ready to surrender any dogma, however dear, at the bidding of any real truth, come whence it may.
—*Rev. W. E. Ijams.*

144. THE SPIRITUAL FEELING.—Let a man once realize the full sense of the truth that he is a spirit, and he will begin to act like an immortal child of an Infinite Father. Let him feel that this earth is only a nursery of souls, that here he learns the mere alphabet of God's great volume of everlasting truth, that this is merely a short space in his whole career, and he will begin to rise out of the filth, how deeply soever he may be sunk in it; he will begin to stir himself, he will begin to lift his head up among the stars, he will begin to open his bosom to the inspiring music of the heavens, and to realize his affinity with all that is beautiful, glorious and divine. We will no longer build our religious temples of philosophy out of the old debris of the dead centuries; we will build them out of the blocks of solid light which science has quarried out of the eternal deeps of nature. We will build their crystal walls of the pure, transparent and dazzling beams drawn from nature's

entire compass. They shall go up grandly, until the domes shall pierce the heavens, and all mankind worship around their altars—sacred to the rights, liberties and progress of all. We will have no spiritual hierarchy, but inspired men and women shall receive their commissions from the Genius of Nature; and we will have for a ritual the repetition of the order and harmony and beauty that print themselves in letters of blazing light on the face of the midnight sky. We will have for members all humanity that carries in its bosom faith and hope, and would fain get rid, some day, of this encompassing and cramping flesh which, when we are once fairly out of it, will enable us all the more to enjoy the freedom of the spiritual republic in Heaven. All the truths of the past are ours; science is their handmaiden; it teaches the tender sympathies of the soul to blossom with more than their usual freedom and beauty; it has a smile for the faithful, encouragement for the disappointed, inspiration for the dull, and hope for all mankind.—*Selden J. Finney.*

THE CORRUPTING INFLUENCE OF REVIVALS.

145. I. REVIVAL METHODS ARE RADICALLY VICIOUS.—The speeches and prayers, limited to three minutes, and stopped by a tinkle of the conductor's bell; the reading of piles of notes for the conversion of indicated persons, and the offering of supplication for them, as though prayer were a method of sacred sorcery; the asking of young persons if they "know the Lord;" the solicitation of people to publish their most sacred feelings of penitence, or their equally sacred glooms and distrusts and scepticism; the flitting about of experts in the system of evangelical pathology—if one can contemplate such methods of dealing with the religious nature, in a season of excitement, without feeling that permanent harm must result to those who conduct the system and those who are the victims of it, he must hold a conception of religion and religious sensibilities that needs, I think, to be enlarged and refined. *Safety* is still the word and motive that is executed with all possible modulations and variations in the whole fantasia of praying, note-reading, and appeal. "Come to Christ;" "get an interest in Christ;" "fly to the cross;" "find the Saviour;" "delay is dangerous, for death may overtake you to-morrow;"—these are the characteristic calls and warnings of the movement.

This shows its radical vice. Its working-force, so far as the instruction and the teachers give it character, is not the glory of truth, the beauty of holiness, the need of human nature, for its health, to begin to serve God and be educated in a spiritual estimate of all nature and all life. The long arm of its lever is selfish fear. Its fulcrum is the death-bed. Its aim is the swinging of men, from the edge of the grave, over the abyss, into a mechanical heaven.

II. REVIVALS POISON MANHOOD.—I cannot do any thing else than say that this is *poison*. The religious emotion that goes to the meetings may be pure and hopeful. But when it is met by this kind of instruction, or is stimulated thus to more intense vitality, a bane is taken into the spiritual blood that I believe almost neutralizes the good effect of a renunciation of open sins. Just to the extent that this doctrine is absorbed into character, the manhood is injured. The person may not be a gross offender, as before, against the commandments, he may be a frequenter of prayer-meetings, and a sincere exhorter to flee from the wrath to come, but he is converted to be stunted; he is innoculated with a virus that chills and shrivels his humanity; he is turned from a careless and perhaps generous-hearted sinner, into a miserable, starveling dwarf of the spiritual order, on the side of the Lord.

III. REVIVALS CORRUPT YOUTH.—Not long ago I read a volume containing twenty-five sermons, recently preached in New York and Brooklyn with reference to the revival, by the most distinguished and cultivated ministers of those cities. Some of the most powerful of the discourses, I read in my library till past midnight. The air at last seemed full of infernal terrors and woe, and I shut the dreadful book. In a room up stairs, my little daughter, six years old, was sleeping, with whom I have often the most sweet conversation upon God and Christ, and the life hereafter.

But I said to myself then, in excitement of soul, what I will say here with seriousness and deliberation, that rather than my child should have the awful theology of the average of that book stamped upon her heart, I should unspeakably prefer that she should grow up an atheist. As an atheist, the best currents of human nature would not be corrupted in her. Believing what that book teaches, and having her whole nature cramped and distorted into its mould, it would not be possible that her spirit could have any religious beauty, cheer, or peace.

IV. REVIVALS DISHONOR THE DEITY.—A large number of men and women, no doubt, do reject most of this venom. They are sound and noble in spite of their theology. Their spiritual sense is instinctively so delicate and healthy, that this leaven of Satan in the bread of life offered to them, is quietly cast out before it can pass into their moral blood. But the majority take it into their constitution. It becomes their wisdom, their motive, their measure of God's character. And then what can they know of the Infinite Perfectness? Believing that God has appointed a terrible and irreversible final doom, that yawns just beyond the sepulchre, for every man that has misused the opportunities of this life; that he will never pity or forgive any spirit he has made, on the most thorough repentance, through eternity—what can they know, under such instruction, of that perfectness of God which is more than the sum of all the holy and lovely qualities of human character on earth?

Make God just as good in eternity as he is in time. Put religion on its *natural* basis, and you kill the revivals, you shrivel the inquiry-meetings.

V. REVIVALS REPEL FROM RELIGION THE YOUNG LIFE AND THE BEST INTELLECT OF THE LAND.—Let any man go through the West, and talk with the men who represent the energy and future of the great rising States; let him hear their lamentations over the dreariness and huskiness of the theology that is poured from the pulpits, their confessions of the inward rebellion and loathing which, when they go to church, they listen to its effete traditions, its ghastly philosophy of life, its artificial terrors, its theories of the government of the moral world, so discordant with the simplicity of science, so foreign from the clearest insight which our best literature reveals; let him hear them utter their fears for the effect on society, after two generations more of this dismal parody of a gospel, and ask if some nobler administration of truth cannot be inaugurated soon and widely.

The awakening in this country by which hopes will be re-animated, and fresh light poured into the popular heart, will flow from the silent stealing of new truth into our theology. We want such an access of truth that the general mind can be fed with a worthier conception of God, that will make every thought of him inspiring as the dawn of the morning, and will banish the superstition that this life is the final state of probation, as an insult to his plan of eternal education, and a chimera of a barbarous age.—*Thomas Starr King.*

THIS LIFE THE AVENUE TO ANOTHER.

146. Political Economy has been called the dismal science, and, as currently taught, *is* hopeless and despairing. But this is solely because she has been shackled and degraded; her truths dislocated; her harmonies ignored; the words she would utter gagged in her mouth, and her protest against wrong turned into an endorsement of injustice. Freed in her own proper symmetry, Political Economy is radiant with hope. Properly understood, the laws which govern the production and distribution of wealth show that the want and injustice of the present social state are not necessary; but that, on the contrary, a social state is possible in which poverty would be unknown, and all the better qualities and higher powers of human nature would have opportunity for full development. Further than this, when we see that social development is governed neither by a Special Providence nor by a merciless fate, but by law, at once unchangeable and beneficent; when we see that human will is the great factor, and that, taking men in the aggregate, their condition is as they make it; when we see that economic law and moral law are essentially one, and that the truth which the intellect grasps after toilsome effort, is but that which the moral sense reaches by a quick intuition, a flood of light breaks in upon the problem of individual life. These countless millions like ourselves, who, on this earth of ours have passed and still are passing, with their joys and sorrows, their toil and their striving, their aspirations and their fears, their strong perceptions of things deeper than sense, their common feelings which form the basis even of the most divergent creeds —their little lives do not seem so much like meaningless waste.

The great fact which Science in all her branches shows is the universality of law. Wherever he can trace it, whether in the fall of an apple or in the revolution of binary suns, the astronomer sees the working of the same law, which operates in the minutest divisions in which we may distinguish space, as it does in the immeasurable distances with which his science deals. Out of that which lies beyond his telescope comes a moving body, and again it disappears. So far as he can trace its course the law is ignored. Does he say that this is an exception? On the contrary, he says that this is merely a part of its orbit that he has seen; that beyond the reach of his telescope the law holds good. He makes his calculations, and after centuries they are proved.

Now, if we trace out the laws which govern human life in society, we find that in the largest as in the smallest community they are the same. We find that what seem at first sight like divergences and exceptions, are but manifestations of the same principles. And we find that everywhere we can trace it, the social law runs into and conforms with the moral law; that in the life of a community, justice infallibly brings its reward, and injustice its punishment. But this we cannot see in individual life. If we look merely at individual life, we cannot see that the laws of the universe have the slightest relation to good or bad, to right or wrong, to just or unjust. Shall we then say that the law which is manifest in social life is not true of individual life? It is not scientific to say so. We would not say so in reference to anything else. Shall we not rather say this simply proves that we do not see the whole of individual life?

The laws which Political Economy discovers, like the facts and relations of physical nature, harmonize with what seems to be the law of mental development —not a necessary and involuntary progress, but a progress in which the human will is an initiatory force. But in life, as we are cognizant of it, mental development can go but a little ways. The mind hardly begins to awake ere the bodily powers decline—it but becomes dimly conscious of the vast fields before it, but begins to learn and to use its strength—to recognize relations and extend its sympathies—when, with the death of the body, it passes away. Unless there is something more, there seems here a break, a failure. Whether it be a Humboldt or a Herschel, a Moses who looks from Pisgah, a Joshua who leads the host, or one of those sweet and patient souls who in narrow circles live radiant lives, there seems, if mind and character here developed can go no further, a purposelessness inconsistent with what we can see of the linked sequence of the universe.

By a fundamental law of our minds—the law, in fact, upon which Political Economy relies in all her deductions—we cannot conceive of a means without an end, a contrivance without an object. Now, to all nature, so far as we come in contact with it in this world, the support and employment of the intelligence that is in man furnishes such an end and object. But unless man himself may rise to or bring forth something higher, his existence is unintelligible. So strong is this metaphysical necessity, that those who deny to the individual anything more than this life, are compelled to transfer the idea of perfectibility to the race. But there is nothing whatever to show any essential race improvement. Human progress is not the improvement of human nature. The advances in which civilization consists are not secured in the constitution of man, but in the constitution of society. They are thus not fixed and permanent, but may at any time be lost, nay, are constantly tending to be lost. And further than this, if human life does not continue beyond what we see of it here, then we are confronted, with regard to the race, with the same difficulty as with the individual. For it is as certain that the race must die as it is that the individual must die. We know that there have been geologic conditions under which human life was impossible on this earth. We know that they must return again. Even now, as the earth circles on her appointed orbit, the northern ice-cap slowly thickens, and the time gradually approaches when glaciers will flow again, and austral seas, sweeping northward, bury the seats of present civilization under ocean wastes, as, it may be, they now bury what was once as high a civilization as our own. And beyond these periods, science discerns a dead earth, an exhausted sun—a time when, clashing together, the solar system shall resolve itself into a gaseous form, again to begin immeasurable mutations.

What, then, is the meaning of life—of life absolutely and inevitably bounded by death? To me it only seems intelligible as the avenue and vestibule to another life.
—*Henry George.*

V.

THE FARM AND GARDEN.

PART V.

THE FARM AND GARDEN.

147. THE INTELLECT must be plowed deeper than the furrows of the field, or the farmer is a mere serf of the soil—a superior kind of dray-horse—a kind of clown, but without his suppleness of wit or limb.
—*Samuel B. Bell.*

148. THE FARMER THAT PAYS HIS DEBTS can't get rich dishonestly, in the sight of heaven. There can't be too much wheat, too many noble cattle, too much wool, an excess of excellent peaches and pears, too many pumpkins, or even too great a crowd of cabbages, if they are not eaten so immoderately as to come to a head again on human shoulders.—*Thos. Starr King.*

149. THE FIRST MAN, being historically and traditionally perfect, had a garden as his noblest allotment The farther the race drifts away from the cultivation of the soil, the nearer it gets to barbarism. The Apache is not a good horticulturalist, and therefore there is no gentleness in his blood. Teach him to love and cultivate a garden, and he is no longer a savage. The best thought and the best inspiration may come to one when all the gentle ministries of his garden wait upon him;

when the soul of things is concurrent with his own; and bee and almond-blossom, the rose, and the smallest song-sparrow in the tree-top, are revelators and instructors.—*W. C. Bartlett.*

150. ECONOMY IN AGRICULTURE.—The Creator, who gave the globe to Adam, with the command to dress and keep it, has connected economy with its fertility. Economy lies at the base of high and permanent civilization. Where a river rises every year, overflows its banks, and renews the elements which the land has expended into crops, men are absolved from the duty and need of caring for the soil. God takes the capital unto his own keeping, and notifies man that he will prevent its waste. But where this is not done, men are notified just as plainly that they must repair the capital and preserve it at a point where the returns will be generous and perpetual. The interests of the human race repose on agriculture, and agriculture reposes on this law. To fulfill it, requires immense knowledge, and a reverent and persistent thrift. The farmer that understands it, and acts upon it, stands at the head of all workers on the planet.—*Thos. Starr King.*

151. AGRICULTURE STIMULATES PATRIOTISM.—As the roots of a tree derive their nourishment, so the foundations of society derive their strength from the culture of the soil. It was her devotion to agricultural pursuits that rendered Poland so glorious in her struggle against tyranny—so deeply imbued with the spirit of freedom that the whole civilized world grew sympa-

thetic in her cause, until the very name of Pole, whether applied to those who chafed at home under the thrall of despotism, or those who were sorrowing abroad in exile, became a symbol of the love of country. The spread of farms is fatal to the growth of penitentiaries.
—*Joseph W. Winans.*

152. CONDITIONS OF SUCCESSFUL FARMING.—Agriculture can be successful only where the people are moral; where they try diligently to learn the conditions of success in treating the land, and will receive it as a trust; and where, too, the State is so well and justly organized that near markets are afforded, so that the soil can receive back the aliments received from it and essential to its fertility. As yet in history the kingdoms have been very few that could take care of and develop their richest soils. They have known enough to be warriors and conquerors, to create literature, to gem magnificent temples and museums with trophies of art; but they have not known enough to be successful farmers, to insure the fir tree for the thorn and the myrtle tree for the brier, to bring out and keep out the beauty on the land which Providence designed, and to base a permanent civilization on fields thoroughly plowed and refreshed, and on meadows and morasses dried, diked, and guarded by watchful energy and thrift.
—*Thomas Starr King.*

153. THE TRUE NOBLEMAN.—The farmer is the true nobleman of nature. He enjoys a rank superior to that of the patricians of all other orders. The chief

nobles of every country in Europe derive their titles from their estates; as if the battle-fields, reeking with their red glories, could afford no appellation so endearing and honorable as the little farm upon which a hero was born. His avocation renders him tolerant and kind, industrious and hospitable, independent and free. In peace, he is amicable, in war, invincible. Every blow that he strikes, either with his sword or his hoe, is struck for mankind. The farm-house is the true Temple of Liberty, the Shrine of Virtue, the Altar of Patriotism.—*William H. Rhodes.*

154. THE FARMER FACE TO FACE WITH GOD.— Abandoned, indeed, must be the heart of that man whose tongue could blaspheme or refuse to honor the name of the Most High, while the very birds are thrilling the air with the notes of His praise. Every occupation of the farmer brings him, as it were, face to face with his Maker, and teaches him lessons of truth, justice and piety. When he plows his ground and sows his seed, he relies not upon the slippery promises of men, but upon God himself, to supply the moisture and to so temper the atmosphere as to sprout the seed and mature the crop. Every flower that blooms, every blade of grass that grows, and every insect that crawls, tell him of the wisdom, power, goodness, justice, and mercy of the Almighty. When he plucks from the tree the rich, ripe fruit, as it hangs in tempting clusters around the parent stem, how sublime the thought that he receives this luscious food direct from God, no mortal hand intruding between the giver and the receiver

to break the charm which Divinity throws around the precious gift. Accustomed as he is to rely upon God and his own strong arm for what he eats, drinks and wears, he dares to think what is right, and to speak and act as he thinks.—*Zachary Montgomery.*

155. THE FARMER THE UNIVERSAL MASTER.—We could strike from society the merchant, lawyer, doctor, manufacturer and mechanic, and still the human family could be sustained in the enjoyment of life; still the great work of moral and mental improvement could go on. But strike from society the farmer's calling, paralyze the farmer's hand, and society would not alone be shaken to its base, but its very foundations would be swept away so utterly as to leave not a wreck behind. Let the seasons but for one year cease to yield their fertilizing influence, the husbandman's labors throughout the world fail for one year, and wherever civilized man exists would be exhibited a scene of desolation and woe, such as was felt in Egypt when the angel of death went forth and struck down the eldest-born in every household. The worst scenes of the French Revolution, the hour of its deepest and darkest orgies, would everywhere appear; death would be on every hand; suffering at every door. Every father would mourn the death of his first-born; every mother would be a Rachel, weeping for her children, because they were not. * * * Three-quarters of all the people in the United States are engaged in farming. The farmer alone is independent; he alone is master of the labor and the talents of every other class. His avocation is the highest of all arts. Has the plodding plowman ever thought of that? It is not only a higher pursuit, being independent of all others, but it is the highest of all arts. It is even given to the farmer and gardener to do that which in poetical conception, was considered impossible—"to paint the lily and add fresh perfume to the violet."

It is most singular that this pursuit, that employs the greatest part of our population, the most important in its interests, upon which all other pursuits depend and on which society itself exists, has never been fostered by the Government, which also depends upon it for its own maintenance. No statesman has taken a large view of the agricultural interest, to make it the basis of an extensive political economy. But such is the fortunate position of the farming interest that it needs not this support. It is one of its greatest triumphs, one of its noblest encomiums, that it can say: "I care not for the protection of the Government. All I ask of Government is to let me alone; let me take care of myself, and I will take care of myself and you, too."

—*Tod Robinson.*

156. THE FARM THE ABODE OF CONTENT.—The judicious and methodical farmer extracts abundant leisure for domestic duties and home delights. In the good progress of the agricultural art, he can still hover about his domestic circle, and bend upon it the proper amount of regard and attention. He may not, by some hazardous speculation in trade, realize a startling increase to his hoards, but he is ever certain of competence, and can surely calculate on moderate gain. Better than all else, he enjoys the sweet repose of heart and mind. He clusters about him his intelligent friends, and quaffs the nectar of social wisdom. The cares and anxieties and acerbities of the great world never reach his happy home. The diseased excitements and prurient amusements of the great city have no charm for him. He revolves about a world of his own. He has an isolated fireside of his own, virtuous and happy. Gradual old age steals upon him; but it finds him cheerful and vigorous, hemmed in on all sides by the ramparts of intelligence and affection. So I wonder that men of substance linger about a city when the country beckons them to affluent bliss. Old Sam Johnson applauded a city life to the day of his death. But Sam, though a good and a learned man, was wedded to his club and his porter and his coterie of adulators. He was prejudiced against rusticity; and a prejudice with him had the strength that lies in the tail of Leviathan. He loved to bully and swagger over timid city gentlemen. Old Falstaff, bloated with sack to elephantine rotundity, bubbling with civic wit, and oozing the lard of metropolitan repartee as a wounded whale its blubber, had yet a green cleft amid the sterile crags of his memory. Disease, as winnowing wind, often puffs aside the chaff of lecherous thought and worldly humors, and reveals the grain of earnest and truthful nature. Dying in penury and disgrace, his mind flew back to his gambols of boyhood upon the green sward. He babbled of green fields. The creations of Shakespeare are humanity in its truth and fervor and condensation.—*James G. Howard.*

157. SANITARY INFLUENCE OF TREES.—Rich, moist, prolific land, with decaying vegetation, in a climate like that of portions of the interior of California, will produce miasma; and the more favorable the conditions for vigorous and abundant growth and consequent abundance of vegetation to decay, the larger the amount of miasma generated or given off. Such lands will always be sought because profitable for cultivation, notwithstanding the penalty attached to residing upon them. This penalty may be mitigated or perhaps avoided by a knowledge of what has been observed of the laws governing this cause of disease.

While miasma is given off by decaying vegetation, it is absorbed or arrested by growing vegetation. No other fact seems to be so universally conceded as this. Primitive forests, when left to the undisturbed operations of nature, preserve the balance between growth and decay, and do not largely generate miasma. It does not prevail in the bogs of Ireland, nor in the Dismal Swamp of Virginia and North Carolina, while their surfaces are covered by perpetually growing mosses and other vegetation.

When forests are cut down and the balance destroyed between growth and decay, the means provided by nature for the absorption of miasma are removed, and it is left free to poison the air. This law cannot be better illustrated than in the history of the Campagna near Rome. At the commencement of the Christian era it was covered with forests of trees and gardens. On it were erected the magnificent villas of the Emperors Domitian and Hadrian.

The effect of the destruction of the trees in changing this paradise to a pestilential desert is observed by every traveler. It is now so terribly stricken by malaria that beyond the Church of St. Paul, about two miles from the walls of Rome, I could not see a human habitation to break the utter solitude. The people who cultivate small portions of it, go down from the hills each day, long after the sun has risen, do their work in the heat of the day, and escape back to the hills again before the sun has set.

It will be seen how great is the benefit to be derived from the planting of forest trees, and how great is the crime in the wanton and needless destruction of the trees on the borders of our rivers, sloughs and overflowed lands, and the certain penalty that follows this crime.—*B. B. Redding.*

158. THE FARMER A CO-CREATOR WITH THE INFINITE.— What honor the highest human intelligence pays to a painter like Landseer, who puts a superb mimic sheep on canvas; or to Troyon, who makes a dreamy-eyed beneficent cow look at us from his colors; or to Rosa Bonheur, who startles us with tableaux of horses clothed with thunder, and bulls whose look makes the room unsafe! This is right. But what shall we say of the farmers who push out of existence the tribes and very types of imperfect or degenerate cattle, and call up the actual horses that make the verses of

Job sing in the brain, and sheep fit to be clad in the finest merino, and herds whose very attitude is a new masterpiece of lordliness or beauty?

In looking at such stock I can easily understand the enthusiasm which leads people to invest thousands and tens of thousands in the experiments of model farms. And then I wonder why anybody is led away by a literary or artistic ambition, if he is not conscious of the first class of powers. Why will a man try to write imperfect rhymes, if he can make a perfect strawberry vine or moss rose? Why put a blundering idea into a book, if you can raise a litter of Suffolk pigs, and thus see a divine idea multiplied in symmetrical pork? Why waste effort with pigments on canvas, when you can put an Alderney calf on a landscape, with eye more poetic than any fawn or gazelle ever gazed with—or can ennoble an acre with an actual pair of young Devons surveying nature in their dumb dignity?

These gems of the annual shows make the farmer's office seem noble, a co-creator with the infinite. They make our average literature and art seem vapid, and in one light make society seem sad; for where are the men and women in society as yet that are as noble in their spheres as these animals—that are fit to own them, that come within a distant range of fulfilling their type in the Creator's mind, as the beasts do that are unstained with sin?—*Thos. Starr King.*

159. THE BEAUTY OF RURAL HOMES.—Whoever in this fair State of ours, has become owner of a little nook of land which, by patient and well directed toil,

may be changed into a garden, must feel in some degree as if he were the master of a new and glorious world. There lie the fresh and smoking furrows, smiling to think of the countless secrets they hide—the fruit and leaves and flowers, the shaded walks and the sloping lawns; there the new maker plans, in faith and patience, for the golden years of a long and useful life. The founding of a home is one of the purest joys left to fallen man; it is the blessing which came softly out of Paradise with Adam, and has followed his wandering children ever since. In the desire for rural homes the perennial freshness of humanity is revealed. As every successive generation of children love to pull corn-silk, and tumble in the hay-fields, so every generation of busy, over-worked men, lawyers, politicians, merchants, editors, love to unfasten the chafing harness at times, and choose some happy spot, by the rippling streams, where they may be new Adams, received again into Paradise—new dwellers in Arcadia. Our modern intense life draws men in early manhood to the centers of activity, where fortunes and reputations are to be won; but their hearts, as they grow older, turn back to the grassy fields, the blooming gardens, the quiet hearth, the country freedom; and they remember with deeper affection the old farm-house of their boyhood, the fruitful orchards, the fragrant garden.

Men have a curious habit of stamping their personality on the clothes they wear, the team they drive, the house they live in, and all their property, real and personal. In a most complete sense the grounds a man lays out, takes care of, and enjoys, become like himself;

or rather, in a very precise way, give us glimpses of his nature and hints of his possibilities. Indeed, I love to notice the constant changes and little improvements in every village through which I pass, and make wondering guesses concerning the owners of each successive cottage. Altheas, lilacs, a damask rose, groups of pansies, and clambering wealth of sweet peas, with perhaps a sugar maple, evidently cherished—it is a suggestion of a New England family. An Irish yew-tree by the gate, a row of black currants along the fence, Shropshire damsons and Kentish cherries in the orchard, box borders and Covent Garden Stocks—this is staid, portly old England, surely. Bottle gourds over the well, balsams and crape myrtle by the door, melons and gumbo in the vegetable garden—here is a picture from the sunny South. Dill, saffron, yellow marrigolds, sun-flowers and horse-beans, in straight rows, in front of a door painted red, yellow and blue—this can only be a Portuguese family from the Azores. It is the charm of California, in the eyes of her children, that so many variations are possible here; so many widely different types of gardening succeed and blend harmoniously in our landscapes. The man who chooses his nook of earth and founds a home there, is justly entitled to that too-often bestowed title of "public benefactor." The tired travelers, plodding wearily along the dusty summer road, look gladly on the waving spires of green, the soft, bright grass, the cool fountains, the flashes of color from the well kept beds, the bending and fruitful boughs, and are made more hopeful by all this beauty and repose. It is for the owner a daily blessing. As the years increase, the hallowed memories of home thickly cluster. The voices of happy children, some of them no longer on earth, and thus eternally young, yet seem to echo beneath the arching trees, which his own hand planted long before. The blue-bells and the violets, the fragrant lilies and the passion-hearted roses—these carry his dreams back to his boyhood, and move his soul to tears. The impulse is justified which led him to found a home.

—*Chas. H. Shinn.*

160. THE FARMER THE MONARCH OF MEN.—Who is nurtured with such an education as the farmer? He is nursed in the strong embrace of prolific, many-handed Nature, our mother who keeps the wisest school, and who is the voice and the hand, the ferule and the prize of Deity. I almost believe that no man can be one of God's great men, unless nurtured in the embrace of our great mother—on the bosom of the earth. All men should, some time in their lives, live out in the midst of nature, and till the soil. He who has been born and reared and lives in a city, debarred from the privilege of communing with Nature, is most unfortunate. He can never be a whole man. He lacks the stern, true, poetic teachings of the Great School. Nothing can compensate for it. An undevout farmer is a monster. Can the husbandman receive his food direct from heaven—its rains and dews and sunshine—its smile over him in the blue and peaceful vault, sun-and-moon-and-star-lit?—all around him the wavy grass and grain, the many tinted flowers, the voices of the

wind and bending trees—underneath him the prolific, fresh-turned soil—and still be a monster, out of tune with Nature? Who lives so far from temptation, so nigh to his Creator, enwrapt all round about with his arms, fed from his dazzling, munificent hand, sleeps between the leaves of God pictured book—the Universe. * * * His tyranny is over barrenness. He smites, and lo! the sterile earth groans—but it is with abundance. He brings his enemies to the faggot and stake—but they are the thorn, the thistle and the brier. He overruns and subdues the territories of his foes—but they are the swamp, the fen, and the quagmire. He plows up the very foundations of the strongholds of his destroyers—but they are the deadly malaria, the stinging insect, and the fanged, poisonous reptile. The Earth is his slave, but it is the slavery of love, for it buds and blossoms before him, and its trees clap their hands for joy of him. He chains his servants to do his will, but they are the elements, they are the huge and willing ox, the majestic horse, impatient to do his bidding, and champing for the word that bids him go. When he stretches his scepter abroad, cities spring up under its shadow. The sounds of the spindle, the loom and the anvil, and the ponderous foundry and mill, are heard. The hum of industry comes like the noise of many waters; white-winged ships fly over the unstable main; men cast aside their hides and fig leaves, and put on imperial garments; women are arrayed in fabrics fine as gossamer, and many tinted as the sun-set cloud. Penury, pestilence and famine he keeps bound in his prison house. Labor stands in the door of his magazine, and in his stalwart hands he holds scales of human life, and weighs out the supplies of Trade and Art and Armies; of School and Church and State; Food and Raiment; Abundance and Luxury. He deals out the Progress of Human Kind! He is the Monarch of Men!—*Samuel B. Bell.*

161. A VAST FIELD OF KNOWLEDGE.—Agriculture to the active intellect is fruitful in subjects of thought and contemplation, and, when intelligently pursued, the whole being is enriched by the vast field of knowledge it unfolds. It is an occupation that elevates the mind to a genial communion with surrounding nature; it is closely connected with the material wants of the whole human family; it develops and beautifies the earth; it produces a healthy, thrifty and virtuous population; and, more than any other pursuit known to man, adds to the pride, prosperity and strength of a State. That it is intimately connected with the education and intelligence of a community, is clearly proved in the history of our country as well as the history of the world. To man's necessities, comfort and happiness, the tillage and yield of the soil are of the first consequence; and an intelligent prosecution of his work requires from the agriculturist a familiarity with the causes and effects of his labor, and a knowledge of botany and chemistry, which aids him in the development of his resources, and elevates his calling to the dignity of a science. The classic authors and orators of Greece and Rome delighted to write and speak of agriculture, and labored to instil a love for it into the mind. In those ancient

times, the highest citizens and most prominent statesmen—the most successful warriors and the most convincing writers—were cultivators of the soil. Even kings and princes have been known to resign their power to become farmers, while farmers have been called from the field to become kings. The familiar story of Cincinnatus, who, in the days of the old Roman Republic, received an embassy from the people while in the very act of plowing in the field, had an illustrious prototype in the example of Elisha, whose mantle of a prophet was urged upon him while working his land with a team of twelve yoke of oxen. Among the great of modern times who have devoted themselves to farming, was he who was "first in peace" as in war. Few probably ever possessed so keen a love for rural pursuits, and a more unyielding pride in the profession of a farmer, than George Washington. Always an early riser, he was enabled to see that the day's work was properly begun, and careful to exact the utmost accuracy and fidelity from those he employed. Before the war his name was known in London as the most reliable planter in Virginia, and the produce of his plantations would command a better price than that of any other in the colonies. "I think," he said, "the life of a husbandman of all others is the most delightful. It is honorable, it is amusing, and with judicious management it is profitable." If it be true, then, that the dignity of a calling depends upon the character of those who pursue it, the status of the agriculturist has been fixed and ennobled from the remotest ages of the world to the present day.

—*Leland Stanford.*

162. The Base of the Whole Fabric of Life.— As we stand and live upon our great mother earth, so the whole fabric of enlightened life stands upon agriculture. Not alone because it feeds and clothes our bodies, but because of its moral and philosophic forces as well as its physical. Egypt was the first cradle of agriculture; it was, therefore, the first cradle of civilization. The Israelites—the chosen people—were no exception to the rule. In their early career, they did not till the soil. They had to be taken down into Egypt to learn Agriculture, or they would have been barbarians. The Greek and the Roman would have been barbarians had they not learned agriculture. Men are mere tribes —hordes—without agriculture. It is the mother of stability, with infinite progression. It is the mother of wealth, of law and order, of manufactures, commerce and the arts. From this source spring the great emotions of the soul, patriotism, social and political order, churches, schools, science and religion, long life, strong life, abundance. Without it the world could not be populated. Pioneering tends to barbarism, because it tends to roving. Pioneering is almost buccaneering. We are pioneers (A. D. 1858) and yet see here this early and devout attention to agriculture. We are the mildest mannered buccaneers of history. What had this State done without agriculture? The present generation might have survived in some sort of repute, from the force of early education; but the generation to come would have been as the present Arab to the ancient Saracen, the present Mexican to the ancient Spanish Cavalier. Gold is not wealth; it is but its con-

venient representative. Commerce is not wealth; it simply exchanges it. Manufactures and art are not wealth; they recombine it. Agriculture is the prolific mother of wealth. The rest simply handle it when it is produced and delivered into their hand. The earth breeds savages; agriculture breeds enlightened nations. It breeds houses and ships, temples and seminaries, manufactories, sculpture, painting and music. It would be folly to speak of the existence, beauty or power of any of these, without agriculture. The thermometer of civilization rises or falls as drives or pauses the plow.
—*Samuel B. Bell.*

163. Nature Enforces Economy Toward The Soil.—Have you read in one of the volumes of "Les Miserables," Victor Hugo's description of the sewer of Paris, and his reflections on it? He tells his countrymen that all that filth is gold, and that they sweep it into the abyss. We fit out convoys of ships, at great expense, to gather up at the south pole the droppings of petrels and penguins, and the incalculable element of wealth which we have under our own hand we send to sea. All the fertilizing substance, human and animal, which the world loses, restored to the land, instead of being thrown into the water, would suffice to nourish the world. These heaps of garbage at the corners of the stone blocks, these tumbrels of mire jolting through the streets at night, these horrid scavengers' carts, these streams of subterranean slime, which the pavement hides from you, do you not know what all this is? It is the flowering meadow; it is the green grass, it is marjoram and thyme and sage; it is game, it is cattle, it is the satisfied low of huge oxen at evening; it is perfumed hay, it is golden corn, it is bread on your table, it is warm blood in your veins, it is health, it is joy, it is life. Thus wills that mysterious creation which is transformation upon earth, and transformation in heaven. There is one thing in which the half-civilized Mongolians can defy their civilized foes to instruct them—the great art of keeping the soil fertile steadily for centuries. Japan is about as large as England and Ireland combined. So much of its area is hilly that hardly more than half is fit for tillage. Great Britain imports food from other countries to the extent of many millions annually. But Japan supports a larger population than England and Ireland. She exports grain now to foreign countries. She maintains the richness of her soil, and has kept it at a high and even rate of productiveness through centuries that stretch back beyond the decay of Greece, beyond the birth of Rome, to the days of Solomon, possibly to the age of Moses. She has done it by careful obedience to the laws of restoration which God has written in the soil. She treats the soil as a factory. Wanting cloth from it, she gives the woof out of which the cloth is woven. She finds that Nature will toil for man forever, if man will give her the elements of her miracles. She reverently offers to the wand of Providence the filth of cities, that it may be transmuted into flowers and bread. California will prove no exception to the general law of nature which enforces economy toward the soil. The Creator gives our land to us as a trust, and if we do not try to pass it over to our children with but little reduction of its vitality, we are simply squandering our capital in our great harvests now, and mortgaging also the patrimony of posterity.—*Thomas Starr King.*

THE GARDENS OF THE PETERSKOI.

164. I spent an evening at the Peterskoi, which I shall long remember as one of the most interesting I ever spent at any place of popular amusement. The gardens of Peterskoi are a favorite place of resort in summer, near Moscow—famous for its chateau built by the Empress Elizabeth, in which Napoleon sought refuge during the burning of Moscow. The weather was charming; neither too warm nor too cool, but of that peculiarly soft and dreamy temperature which predisposes one for the enjoyment of music, flowers, the prattle of children, the fascinations of female beauty, and the luxuries of idleness. In such an atmosphere no man of sentiment can rack his brain with troublesome problems concerning the origin of the human race, or abuse his limbs rambling through dirty streets in search of curiosities, or do any other labor usually allotted to the tourist. Such evenings, and such nights, when the sun lingers dreamily on the horizon, when the long twilight weaves a web of purple and gold that binds the night to the morning; when nature, wearied of the dazzling glare of day, puts on her delicate silver-spangled night robes, and reclining upon her couch, smiles upon her loving worshipers, and tells them to "woo her gently, and with honeyed words," when stubborn hearts are softened and haughty eyes made gentle by the invisible spirits that hover in the air—ah, surely such evenings and such nights were never made for sleep. The veriest monster in human shape cannot be utterly insensible to their inspiring influence. We must make love, sweet ladies, or die.

The gardens of the Peterskoi are still a dream to me. It was night when I first entered their portals. Guards, in imperial livery, glittering from head to foot with richly-wrought embroidery, stood at the gateway and ushered in the company with many profound and elegant bows. Policemen, with cocked hats and glittering epaulettes, were stationed at intervals along the leading thoroughfares, to preserve order. The scene within was singularly rich, glowing and fanciful. In every feature it presented some striking combination of natural and artificial beauties, admirably calculated to fascinate the imagination. I have a vague recollection of shady and undulating walks, winding sometimes over sweeping lawns, dotted with wide-spreading trees, copses of shrubbery and masses of flowers; sometimes over gentle acclivities, surmounted by rustic cottages, or points of rocks overhung with moss and fern; here branching off into cool umbrageous recesses, where caves, with glittering stalactites, invited the wayfarer to linger a while and rest; there driving suddenly into deep glens and retired grottos, where lovers, far hidden from the busy throng, might mingle their vows with the harmony of falling waters.

What a pity we should ever grow old, in this beautiful world, with so many fair ladies in it to be wooed and won! Who could be insensible to their charms on such a night and amid such scenes, when the very flowers are whispering love to each other, and the lights and shadows are wrought into bridal wreaths? Here one can fancy the material world has ceased. Reality is merged into the realms of enchantment. Marble statues, representing the Graces, winged Mercuries and Cupids, with their bows and arrows, are so cunningly displayed in relief against the green banks of foliage, that they seem the natural inhabitants of the place. Snow-spirits, too, with outspread wings, hover in the air, as if to waft cooling zephyrs through the soft, summer night. Fountains dash their sparkling waters high into the moonlight, spreading a mystic spray over the rich green sward. Through vistas of shrubbery gleam the bright waters of a lake, overhung by cliffs and embattled towers and the drooping foliage of trees. On an elevated plateau stand Asiatic temples and pagodas, in which the chief entertainments are held. The approaching avenues are illuminated with brilliant and many colored lights, hung from the branches of trees, and wind under triumphal arches overhung with flowers. Theaters present open fronts, richly and curiously decorated. Artificial grottoes and fountains, that seem to cast forth glittering gems; temples and embattled towers, palaces and ruins—all aglow with brilliant and mysterious lights, are scattered in sumptuous profusion over the grounds. The open spaces in front of the theaters are filled with the rank and fashion of the city, in all the glory of jeweled head dresses, brilliant costumes, and decorations of Orders. Festoons of variegated lights swing from the trees over the audience. Painted figures of dragons and genii guard every avenue. Rustic seats and elegant divans are scattered in the most inviting nooks, and tables, overshadowed by hanging rocks, spangled with stalactites of silver, indicate where rest and refreshment lend their aid to the varied pleasures of the eye. The gorgeous profusion of lights and glittering ornaments, the endless variety of colors, the Asiatic character of the various temples of pleasure, the tropical luxuriance of the foliage; the gleaming white statuary; the gay company; the soft strains of music—all combine to make a scene of wonderful enchantment. High, overhead, dimly visible through the tops of the trees, the sky wears a rich, strange, almost preternatural aspect, in the short summer nights. A soft, golden glow, flushes upward from the horizon, and lying outspread over the firmament, gives a peculiar spectral effect to the gentler and more delicate sheen of the moon. The stars shrink back into the dim infinity, as if unable to contend with the grander and more glowing effulgence of the great orb that rules the night; and the rapt spectator is unconscious whether the day is waning into the night or the night into the morning. All is a grand anomaly—a rich, strange, and inexplicable combination of the glories of art with the wonders of nature.—*J. Ross Browne.*

VI.

SOCIETY AND THE STATE.

PART VI.

SOCIETY AND THE STATE.

165. Dueling.—I utter my unqualified condemnature of the code which offers to personal vindictiveness a life due only to a country, a family, and to God. If I were, under any circumstances, an advocate for a duel, it should be at least a fair, equal and honorable duel. If, as was said by an eloquent advocate in its favor, "it was the light of past ages, which shed its radiance upon the hill-tops of civilization, although its light might be lost in the dark shade of the valleys below," I still maintain that a duel should be fair and equal; that skill should not be matched against ignorance, practical training against its absence. No duel should stand the test of public opinion, independent of the law, except the great element of equality is there. In the pursuits of common life, no one not trained to a profession is supposed to be a match for a professional man in the duties of his profession. I am no match for a physician in any matters connected with his pursuits, nor would a physician be a match for me in a legal argument. The civilian not trained to the use of arms is no match for the soldier; nor, although his courage is equal, and he may have a profound conviction that he is right, will, therefore, the contest be rendered equal and just. I denounce the system itself, because it loses annually hundreds of valuable lives, and, in the present state of civilization, it does no good, profits nothing, arrests no evil, but impels a thousand evils; but, above all, do I protest against any contests of this nature where, in skill, knowledge of weapons, or from any cause, the parties are not equal in all the conditions of that stern debate.

The code of honor is a delusion and a snare. It palters with the hope of a true courage, and binds it at the feet of crafty and cruel skill. It surrounds its victim with the pomp and grace of the procession, but leaves him bleeding on the altar. It substitutes cold and deliberate preparation for courageous and manly impulse, and arms the one to disarm the other. It may prevent fraud between practiced duelists, who should be forever without its pale; but it makes the mere "trick of the weapon" superior to the noblest cause and the truest courage. Its pretence of equality is a lie. It is equal in all the form, it is unequal in all the substance. The habitude of arms, the early training, the frontier life, the border war, the sectional custom, the life of leisure—all these are advantages which no negotiation can neutralize and which no courage can overcome.

Whatever there is, in the code of honor or out of it, that demands or allows a deadly combat where there is not in all things entire and certain equality, is a prostitution of the name, is an evasion of the substance, and is a shield, blazoned with the name of Chivalry, to cover the malignity of murder.—*Gen. E. D. Baker.*

166. POPULAR CORRUPTION.—For a lying press, for iniquitous politicians, and an ignorant pulpit, for the absurdities of fashion and the injustice of society, for prostitution, for gambling, for thieving, for the knaveries of the scheming capitalist, the grinding of monopolists, and the swindlings of corporations, the people have only themselves to blame, for all these enormities spring from the people and exist only on the sufferance of the people.—*Hubert H. Bancroft.*

167. POPULAR JUSTICE.—I have the fullest confidence in the ultimate justice and judgment of the people. I am not afraid of them at all. Sometimes, when they do not understand, they stone the prophets, revile earnest reformers, and hang innocent men; but when, too late, they discover their error, they return in surging multitudes, build costly monuments over the victims of their phrenzy, plant sweet blooming flowers, and water them with their tears. When the Athenian populace had accused Aristides of conspiracy, and had banished him from the Capital, they found out their mistake, and called him back with acclamation; and when, in the theater that night, the actor spoke of a true patriot and a just man, the whole audience rose and turned toward the exile. That was the most triumphant hour in the life of the warrior and statesman—grander, more glorious, more exultant than that of Marathon. Some years ago the people of San

Francisco chased away an eloquent old man, (Gen. E. D. Baker—Editor,) who took refuge in the mountains of Nevada. He was afterwards brought back from the sacrificial heights of Stone River, a mangled and speechless prophet of freedom, and fifty thousand people laid him tenderly on the altitudes of Lone Mountain, within hearing of the eternal dirges of the ocean—while his glorious declaration echoed and still echoes in the valleys and mountains from the fountains of the San Joaquin to the sources of the Columbia: "Years, years ago, I took my stand by Freedom, and where in youth my feet were planted, there my manhood and my age shall march."—*Gen. John A. Collins.*

168. Catholicity of Spirit. — Momus blamed Jupiter because, when he made man he put no window in his breast through which the heart might be seen. Momus was a sleepy god; and we mortals are likewise troubled with a lack of insight into human character. No doubt Jupiter should have done better. Man is far from a perfect creation. But as the gods saw fit to do no more for us, thanking them for what they have done, may we not now do something for ourselves? Were not the eyes of Momus somewhat at fault, as well as the fingers of Jupiter? If we lay aside the narrowing prejudices of birth and education, under the influences of which it is impossible to balance nicely the actions of men, may we not discover here and there openings into the soul? The homily of glowing patriot or zealous sectarian, is not history, but verbiage. Let all that is worthy of censure in state, church and society,

be condemned; let all that is worthy of praise be extolled; but let not censure and praise be meted out according to the maxims of country or creed. Let us meet every age and nation upon the broad platform of humanity, measuring no man's conscience by our own, but by the conscience of nature, and condemning cruelty and injustice wherever we find it, whether in Hebrew, Turk, Christian, Spaniard, or Anglo-Saxon. I hold it to be no less unwise than dishonest to wage vituperative warfare against any nation or sect, as such. Would he keep pellucid the stream of thought, with his piety and patriotism, the writer of history will have little to do.—*Hubert H. Bancroft.*

169. SOCIAL ARTIFICES.—It is all very well for those who are perched upon the highest pinnacles to fling out the old aphorism, that water will always reach its level. They forget, for the nonce, that it is quite possible to force water above its level by artificial appliances, and to keep it there, for a time, at least. Hydraulic pressure lends a momentum quite equal to the attainment of such results. Not more difficult is it to prevent water from reaching its level, by shutting it out almost entirely, by the construction of coffer dams. There are hydraulic rams constantly at work amid the complicated machinery of society; and their potent moving force is felt in the uplifting of many a dead weight into a hateful prominence, that would otherwise lie prone at the bottom.—*Sarah B. Cooper.*

170. MODERN CIVILIZATION.—It may be a contested point whether modern civilization is more pro-

ductive of human happiness and morality than of vice and misery. It is true that culture and refinement, while they broaden the scope of joys and duties, and stimulate the moral and intellectual attributes, must increase the capabilities of crime. The educated villain can accomplish more evil than the ignorant knave can conceive. The heart of the cultivated and refined man can feel keener pangs than the benighted and blunted sensibilities of the primitive boor can imagine. But herein may lie the fallacy: It is not that enlightenment increases disproportionately crime over virtue, sorrow over gladness, but that it illuminates, and brings into such hideous contrast, the extremes, so that we forget the bright, while we look lamentingly on the dark side of the picture. Those of us who are of the Pioneers of '50 and '52, know from experience, without the aid of rhetoric or logic, the change for good which the humanizing influences of cultivated, social and intellectual society has wrought here in California. Where once the jingling of gold in the gambling dens constituted the Sabbath music, broken now and then by the muttered oath or the shrieks of dying men, are now heard the swelling tones of the organ mingling with the voices of the worshipers of God.—*Nathaniel Bennett.*

171. CONTINUOUS SOCIAL ADVANCE.—In the present state of knowledge, the mystery of civilization, or social progress, like all the phenomena of evolution, is unexplainable; and whatever opinion we may hold as to natural agencies, and supernatural interpositions, we

can best see marked by the centuries, a permanent and continuous unfolding and improvement, acting under laws as fixed as those which regulate siderial systems. Yet though predetermined and fixed in its efforts and results, like the plant artificially dwarfed or improved, progress may be hindered or accelerated by the character of individuals and the politics of society. Social disruptions, moral earthquakes, mobs, murders, and outraged law, no less than literature, art, industry, and wealth, in their action and reaction on each other, fertilize intellect and stimulate intellectual growth.
—*Hubert H. Bancroft.*

172. OUR MORAL INHERITANCE.—The geologists say that the earth's surface is made up of layers of sandstone, limestone, chalk and marl, the products of successive deposits. The moral world is as truly made up of layers of opinions hardened into beliefs; of sentiments, and thoughts. The best father of most of us is our great past. A man endowed with millions and with boundless square leagues of real estate, but with the civilization that he inherits all cancelled, is poorer than the poorest citizen surrounded by, and partaking in, our civilization. Better for us to lose the whole of our army and navy, and that all our ports be laid waste, than that one per cent. be abated of our respect for the forms of a public meeting, of our regard for law, of our love of home, of our dread of riot and anarchy. In the one case we part with the evidences and immediate instruments of our power, which may be replenished; in the other we part with the forces that we have inherited from ages.—*Thomas Starr King.*

173. Wine.—This conglomerate which you call society is hanging out a great many flags of distress. It babbles incoherently of perfectibility, and goes straightway to the bad. Are those reformers going to save the world, who, either through intemperance of speech or drink, must needs be moderated by a padlock put upon their mouths? Nor is it safe, just now, to calculate the results of this feminine gospel of vituperation. The back of the body politic may be the better for having a fly-blister laid on; and it might, perhaps, as well be done by feminine hands as by any other. But there are some evils too deep for surface remedies. If, for instance, vineyards are going to curse the people, as my moralizing friend insists, then humanity hereabout is in a bad way, and needs reconstructing from the nethermost parts to the bald crown of the head. Why, a little generous wine ought to enrich the blood and inspire nobility of thought. If it does more than this—if it becomes a demon to drive men and hogs into the sea—then it is evident that both were on too low a plane of existence for any safe exaltation. But shall the vineyards be rooted up for all this? It is better to drown the swine, and let the grapes still grow purple upon the hill-sides. Oh, my friend, with thin and impoverished blood! do not pinch this question up in the vise of your morality. No doubt there was a vineyard in Eden, and there were ripe clusters close by the fig leaves. You cannot prove to me that sinless hands have not plucked the grapes, and that millions will not do it again. What we need is not a greater company of wailing prophets, but men who will reveal to us the higher and nobler use of things.—*Rev. W. C. Bartlett.*

174. CONSERVATIVES AND RADICALS.—How constantly the different classes of mind are supplied. Conservatives and radicals are made so more by nature than by argument. Some are born to hark for the tramp of new truths, to watch for gleams of new revelations; others are born to live with their faces nobly turned to the past. No nation is without her progressive party, and no community, however fast, without its party of conservatives. If all were bound to go ahead, our growth would be like the gourds. If the Hunker element were in excess, the tree would be all gnarls and knots. Where both are present, we have society like an oak, believing in air and leaves, with tough, wide-spreading limbs and twigs that respond to every breeze, and coarse, rough bark and roots that mine the earth and fill the soil. If the bold critics of governments, if the agitators were all lost from the community for a century, we should be like a train of cars without an engine, rotting on the track; but with nothing but agitators in a State, we are like a line of locomotives without a car, bound to tear on, so long as fuel and track hold out.—*Thos. Starr King.*

175. THE CAUSE CALLS FORTH THE MAN.—All the efforts of Science have failed to trace back of itself the springs and sources of that subtle thing that we call life and know not what it is. So far as we can go is to discern back of each living thing some other living

thing. Yet so widely are its germs scattered, that, given but the conditions that support it, and there will life appear. And so it seems in the moral world. Whenever in human history occasion and opportunity wait the man, forth he steps, and as the common worker is on need transformed into a queen bee, so when circumstances are favorable, what might otherwise pass for a common man, rises into hero or leader, sage or saint. So widely has the sower scattered the good seed; so strong is the germinative force that bids it bud and blossom. But, alas! for the stony ground, and the weeds and the tares! For one who attains his full stature, how many are stunted and deformed!
—*Henry George.*

176. ONE-SIDED PROGRESS.—The winds do our bidding, and the occult pulses of the earth carry our words; we weigh the sun and analyze the stars. One after another, mightier genii than those that arise in Arabian Story have bowed to the call of the lamp of knowledge. And yet they throng and come, powers more vast, in shapes more towering. But to what end? Look to the van of progress, where the conditions to which all progressive countries are tending are most fully realized, where wealth is most abundant and population densest—the great cities, where one may walk through miles of palaces, where are the grandest churches, the greatest libraries, the highest levels of luxury, and refinement, and education, and culture. Amid the greatest accumulations of wealth men die of starvation, and women prowl the streets to buy bread

with shame; in factories, where labor-saving machinery shows the last march of ingenuity, little children are at work who ought to be at play; where the new forces are most fully realized, large classes are doomed to pauperism or live just on its verge, while everywhere the all-absorbing chase of wealth, shows the force of the fear of want, and from altars dedicated to the Living God leers the molten image of the Golden Calf.

Progress thus one-sided is not real, and cannot last. No chain is stronger than its weakest link. If the low are not brought up, the high shall be pulled down. This is the attraction of gravitation of the moral universe; it is the fiat of the eternal justice that rules the world. It stands forth in the history of every civilization that has had its day and run its course. It is what the Sphinx says to us as she sitteth in desert sand, while the winged bulls of Nineveh bear her witness! It is written in the undecipherable hieroglyphics of Yucatan, in the brick mounds of Babylon, in the prostrate Columns of Persepolis, in the salt-sown plain of Carthage. It speaks to us from the shattered relics of Grecian art, from the ruins of the Coliseum!—*Henry George*.

177. THE DECAY OF EMPIRES.—Science teaches that invisible things are more substantial than visible, and truth is the food of all that is substantial. Nations have seldom been drawn and quartered while in good health; they generally die of disease. If true coroners' verdicts were written on the tombstones of kingdoms, the theories of sensuous history would be sadly contradicted. Babylon died of delirium tremens; rum did it;

in a single night she staggered to her ruin. Nineveh was killed by apoplexy; Macedon died of a raging fever; Egypt of gluttony and gout; Rome of dropsy. We might go further, and make the diagnoses of diseases that are threatening living nations.—*Thos. Starr King.*

178. PATRIOTISM.—The life-and-death-struggle of a free people to preserve their country is an event angels might weep and yet exult to see. Heroism defying wounds and death, pouring out its life blood freely, is the inspiration of country. Two ideas there are which, above all others, elevate and dignify a race, the idea of God and the idea of Country. How imperishable is the idea of country! How does it live within and ennoble the heart in spite of persecutions and trials, and difficulties and dangers! After two thousand years of wandering, it makes the Jew a sharer in the glory of the prophets, the lawgivers, the warriors and poets, who lived in the morning of time. How does it toughen every fiber of an Englishman's frame, and imbue the spirit of Frenchmen with Napoleonic enthusiasm. How does the German carry with him even the old house furniture of the Rhine, surround himself with the sweet and tender associations of Fatherland, and, wheresoever he may be, the great names of German history shine like stars in the heaven above him. And the Irishman, though the political existence of his country is merged in a kingdom whose rule he may abhor, yet still do the chords of his heart vibrate reponsive to the tones of the harp of Erin, and the lowly shamrock is dearer to his soul than the fame-crowning laurel, the love-breathing myrtle, or the storm-daring pine. What is our country? Not alone the land and the sea, the lakes and rivers, and valleys and mountains—not alone the people, their customs and laws—not alone the memories of the past, the hopes of the future; it is something more than all these combined. It is a divine abstraction. You cannot tell what it is, but let its flag rustle above your head, you feel its living presence in your hearts. They tell us that our country must die; that the sun and stars will look down upon the Great Republic no more; that already (A. D. 1862—EDITOR) the black eagles of despotism are gathering in our political sky. That even now kings and emperors are casting lots for the garments of our national glory. It shall not be! Not yet, not yet, shall the nations lay the bleeding corpse of our country in the tomb. If they could, angels would roll the stone from the mouth of the sepulcher. It would burst the casements of the grave, and come forth a living presence, redeemed, regenerated, disenthralled. Not yet, not yet, shall the Republic die. The heavens are not darkened, the stones are not rent! It shall live—it shall live, the incarnation of freedom, it shall live the embodiment of the power and majesty of the people. Baptized anew, it shall live a thousand years to come, the Colossus of the nations—its feet upon the continents, its scepter over the seas, its forehead among the stars!—*Newton Booth.*

179. PATRIOTISM is but a reflex of egoism, and respect for statutes and constitutions is but another form

of loyalty. And as excessive love of country is simply excessive self-love, so undue worship of forms of law is nothing more than a part of that superstitious loyalty which of old held to the doctrine of divine kingship. If reverence is anywhose due, whatever good there may be in loyalty, in that sentiment which unites individuals under a common head, it is not the power of law which should be reverenced, but the power which creates and sustains law. This doctrine of divine kingship appears in a sort of inverted form in the mind of the Athenian who held it wrong for a man to rise above his fellows—whence ostracism, or oyster-shell voting a great man out of the country.—*Hubert H. Bancroft.*

180. POLITICS.—The pursuit of politics is delusive and full of temptation. No man should forget the duty he owes his country, but all should remember that they owe a duty to themselves. When men, more particularly young men, see a great statesman stand forth in the midst of a listening senate, and mark the stamp which he makes upon the public mind, and upon the policy of the country, by the force of his intellectual vigor, they are apt to forget the labors by which that proud position has been achieved; to forget how many have sought to attain such a lofty place and have failed; and to forget that he who is filling their minds with admiration may be on the eve of a sudden fall. Politics should not be the pursuit, I mean the only pursuit, of any man. Representative honors, official station, should only be the occasional reward, or the occasional sacrifice; and if, forgetting this rule, young

men attempt to make politics their only hope, with the probability that in many cases they will fail, and that, if successful, they will surely be exposed to a thousand temptations; if they love excitement for its own sake—the noisy meetings, the conventions, the elections—this love for excitement will grow upon them, and they will soon be upon the high road to ruin. If anyone is determined to achieve distinction in politics, let him first obtain a competency in some trade, profession, or pursuit, and then, even if unsuccessful in politics, the misstep will not be irretrievable.—*Gen. E. D. Baker.*

181. FREE TRADE.—Free trade, the right to buy in the cheapest and sell in the dearest market, is based upon a fundamental law, as inexorable as death, and the violation of which is inevitably followed by severe retribution. This law no nation can overlook. It is the same law which gives to a man the right to enjoy life and to hold property without restrictions, except such as are absolutely needed for the benefit of the whole community of which he forms a part. When a government oversteps these limits, for the benefit of a particular class, it in effect destroys rights which are inherent in the people, and with which no interference can be justified. Commerce should be as free as the air we breathe. Its arms should extend to every spot upon the globe where human beings exist; and should have the right to grasp, unchecked, whatever can contribute to the happiness of men. The only regulations it requires are those which spring from the natural laws of supply and demand. Beyond these, all interference with its

operation is simply proscriptive and semi-barbarous; because, in addition to other arguments, it checks the progress of civilization. Commerce is the great civilizer of the world. By facilitating intercourse and the free interchange of commodities, it conveys the great truths of progress into every land and over every sea. It knits humanity together; and by the very sympathies and interests it generates, tends to render war, which destroys what peace creates, impossible. That commerce must be free, is a decree of nature, before which all must bow; so that as it scatters broadcast the blessings of liberty, science and the arts may cause knowledge to spread, until it shall cover the earth as the waters cover the great deep.—*Henry E. Highton.*

182. NATIONAL CHARACTER.—The great thing for statesmen to learn as a primitive fundamental truth is this simple fact—that the organization of a State is not effected by its paper bonds, but by its moral bonds. The Creator always deals with a state as a great person. Laws are ever at work beneath the changes of its inhabitants and the struggles of its parties, weaving into stable character its passing experiences—character which is the noblest national reward, or the sternest retribution. Individuals are never conscious of this law. Very often they think that the forces of a nation's life are playing at haphazard. But the law plays around them, uses them, and no more permits a state to begin its life anew with each generation than it allows a man to begin his life anew after each night's sleep. It is the glory of the human intellect that it can detect law in the process

of the universe, and see at least in countless threads of order, the habits, purposes, and expressions of a creative power. Everywhere we turn there is law, and the most striking expressions of it are in what we often consider to be the region of chance or lawlessness. Running up through the realm of science to society, and to the life of nations, we find that the apex-truth which the intellect discovers, is this: Character is of supreme importance for national growth, prosperity and stability. How impressive does history seem as a study, when we find that every country is a huge pedestal, lifting up one national figure, which symbolizes the prospects and the perils of the millions that dwell around its base.—*Thomas Starr King.*

CAPITAL AND LABOR.

183. Slavery is not dead, though its grosssst form be gone. What is the difference, whether my body is legally held by another, or whether he legally holds that by which alone I can live? Hunger is as cruel as the lash. The essence of slavery consists in taking from a man all the fruits of his labor except a bare living, and of how many thousands miscalled free is this the lot? Where wealth most abounds there are classes with whom the average plantation negro would have lost in comfort by exchanging. English villeins in the Fourteenth Century were better off than English agricultural laborers of the Nineteenth. There is slavery and slavery. "The widow," says Carlyle, "is gathering nettles for her children's dinner; a perfumed seigneur, delicately lounging in the Œil de Bœuf, has an alchemy whereby he will extract from her the third nettle, and call it rent!"

Let us not be deluded by names. What is the use of a republic if labor must stand with its hat off, begging leave to work; if "tramps" must throng the highways and children grow up in squalid tenement houses? Political institutions are but means to an end—the freedom and happiness of the individual; and just so far as they fail in that, call them what you will, they are condemned.

Our conditions are changing. The laws which impel nations to seek a larger measure of liberty, or else take from them what they have, are working silently but with irresistible force. If we would perpetuate the Republic, we must come up to the spirit of the Declaration, and fully recognize the equal rights of all men. We must free labor from its burdens and trade from its fetters; we must cease to make government an excuse for enriching the few at the expense of the many, and confine it to necessary functions. We must cease to permit the monopolization of land and water by non-users, and apply the just rule, "no seat reserved unless occupied." We must cease the cruel wrong which, by first denying their natural rights, reduces laborers to the wages of competition, and then, under pretence of asserting the rights of another race, compels them to a competition that will not merely force them to a standard of comfort unworthy the citizen of a free Republic, but ultimately deprive them of their equal right to live.

Here is the test: whatever conduces to their equal and inalienable rights to men is good—let us preserve it. Whatever denies or interferes with those equal rights is bad—let us sweep it away. If we thus make our institutions consistent with their theory, all difficulties must vanish. We will not merely have a republic, but social conditions consistent with a republic. If we will not do this, we surrender the Republic, either to be torn by the volcanic forces that already shake the ground beneath the standing armies of Europe, or to rot by slow degrees, and in its turn undergo the fate of all its predecessors.—*Henry George.*

184. THE NECESSITIES of life, the wants of advancing civilization, open a scope for employment wide as humanity. They demand the fullest exercise of the highest energies of every member of the human race. Let Society and Government seek to attain an organization wherein Labor shall be elevated to its true position, and its claims recognized and rewarded. Government taxed to furnish employment? Why, national prosperity must be vitalized every moment by increasing toil, or the value that capital represents would perish, and money become as worthless as the mere pictures on the coins. The roots of the tree of wealth must be continually watered by the sweat of the laborer's brow, or its branches would die, its leaves wither, and its golden fruit turn to ashes on the lips of its possessor. Let labor suspend for a day, and the world would feel the shock. Let it cease for a month, and a crisis would come, such as commerce never felt, involv-

ing banks, moneyed institutions, and national credit in common ruin. Let it be idle for a single summer, and terror would come down on the strong and the weak, beauty would turn pale at the toilet, eloquence become dumb in the Senate, ships would open their seams, the grass grow in the market-place, and the nations be shaken to their foundations. Anarchy, bloody-handed revolution, grim and ghastly famine, would shake their snaky locks in every land. Let it be paralyzed for a single year, and the world would be smitten as with the wrath of God. Jehovah, in his awful omnipotence, could devise no curse that would more blast, and scorch, and desolate the earth. Not Cotton is King; nor Gold. Labor is the true Monarch of the world! With stalwart frame and sinewy arm, and face bronzed and scarred, but still with "front of Jove and eye like Mars," he must be recrowned—crowned in the starry temple of science—with power for his throne, art his sceptre, and wealth his sparkling diadem.—*Newton Booth.*

185. THERE IS NO DOGMA, nor theory, nor device under the sun, upon which men have been so universally agreed as that the right of property underlies all true religion, government and civilization. Without it, deprived of all motive to acquire beyond the most absolute necessity, man would sink into the savagedom from which it has taken five thousand years to raise him. The justice of allowing unlimited acquisition is evidenced by the fact that the desire is univer-

sal. No natural inherent quality or passion is ours without there is lying behind it a benign purpose.

—*James McM. Shafter.*

186. IT WOULD BE USELESS, vicious and insane to declaim with Proudhon against the rights of property. Property is the incentive to exertion. It is the stimulant which is the preventive of idleness, and its enjoyment should be the just reward of honest industry. Its security is the very foundation of order. Take it away, and society would relapse into that anarchy which is worse than despotism. It would be idle and visionary to join with Rousseau in his sentimental praises of barbarism. One Shakespeare, or Newton, or Fulton, or Washington, were worth all the savage tribes that ever lived. The world was not made for savages, but for men. We must not recede to a lower civilization, but advance to a higher; the type must not be broken, but improved. The means of production must continue to increase, but the principles of distribution must become fair and equitable; the paradox that riches and poverty increase in the same ratio must be disproved. Wealth must not be diverted into reservoirs to stagnate, but flow out in living streams, perpetual rivers of abundance, making the landscape beautiful, the fields green and fruitful, and all the people glad. Communists, socialists and Fourierists, have grappled with these difficulties in vain. Associations, phalanxes and communities, however beautiful in theory, have failed in their application to the facts of human nature. Society can never be modeled upon an invented plan;

it always casts itself in the mould of necessity—it obeys its own laws. We must seek in itself, in the ingredients as they are, for the powers and agencies that shall evolve its improvements. Among these powers, whatever tends to diffuse the privileges that have been concentrated, to scatter broadcast the blessings that have been garnered up, will be a noble and efficient instrumentality for good. A free pulpit, speaking to the great heart of the people, a religion that goes into the highways and byways, free schools whose doors are open to the children of all, a free press sending its streams of literature to every man's home, science popularized until its great truths blend with the public mind, mechanical arts approaching that perfection that will so cheapen the commodities they manufacture as to place them within the reach of all; life and health assurances and insurances, enabling the laborer to free himself and family from the crushing fear of want in the hour of sickness and calamity; saving societies, whereby small sums can be made productive, and by their aggregation compete with individual wealth, are all remedial agencies whose influence will widen and deepen as they become more universal and permanent. And if, while new inventions continue to increase man's individual ability, the laws of distribution are made active, just as the powers of production are active, and labor receive its fair reward, there need be no fear that society will lapse towards barbarism in the pursuit of happiness, no fear that phrenzied passions will destroy the rights of property in vindication of the rights of man, no fear that the seats at the table of life will all be taken.

There will be room for all who come, at the bountiful board which nature will continue to spread, until the last syllable of recorded time.—*Newton Booth.*

187. So FAR as the labor question, as it is called, or labor and capital, is concerned with social discontent, there can be no settlement on any present terms of labor and capital. It is no local question, but of universal human interest, and pervades Christendom. The only reconciliation of that difficulty is in moving forward on to a new ground, where the moral relations of employer and workman are recognized as clearly as the politico-economic relation. What men want is a respectful consideration of their welfare. It does not consist in the government taking them up, and finding work for all who want it. A parental government is a monarchy or a despotism where men cannot take care of themselves; but in a free State men are supposed to be of age and able to take care of themselves. Capital and labor will never be at peace, nor will they ever reap their full rewards until they have a material and moral interest in each other's welfare over and above the wages paid on the one hand, or the service rendered on the other. The final goal is not parental government, nor socialism, nor communism, nor trades-unions, but co-operation. This will not be accomplished primarily by legislation, but it will be begun here and there by enlightened men of comprehensive and liberal views, who understand that good workmen must be the allies of their employers. A writer from that part of the country which we call The West—evidently a proprietor and influential director of railroad management, sent a letter to a distinguished journal, setting forth in a clear and forcible way that owners, directors and managers of railroads should adopt some method of helping their workmen, outside the duties for which they are paid, in their private lives. He is a man of experience and ability. His view I will not discuss; it is the spirit of it that I notice. It is the appearance of the moral element in political economy which, until recently, has been altogether ignored. Such movements will get into form after a while. All intelligent and thoughtful men should inform themselves on these things, and know what is being done, and with what success. It is, according to my way of thinking and feeling, one of the most interesting and important subjects that our modern society presents. If intelligent and wise men do not take it up, passionate and ignorant men will. Men who can only feel a wrong need to be guided by those who can see it. If there is anything in the future that seems to me certain in the unfolding of principles, it is that labor and capital can never settle down on the old bare political-economy proposition of demand and supply. The matter can never rest, so it seems to me, save on terms of mutual moral support. In the mean time, the man who talks only to human passions, who talks carelessly about the rights of property, and only disturbs men where they are, before they can do better, is a moral incendiary, and deserves condign punishment.—*Rev. Horatio Stebbins.*

THE REARING OF CHILDREN.

188. THERE CAN be no doubt that the gradual impairment and loss of parental authority and influence is one of the most serious and momentous evils which beset the American civilization. It undermines the very foundations of the family—the essential unit of society.—*Prof. John LeConte.*

189. OUR MORTUARY reports show that about forty per cent. of our children die before they attain their fifth year. If stock-raisers were no more successful in rearing brutes than parents are in raising children, they would soon become bankrupt. If beautiful and healthy children at the age of fifteen years should command a high money premium from society or the State, or if families rearing children without loss, and at the same time possessing health and beauty, should be entitled to honors and pecuniary rewards, it is very probable that the present system of slaughtering children would not long continue. A money consideration would prompt the discovery of laws and lead to the adoption of proper food, clothing, exercise, and habits favoring health, development, symmetry of form, beauty of feature, and longevity. Great is the Almighty Dollar!
—*Gen. John A. Collins.*

190. LET NO WOMAN dare invoke an immortal life until she feels herself worthy to develop it and lead it forth into all its appointed good. Let her never enter that "holy of holies"—the confidence of the young heart that has been nurtured beneath her own—without trying herself, whether she be worthy of that high prerogative; without a tender, deep and prayerful determination to make this one duty paramount to all others, so that she may invest maternity with that divine intelligence that can instruct, with that beautiful love which can feel no sacrifice, with that sweet forbearance which knows no impatience, with that sublime devotion which can make even suffering itself a joy.—*Gen. John A. Collins.*

191. THE MINDS of children, like their bodies, can safely bear but a limited amount of exercise. During the tender years, mental as well as physical culture should partake more of the character of amusement than of labor. Physical weakness, retarded and stunted growth, and deformity, are common among the factory children of Europe. Nervous irritability, dyspepsia, stunted and imbecile minds, are among the youth of our American schools. Men whose frames have attained their natural growth, whose bones are matured and hardened, complain, protest, and rebel against ten hours' daily labor, as being too much and too long for healthful endurance; and yet we confine our children in schools from five to six hours daily, and then many of the lessons must be acquired out of school. This is an outrage upon our youth, and downright robbery of the coming generations of their rightful physical strength, and mental and moral powers. No pupil under fourteen should be allowed, under ordinary circumstances,

to take home a book from the school room. There are always a gifted few who possess enormous capacity for endurance and study, but to make the ability of these the standard, is unwise and unjust. Our youth have something to learn besides abstract mental studies. The heart, or morals and manners, as well as mind, demand culture, expansion, pruning and direction.
—*Gen. John A. Collins.*

192. PARENTS COMMIT a sad and almost remediless error when they bring up their children in bookless, pictureless homes. A forlorn looking house, with dusty grain fields sweeping to the very door, no orchard or garden, no picturesque porches or balconies, is not apt to be very dear to the memories of after years. It does not take much money to brighten home, but it does take patience and forethought. A few books of permanent value—the master-pieces of English literature; a few engravings of pure outline and refined beauty, which shall daily refine the children's faces; a few papers of good morals and practical ability; a bit of color here, a home-made bracket there, an air of neatness everywhere—are these costly requirements? In this age of toil, ambition, and wealth-getting, we cannot too strongly emphasize the fact that it is not sufficient for a man to feed, clothe, and technically educate his children. He must forge links to bind their hearts to the paternal acres and to the family calling: gardens, shrubberies, clinging vines, pictures, low voices of loving parents—these shall far out-bid the attractions of saloons, billiard tables, races, and licentiousness. Your

sons, under proper home-influences, shall become sinewy and truth loving, your daughters fair and stately; their names shall be unsullied, and their lives sweet and rare.—*Charles H. Shinn.*

FREEDOM.

198. Freedom is, and ever must be while the earth turns round, mankind's inalienable inheritance, and manhood's strength and pride and glory. Her snowy raiment has oft been stained with blood. Her mild, sweet eyes have kindled with frenzy; her hymn of deliverence has mingled with the wild scream of plasphemy, the howl of livid fury and infernal hate, but she is still an angel of more than mortal light and beauty to the nations. To win her recognition and receive her benediction humanity, from immemorial ages; has wandered in burning sandy deserts, climbed with bleeding feet the rocky gorge and flinty mountain, endured the pangs of hunger and the agonies of thirst, borne the blast of the merciless hurricane, the whirlwind of pitiless fire. Our country had nobility stamped upon its origin! It sprang into luminous being from the throes of a bloody revolution, with the deathless, thrilling word of Freedom blazoned on her shining forehead—Freedom, whose every look was wisdom, whose every word was love. Won by ancestors, whose thought by day and dream by night, was freedom, whose only august alternative was death! Our country!

with an outlook of promise, grander than which never bewildered the eye of fancy; with a destiny so peerless that the reckless enthusiast, urged he never so wildly the steeds of thought, might never hope to reach its uitimate development or attain its final grandeur, when in consummate perfection with the realization of all its extrinsic and intrinsic possibilities it shall present itself to the muse of history as the grandest government ever witnessed by humanity, the strongest and happiest republic built by man, feared by tyrants, and blessed by God.—*Dr. J. Campbell Shorb.*

194. OFTEN HAS the death of freedom been foretold, and her grave prepared. Once and again has despotism sat down, amidst the pomp and glare of victory, to write her epitaph. Prostrate upon the bloody field, her foes have mistaken her trance of agony for the pangs of dissolution. But now she has leaped from the dust, called her warriors to battle, bared her shining blade to the foe, and shouting at the head of her charging columns, she has converted the dark hour of her fancied extinction into the dawn of an immortal day. Such were the days of Marathon and Thermopylæ; and the preservation of freedom is as much more glorious now than then as American liberty in the nineteenth century is superior to the tumultuous democracy of Athens, or the cruel and gloomy republicanism of Rome. No, Freedom cannot die. She may be prostrated upon a hundred fields of blood, but she will rise crowned with light and radiant with immortality.

—George Barstow.

195. LONG YEARS ago, I took my stand by Freedom, and where in youth my feet were planted, there my manhood and my age shall march. And, for one, I am not ashamed of Freedom. I know her power; I rejoice in her majesty; I walk beneath her banner; I glory in her strength. I have seen her again and again struck down on a hundred chosen fields of battle; I have seen her friends fly from her; I have seen her foes gather around her; I have seen them bind her to the stake; I have seen them give her ashes to the winds, regathering them that they might scatter them yet more widely; but when they turned to exult, I have seen her again meet them, face to face, clad in complete steel, and brandishing in her strong right hand a flaming sword, red with insufferable light.—*Gen. E. D. Baker.*

196. AGAIN, forth from the wrecks of empire, amid tumbling thrones and tottering dynasties (as the Acanthus bursts in bloom and beauty from the ruins of Egyptian graves) rises man, the lord vicarious of earth, proud and imposing in the majesty of manhood. Again Freedom stalks above the mountain tops, singing her song of triumph and brandishing her flaming spear. So strode the daughter of Jeptha, as she advanced unto the sacrifice; so sang Deborah, as she chanted the conquests of her people; so flamed the sword of Judith, red with the blood of Holofernes.

—*Jos. W. Winans.*

197. THEY WHO look upon Liberty as having accomplished her mission, when she has abolished hereditary privileges and given men the ballot, who think of her as having no further relations to the every-day affairs of life, have not seen her real grandeur—to them the poets who have sung of her must seem rhapsodists, and her martyrs fools! As the sun is the lord of life, as well as of light, as his beams not merely pierce the clouds, but support all growth, supply all motion, and call forth from what would otherwise be a cold and inert mass, all the infinite diversities of being and beauty, so is liberty to mankind. It is not for an abstraction that men have toiled and died; that in every age the witnesses of liberty have stood forth, and the martyrs of liberty have suffered. It was for more than this that matrons handed the Queen Anne musket from its rest, and that maids bid their lovers go to death!

We speak of liberty as one thing, and of virtue, wealth, knowledge, invention, national strength and national independence as other things. But, of all these, Liberty is the source, the mother, the necessary condition. She is to virtue what light is to color, to wealth what sunshine is to grain, to knowledge what eyes are to the sight. She is the genius of invention, the brawn of national strength, the spirit of national independence! Where Liberty rises, there virtue grows, wealth increases, knowledge expands, invention multiplies human powers, and in strength and spirit the freer nation rises among her neighbors as Saul amid his brethren—taller and fairer. Where liberty sinks, there virtue fades, wealth diminishes, knowledge is forgotten, invention ceases, and empires, once mighty in arms and arts, become a helpless prey to freer barbarians.

—*Henry George.*

198. AMERICANS, in their excusable pride and enthusiasm, are often prone to claim for themselves solely, the glory of having first enunciated, in distinct form, those grand maxims and principles which constitute the chief corner-stone of our temple of freedom. We forget that, under a great law of nature, nothing seems to be created and perfected at the same time. The great globe on which we stand—this broad and beautiful earth—was, in the beginning, without form, and void. After it took up its grand march, to the music of the spheres, around the blazing pivotal sun, thousands and thousands of ages passed away before it emerged from its primeval state of chaos, and gradually became prepared for the purposes designed by its great Creator—crested with mountains, silvered with oceans, shadowed by forests, gilded and spangled with flowers, and finally consecrated by the presence of God-like man.

The homely fragment of carbon lay, rude and neglected, in the hidden gorges of Golconda, for myriads of centuries before the magic influences of time endowed it with that lustrous radiance which adds splendor to the most gorgeous diadem of royalty, and which the brilliancy of Beauty's eye alone exceeds.

Countless centuries have passed away since, on the sanded floors of the ocean, were laid the first foundations of those coral-islands, which have risen proudly above the dashing wave, and gleam in their velvet verdure, like stars on the breast of the sea.

So, in like manner, we are to look far beyond the Fourth day of July, 1776, for the primitive sources of those sacred sentiments and principles which, like multitudinous rivulets gathering from far distant mountain peaks, have converged, and at length united in one noble, generous, broad-rushing stream, that gives life and happiness to all the dwellers in the land.

From Palestine, from Greece and from Rome, from Germany, France and from England, have descended to us through centuries, the chief axioms of liberty, and many of the weapons of its defence. Chiefly, however, to our mother-land, we owe a debt of gratitude for a great share of our immunities as freemen; she gave to us the Magna Charta, the right of trial by jury, the writ of Habeas Corpus, and the guarantees of religious liberty. And though the mother and daughter, subsequently quarreling about matters of taxation and representation, dissolved their political connections and became permanently separated, yet no candid and liberal mind will deny, that we owe a very large share of our inestimable civil and religious privileges, to that sturdy and imperishable love of freedom and hatred of tyranny, which have ever been a marked feature of the English character, and which have descended to us on the western shore of the Atlantic.

Jefferson, in writing the Declaration of Independence, drew his inspiration from these various sources; the wise and patriotic statesmen who assembled to frame the Constitution of the United States, found no higher or purer springs at which to slake their quenchless thirst for freedom. While we scan the luminous records of the past, and glorify the names of the fathers of the Republic, let us not, in thoughtless selfishness, forget the services rendered to us, in common with the rest of mankind, by the patriots, soldiers and sages of generations long departed.

The Constitution of the United States may aptly be compared to a grand and mighty temple, built of the rarest and choicest materials, collected and preserved by the heroes of the human race through all the ages of the world's history, and handed down to our fathers for the benefit of themselves and their posterity forever. While we praise the architects who composed the edifice, and exhaust panegyric in expressing our admiration of their skill and fidelity, we must not forget the long train of immortal co-laborers, who, from the distant realms of Time, brought column and architrave, cornice and spire and firm foundation stone, to aid us in the erection of a fabric that should defy the corroding tooth of age, the earthquake shock of civil commotion, the thunder bolts of foreign invasion, the silent but fatal influences of human corruption and degeneracy, and become the eternal abiding-place of the spirit of liberty; a fabric beneath whose broad and hospitable roof all the warring and diverse nations of Europe might find shelter and peace; amid whose stately corridors and spacious aisles, beneath whose majestic domes, the humblest citizen and the proudest dignitary should find their legal and political rights held in exact equipoise.—*Judge E. C. Winchell.*

199. POPULAR SOVEREIGNTY, in some shape or other, lies at the foundation of all free governments. Whether a constitution is written or traditional, wherever free government obtains, it must rest upon that great basis; that must be the bed-rock, below which you cannot go. All the expressions upon that subject which men believe in and love in any country, emanate from that point—the right of self-government, the power in the people to regulate and control their own domestic affairs, 'limited by or manifested through constitutional provisions or legislative enactments—expressions more or less deliberate of the popular will. The American people have shown their love of this doctrine from the time of the Revolution down to this day. We derived the idea from the land far across the waves, and from the ages in which such men as Hampden and Russell and Sydney, the patriots and warriors and martyrs of that faith, struggled for it on the field of battle, pined for it in the dungeon, or bled for it on the scaffold. Are you a German? Is not the idea of universal personal independence a favorite of yours? Whether ruled by a duke or a monarch, still the idea of personal liberty is dear to the German heart. So with the Frenchman. Whether fighting under a despot in Italy, or barricading the streets of Paris during a revolution, he loves the idea of personal liberty, and it is equally present in his heart. So with the Englishman. Dear to him are the recollections of the great English Revolution of

1688. Proudly and affectionately he recalls the time when Cromwell and his psalm-singing Ironsides arrayed themselves against the hosts of a treacherous sovereign, and dragged him ignominiously to the block because he attacked the great principles of popular rights and personal liberty. Who ever heard of any man reciting a poem to slavery? But if you want the noblest and most inspiring poems, save those from heaven, read Milton, read Shelley, read Homer, read Halleck, read Bryant, above all, read SHAKESPEARE. There are poets who sell themselves with venal spirit to fatten in the atmosphere of Courts; but even they, seduced by the pomp and brilliancy of fashion, cannot break into praise of slavery. They may praise the despot himself, but the iniquity of slavish servitude they dare not crown with poetry. The hauteur of the poet will not allow it, and his hand trembles, falters, and is palsied ere he attempts to sweep it in such praise across the lyre of song. But when you talk to him of Freedom, his lip quivers with inspiration, his heart glows, and his numbers break out as the stream dashes from the mountain top to seek the vale below—bright, clear, sparkling, *free*. And are you ashamed to march in that procession? Shall reproach, shall malignant slander, shall base misrepresentation make you hesitate? For me, at least, no. A thousand times, no! I love freedom better than slavery. I will speak her words, I will listen to her music, I will acknowledge her impulses, I will stand beneath her flag, I will fight in her ranks, and when I do so, I shall find myself surrounded by the great, the wise, the good, the brave, the noble—

the noble of every land. If I could stand for a moment upon one of our high mountain-tops, far above all the kingdoms of the world, and see coming up, one after another, the bravest and the wisest of the ancient warriors, and statesmen and kings, and monarchs, and priests, and be permitted to ask their opinion on this theme, with a common voice, and in thundertones, reverberating through all lands and echoing down the ages, they would cry, "Liberty, Freedom, the Universal Brotherhood of Man." I join in that shout; I swell that anthem; I echo that cry forever and forever.

—*Gen. E. D. Baker.*

WAR.

200. War never brings unmitigated evil. When a nation has grown puerile in the lap of peace, it revivifies its torpid dust and rekindles its martial fire at the bloody shrine of war. Even degenerate sons, goaded by shame at witnessing the degradation of their country, arouse themselves at last and draw the swords of their fathers. Bad as war is, there is one thing worse —it is that depth of moral degradation which a nation reaches when it considers that it has nothing worth fighting for.—*George Barstow.*

201. WHAT SHALL be said of those conflicts that shatter empires—the civil contests that deluge mighty States with blood? Viewed as isolated phenomena, they appear to be pure scourges—the incarnate wrath

of God, smiting sinful man. But could we trace events to their germinal cause and ultimate results, might we not discover that wars are normal forces moving along the track of progress? May they not have their appropriate place and office in the evolution of humanity, from the primitive to the perfected state? May they not be looked upon as curative rather than destructive agencies—Nature's heroic method of expelling disorder from the social system? May they not perform the same office for the State that the surgeon's knife performs for the individual stricken with a consuming ulcer? The knife is not an instrument of death, but an instrument of science; it is guided, not by a cruel, but a merciful hand. Its office is not to kill, but to cure—not to destroy, but to save. The blood flows, the frame is racked by torture, but the patient is saved.
—*Samuel Williams.*

202. THE GREAT enemy of commerce, and, indeed, of the human race, is War. Sometimes ennobling to individuals and nations, it is more frequently the offspring of a narrow nationality and inveterate prejudice. If it enlists in its service some of the noblest qualities of the human heart, it too often perverts them to the service of a despot. From the earliest ages a chain of mountains, or a line of a river, made men strangers, if not enemies. Whatever, therefore, opens communication, and creates interchange of ideas, counteracts the sanguinary tendencies of mankind, and does its part to "beat the sword into the plowshare."—*Gen. E. D. Baker.*

203. IT SEEMS strange that in the economy of Providence, war should have been permitted—stranger yet that it should have been made the means of human progress. But He who ordained that physical manhood should be attained by hard contact with external things—that strength of character must come by struggling with difficulties, and that moral excellence must be the result of triumph over vice, also ordained that nations must be baptized in the fires of war before they can wear the crown of national glory. Wars have their hopes and their gains, their debits and their credits. The losses fall heaviest upon the immediate generations, the greatest gains belong to generations to come—often their ever-increasing heritage. Instance the American Revolution. Who would strike its bloody, glorious chapters from history now? How infinitely do the gains preponderate over the losses! See the balance-sheet! *Debit*, eight years of war, cruel, merciless, with sufferings and hardships unparalleled; debit, thousands of lives, millions of dollars in property; debit, homes destroyed, families severed; debit, the cruelties of the cow boys, the murder of innocents, the massacre of Wyoming, the treachery of Arnold; debit a land steeped to the lips in poverty. *Credit*, American Independence, credit the Federal Union, credit the Constitution; credit a material advancement unheard of before; credit the inventions in mechanics, the discoveries in science, great names in literature; credit an impulse to civil liberty throughout the world; credit the idea that while Emperors and Kings are dividing and partitioning Europe, this continent shall belong to the people, and they shall possess it forever. Credit WASHINGTON! and if the Revolution had only served to reveal that name in the brightness of its glory—name among all men and races and ages, most loved, most honored, most revered—its blood would not have been shed in vain. There is nothing that consumes, wastes, destroys, like an army. War is a great maelstrom that draws into its vortex that which is near, and whose eddies and currents disturb the waters of the farthest sea. But there is a deeper, tenderer, sadder loss, that figures cannot represent or imagination conceive, the heart can only bleed over it— the loss of precious, noble lives. And such lives—the brave, the daring, the manly, the self-sacrificing. Nations mourn the fall of the gifted, and history enshrines their names in their annals; but the humble, the lowly, though brave and good, have fallen by tens of thousands, not alone on the field of battle and of glory, where there are shoutings of the captains, the thunder of artillery, and all the pomp and pride of war, but in the sickly camp, the crowded hospital, in the noisome prison—they lie in indiscriminate trenches and in nameless graves, where not even the tear of love can mark their resting place.—*Newton Booth.*

OUR COUNTRY.

204. AMERICAN PATRIOTISM.—We walk the earth at mid-day, and the vast expanse of the blue heavens appears unrelieved by the sparkle of a single star. Our world seems to be the lonely satrap of space, chained to the fiery chariot of the mighty sun. And yet we know that Mars still holds his course; that Venus still whirls through space; that Saturn circles amid his shining rings; that Jupiter and Uranus are flashing on the confines of light; that the blazing belt of Orion and the guiding gleam of the North Star are all there; and that when the centrifugal force of the earth shall whirl us again into the presence of night, we shall again behold our companion worlds, as they journey in shining splendor upon their eternal rounds. So, though we may not always be able to see the patriotism, the honor and the free spirit of the American people, we know they exist, and that when the hour comes, we shall see them once more arrayed in majesty, in beauty and in power.—*Thomas Fitch.*

205. GOVERNMENT.—As yet the American mind governs the American continent, and its most powerful instinct is to appeal to law for the redress of private wrong, and to the ballot for the reform of public grievances. No government can be better than the people, or, for any long period of time, worse than the people. The world is governed too much by remote and centralized power. Minute local administration is always purest and wisest. To thoughtful men the governments of the world seem to be growing better, because they govern less.—*Edward C. Marshall.*

206. WHAT IS OUR COUNTRY?—It is not the land and the sea, the river and the mountain, the people, their history and laws. It is something more than all

these. It is a bright ideal, a living presence in the heart, whose destruction would rob the earth of beauty, the stars of their glory, the sun of its brightness, life of its sweetness, love of its joy. My countrymen! cherish this ideal. It will exalt you, as you exalt it. Make it your cloud by day, your pillar of fire by night. Follow where it leads. Enlarge your horizon. Take counsel of the dead. No martyr ever died in the conflict of ideas, which is one of the conditions of human progress, but pleads for the cause consecrated by his blood. Strive to pierce the future. Listen to the footfall of coming generations. No child to be born on earth but has an interest in the cause of liberty and equality. Rise to the hight of a great occasion. Hear the voice of the ages. Take your reckoning by the stars. Then choose.—*Newton Booth.*

207. You may search through the volume of history, you may study closely, and analyze the charateristics of nations that have passed away, yet of none will you find greater attributes, nobler powers, or deeper capacities than those which surround, adorn and bless the American people. Nowhere else was there such a continent, nowhere else such an empire. Nowhere else is nature so bountiful, holding such stores of agricultural and mineral resources. Nowhere else has there been made such progress in the sciences and in all that benefits the human race.—*Milton S. Latham.*

208. Though neither a zealot nor a dreamer, I have an abiding faith in the fortunes of my country.

Could I stand like a revelator, and gaze upward through the grand visions of the political Apocalypse; could I behold the opening of seal upon seal, and the revelation of glory upon glory, disclosing the future of the nations in a prospect more gorgeous than that which the tempter spread before the Son of Man, I would ascribe all the splendor of the scene to the origin, the progress, the grandeur and the destiny of these United States.
—*Joseph W. Winans.*

209. ONE ESSENTIAL TO NATIONAL LIFE.—It will be well for us to ask ourselves the question, and answer it honestly and frankly, whether our unprecedented material progress has not in a great measure overshadowed our moral and intellectual advancement— whether the sea of material prosperity in which, despite occasional squalls, we continue to float buoyantly and hopefully, does not threaten completely to engulph those moral and intellectual qualities without which a nation cannot long sustain its position and independence. We care not to reply to these interrogatories; they are fraught with painful considerations. But we will suggest that when ingratitude corrupts the moral heart of a people, patriotism is on the decline; and when patriotism ceases to exist, dissension, treachery, and ruin soon follow. The name of Samuel Adams is scarcely known among us to-day, and the memory of our glorious Washington seems to inspire us with little gratitude. It will be well for reflective people to ponder on these things.—*T. W. Freelon.*

210. "A Fair Vestal Throned by the West."
—The sayings of the wise have oftentimes a reach beyond their common meaning. When the dying Webster exclaimed, "I still live," he only meant to indicate that life still fluttered in his veins; but the words had a higher force, and symbolized the immortality of his renown. And so, when Shakespeare spoke of "A Fair Vestal Throned by the West," he simply meant to eulogize Elizabeth, the queenly ruler of earth's proudest realm; but a prophetic meaning gathered in those words, which, stretching to the future, heralded another, mightier than Elizabeth, even the Goddess of Liberty herself, seated on a continent and lifting her head above the stars, and before whose majesty all nations were to bow.—*Jos. W. Winans.*

211. Patriotic Devotion.—I yield to no man in devotion to our common country. I love the North, because the blood of my paternal ancestors watered her soil, and beneath her green sod their bones now moulder. I love her for the good and great, the mighty dead, who once trod her ways. I love her for the good and true men who are within her borders—those men of whom it has been well said, that their loins are strong enough and their shoulders broad enough to bear the load of principle; men who have the earnestness to seek the right, and the moral courage to follow their convictions; attempting to direct, and not drifting with the tide of public sentiment; who, despite the tiger stare of ignorance, unmoved by the rending roar of the lion of fanaticism, heedless of the hungry howl of

the wolves of faction, battle not for Southern rights, battle not for Northern rights, but battle that each and all may have their share of the universal right which is broader than the universe and deeper than the sea. I love the West because it is the land of my adoption. I love her because amid her golden hills and her pacific shore the years of my early manhood have glided into the past. I love her because those flowers of friendship which only flourish in the spring and summer of life, for me have bloomed and blossomed here. I love the South because she is the land of my birth. I love her responsive to a sentiment which finds echo in every true bosom. I love her as a man should love his mother.—*R. D. Crittenden.*

212. COMMEMORATIVE DAYS.—It is a great thing for a nation to have a heroic past. There is hope of imbecile and lawless Greece, so long as the names of Salamis, Thermopylæ and Marathon are spoken among her mountains and by the sea. The golden age of Rome has been a perpetual and keen reproach to the degenerate Italian heart, and made possible a united Italy. The Alpine passes are kept forever against the foot of tyranny by the spirit of the patriot Tell; and all the Scottish hills are hallowed by the memory of the Bruce of Bannockburn. Indeed such names and such memories cease to be national. They become the heritage of humanity, and are quickeners to brave deeds and illustrious lives among all peoples. It is therefore wise and good to keep alive by monument and festival, and speech and song, by any memorial device, those pas-

sages of a nation's story in which she moves and acts in the highest and noblest strain. It is not enough to write them down on the pages of their annals, for scholars to read amid the quiet of their books. They should be rehearsed before popular assemblies, made visible and vocal to the popular eye and heart, be re-enacted as in a living drama, and press their moulding influence upon the whole current life of the people. It is especially needful for us in this land, that we keep commemorative days, for we are on such a swift and hurrying tide—we drift so rapidly on to the new—fresh issues are continually calling to us out of the future—we rush forward with headlong eagerness to seize more splendid prizes—we have no time to look back—we cannot call a halt in our career to estimate the cost of what we have gained, and pay our reverent and grateful debt to the past.—*Rev. Dr. A. L. Stone.*

213. NO NORTH, NO SOUTH.—I know no distinction between North and South, in the just and legal enforcement of the laws. I believe in the Constitution of the United States, and by the compact which our fathers made I am willing to stand to the death. With the institutions of the South I have nothing to do (A. D. 1861—EDITOR.) They are local in their character, and there let them remain. But I was reared in a State which was consecrated to liberty long before the cornerstone of the Republic was laid; whose free soil, unpolluted by a bondsman's tread, nurtured a happy and independent people. Then be not surprised if, having been reared among the free, I feel no great admiration

for the political system which would condemn the meanest of God's creatures to hopeless and endless captivity. If God in his wisdom has doomed this nation to destruction—if her mission is fulfilled and her glory is to pass away—let the throes of her dissolution resemble the agony of her birth, and as she was born, so let her expire: amidst the shock of conflicting armies, the roar of battle, the thunder of cannon, and the groans of the dying. Let her live no longer, a cheat and a lie, to deceive mankind with false beacons of freedom. Let her punishment be an example so terrible that posterity, for a thousand years to come, shall tremble at the story of her ruin. If man cannot appreciate the blessings of freedom and learn the secret of governing himself, let her name be blotted out from the nations of the earth, and the smoke of her expiring fires darken the broad heavens like the folds of a funeral pall. But this extremity has not yet come. High above the dark clouds of war I see the sweet vistas of peace—peace purchased, perhaps, on the blood-stained battle-field, but which will endure when the conflict is past, and the cries of the combatants are hushed in the stillness of death.—*J. H. Warwick.*

214. A PERMANENT UNION.—When we think what men builded these structures (the several States of the Union); when we think what principles cement them; when we think what blood bought and protected them, we feel that there is but one power on this earth that can dissolve the American Union. And what is that power? It is the will of the whole American people.

Until that mighty fiat goes forth the Union will never be dissolved, unless this great globe itself and all upon it shall also be dissolved. Those living forms of our liberties, the American Union and American Constitution, will not perish from the earth. Spirits that live throughout, vital in every part, cannot but by annihilation die. Our flag is the flower of our nationality—there is not a thread in it which has not been bought and drenched by the blood of the first races of the world. To the millions of the Old World, in their deepest gloom, it gleams in the Western sky like a star of hope. The exile from the banks of the Rhine, from the sunny Garonne, and from the broad Shannon, sits down under its ample folds for protection, and perchance hoists beneath it the trampled emblem of his own nationality, and looks upon it with joy and pride. It is the sign, the seal, the symbol, the pledge, the bond of our nationality. May that flag and nationality be eternal. We Californians are in a land of which Allen and Putnam never heard, and over which the wildest visionaries of those early days never dreamed that our eagles would soar, but though remote we are not indifferent. I am an American citizen. The first lesson which my dawning reason learned from the lips of a patriot father, was that there was no title which any rank or order, or class, in any country, could give me, prouder than that of an American Citizen. The enthusiasm of my youth, and the judgment and experience of my manhood, have confirmed that truth, and I will never surrender that proud title that I may decline upon any paltry provincial appellation.—*Eugene Casserly.*

215. RECUPERATIVE POWER OF THE NATION.—The mission of the Pioneer has well nigh ended. He has nowhere to retreat beyond the companionship of his fellows or the far stretching antennæ of a zeal which reaches him, and holds him, and civilizes him, whether he will or no. He has no more solitudes to conquer. Faster and faster upon his retiring footsteps the massed columns of enterprise and capital have advanced, and made his most secret haunts their abiding place. The deserts no longer protect him; the mountains give him no shelter. The vast plains that since primeval hours had borne little more than impressions of sweeping clouds, that shut out the sunshine from their mighty desolation, have trembled and been burdened with the hurrying vanguard of the commerce of Occident and Orient; and the White Death that sat upon the brow of the Sierras has been transmuted into glowing life by the irresistible touch of the gods of steam and electricity. Far to the north, peaceful acquisitions of territory have increased the nation's three millions of square miles to hundreds of thousands more. Thirty millions of people have increased to more than forty millions; and the sun, as he throws his benignant smiles from ocean to ocean, from the poles to the tropic savannahs, does not behold the unrewarded toil of a single slave, or see the face of one not rich in hope. Upon the surface of this momentous progression, the Nation has endured and triumphed over the scourge of civil war. Cities have been burned to ashes. Almost whole States have been devastated, and apparently left to the horrors of a lingering decay; and all industries and arts of peace have seemed at times unsettled and paralyzed by the anxieties and uncertainties of the most terrible of intestine dissensions. Even when the last battle had been fought and the last physical wound inflicted, it seemed as if generations must be born and buried before the nation's wounds would heal, and that it must always bear unsightly scars. Yet the impetus of progress has been so universal and powerful, that no evils, real or anticipated, have materially checked the national growth. It hardly feels the five years of civil war. Our personal recollections almost fail to preserve a memory of its awful experiences. The occasional crippled veteran who solicits charity in the streets, or struggles bravely with a mutilated body to gain his poor livelihood; or the social sympathies aroused by the sight of some widowed woman, or fatherless child, are almost our only reminders of the bloodiest and most desperate conflict the historian has ever had, or I believe ever will have, presented to his pen. The very States most harassed by the visible presence of war, still more embarrassed by the unsolved problem of free labor imposed upon a servile race, and the almost total destruction of commercial values, and, most of all, cursed in the effort to recuperate by a devouring and insatiable breed of political locusts—now yearly add to the nation's wealth more than they ever contributed in any one year of their former prosperity, and are solvent and financially secure. I am proud to recognize this fact, so much more calculated to exalt the prestige of the Southern name than the fearful prodigality with which it sacrificed millions of treasure and hecatombs of valuable lives in vindication of political ideas whose realization would have been their and our national extinction. The moral triumphs of the South have been greater and grander than any she could have won by prevailing over the national government. She has conquered herself; encountered and mastered the most serious social question of the century; and is successfully moulding her opinions and shaping her destinies to meet the requirements of the great future in store for her. Whatever politicians may say—however the pressure of partisan necessity may seek to foster a spirit of distrust in the general political temper of the South, the people firmly believe that with the extinctiion of the causes of sectional dissension, with the abandonment of human slavery, and with the costly but not too dear results of the contest waged over the pestilential dogma of secession, there is securely established between North and South, and for the first time since the Convention of 1787, there exists that more perfect Union, which the Constitution, then adopted, sought to create. The chief dangers have passed away forever, and the evils which remain to be overcome are results, not causes; they diminish of themselves, day by day; as after some mid-night tempest, the perturbed waves still rebellingly upheave the ocean's dark, unfathomable depths, but with an ever decreasing strength, and at last, their foamy crests no longer lifted, the horizon falls upon a high expanse, and the day dawns upon a limitless and golden peace.—*Gen'l W. H. L. Barnes.*

216. THE PERFECTION OF HUMAN WISDOM.—Of this let the world be assured—that the project of

American liberty was a bold one, conceived by gallant spirits, won by the stern determination of a band of heroes, the beneficial results of which can be measured by no standpoint of human conception. And let the world understand this other fact—that it has cost too much of blood and treasure to be lightly sacrificed. Its accomplishment was the result of superhuman exertion. For it, martyrs laid down their lives, and patriots gave themselves willing sacrifices. The blood of these martyrs is the seed of the church of universal liberty. Its accomplishment became a new fact in the history of empires, a new era in the history of the world. Civilization beheld the dawn of a newer and brighter day. Barbarism became involved in a darker and drearier night. Religion caught the mellow lustre of its reflected beauty. Science saw new revelations in its clearer light. Literature turned a new and a more glowing page. Poetry took a loftier flight. Industry became the handmaid of genius, and, bound in the golden chains of honored labor, the son of toil first took his true rank in the family of man. Roman and Grecian liberty was the sport and plaything of a refined and Utopian philosophy, the experiment of a highly cultivated age. It was the growth of a sun-shiny morning in the world's history. It flourished while the dews of philosophy watered it, but when the storms of a sterner era, the tempest of internal faction, and the winds of foreign invasion beat upon it, it fell. American liberty was a real, practical and substantial achievement; its foundations were laid in the recognition of the absolute right of all men to be regarded as equal—of the principle that the government was founded for the benefit of all; that a majority of the people should, by a simple expression of their will through the ballot box, in the choice of law-makers and rulers, govern themselves. It was a wise scheme of government that our fathers conceived, because it was simple; it was a firm government, because it was planted in the rights and interests of all; it is destined to immortal perpetuity, because it is the perfection of human wisdom; it cannot fail, because it is for the interest of the American people to sustain it.—*F. M. Pixley.*

217. THE AMERICAN REVOLUTION.—The sanguinary record of the Revolution is engraved on every patriot heart. From her crumbling thrones and tottering dynasties Europe had gazed aghast upon the spectacle of that young and giant race who, far away upon another hemisphere, strangled the serpent in the cradle, and burst the bonds of tyranny; who grew invincible amid the power, and radiant amid the luster of free institutions; who gave new impulses to science and the arts; and in their grand ambition had resolved to demonstrate the freedom, the intelligence and the equality of universal man. The contest which ensued was not a mere warfare of opinion, not a simple struggle for supremacy, not alone a craving thirst for conquest, but that inevitable strife which from the beginning had been fore-ordained between the independence of the people and the despotism of their rulers. In the sublime yet inscrutable design of the Omnipotent it was ordained that our era should be the time, our continent the thea-

ter, our people the instrument of working out this mighty problem. And so the fathers trod the gory path, and bore the fierce ordeal, not for themselves alone, not alone for us, not for the glory of our country only, and the splendor of its unimaginable future, but that the scepter might be broken and the miter crushed; that the exactions of tyranny and the spirit of intolerance might be resisted, until at last, in the long lapse of time and the grand sweep of revolution, the myriads of earth's benighted men, of every lineage and race and creed and clime, should emerge from the gloom of ages into the lambent light of civil and religious liberty. Well may we too rejoice, as our fathers did, and glory in that day which gave these priceless blessings to mankind.

The events which followed are like the marvels of a dream. Vast in increase, peerless in power, and lustrous with intelligence, the land grew glorious among the nations. Hither came genius, which no more could kennel with the royal hounds. Hither invention, which grew chill beneath the throne; hither came all the energies of mind and thought, to radiate in the free air; hither came enterprise and talent, which had failed to thrive on the caprice of patronage. Up rose a stalwart race, the true nobility of nature. Up sprung an era more splendid than the age Augustan, more enlightened than the age of Pericles. Labor, by its right divine, became King. On white-winged navies Commerce swept the sea. Through every people and to every land, the prowess of our arms and the radiance of our institutions sped, diffusing universal influence and light.

The sword rested in its scabbard, and the arts and sciences usurped the lurid throne of war.—*Joseph W. Winans.*

218. THE SUREST GUARANTY OF OUR PERPETUITY. —Intelligence alone, however general, will not suffice to preserve our republican institutions. The love of morality and virtue, and an abiding respect for the ennobling principles inculcated by the precepts of Christianity, must be firmly rooted in the hearts of the people. The surest guaranty of the perpetuity of the American plan of self-government, lies in the incorruptible character of the mass of the citizens of this Republic. Exceptions to the general rule of integrity can be found in every community; but these do not affect its substantial accuracy, for the great majority of American citizens, north, south, east and west, are, as yet, governed in their private lives, and in their political actions, by their honest convictions of what is just, right, equitable, and conducive to the common welfare; and thereby indicate a recognition of their moral accountability, to an Unseen and Overruling power. So long as these sentiments hold dominion in the hearts of our countrymen, our free institutions must exist in all their pristine purity and vigor. Corrupt, base and designing men will attain official station, but the noxious influences which exhale from their moral rottenness, will be neutralized by the active and imperishable principles of virtue and truth, incarnate in the forms of honest, faithful and capable men, who are their colleagues in duty. Even if it should happen, through any inexplicable combination of circumstances, that the most, or all of the important official positions in the State and Nation, should be held by daring and unscrupulous incumbents, defiant of God, and regardless of their fellow-men, the unshaken integrity and incorruptibility of the people would eventually thwart the lawless machinations of their unworthy rulers, and bring their crafty designs of personal aggrandizement, and public ruin, to a sure and ignominious end.

If, on the other hand, a long and prosperous career, filling the land with wealth, luxury, ease, idleness, and vice, shall at last, slowly and inevitably, like a relentless cancer, eat out the vital virtues of the people, consuming their probity, integrity, honor and truth, destroying their love for, and pride in, their free institutions, and rendering them indifferent to all save their private schemes of selfish exaltation and criminal indulgence, the downfall of our republican fabric will speedily and certainly ensue. Rulers will grasp the reins of power, who excel in flattery, mendacity, dishonesty, and wicked ambition. Unrestrained by any inward monitor, unawed by any fear of future retribution, unchecked by any protest from their negligent and deluded constituents, the constitutional bulwarks which confine their insatiable rapacity will be, stone by stone, turret by turret, bastion by bastion, easily broken down and trampled in the dust, and nothing will remain to shield those God-given rights, the lives, liberties and happiness of the people from capricious, cruel, iron despotism.

—E. C. Winchell.

219. The Founders of our Government.—The science of government is the grandest, most imposing, and most profound that ever employed the genius of the statesman, the speculations of the philosopher, or the wisdom of the sage. Within its giant grasp are held the destinies of nations and the welfare of the race. Constituted as man is, and was from the beginning, a social being, incapable of self-direction, or even of sustaining his existence in isolation from his kind, it became no less essential to his safety than indispensable to his happiness that he should mingle in social communion with his fellow-men. For this, concessions must be made so far as needful, absolute rights renounced so far as inconsistent with the common good. For this the license of a state of nature must give place to the sanctions of social harmony and order. For this a systematic rule of action, now denominated law, must be established, and relative degrees of subordination and authority must be created and enforced. First in order came the formation of families, clans, and tribes, and as these multiplied into nations, they resolved themselves into such forms of municipal combination as accident or choice, or the compulsion of their leaders might prescribe. Hence sprang the organization of States, Kingdoms and Empires, with their different systems of polity, authority and law. The comparative merits of these systems, and their imperfections, have been thoroughly investigated. From the earliest periods of history it has been the highest aim of human intellect to devise a perfect form of government, such as would best secure to the people the largest degree of natural rights consistent with the general welfare, which, while it advanced the true interests of the commonwealth, would equally promote the happiness and protect the liberty of the citizen or subject. For this Aristotle theorized and Plato mused—for this Cicero pondered and More dreamed. Yet the Politica were but the comparison of existing constitutions with an abstract possibility, the Republics of Plato and Cicero were perfectly ideal, and the Utopia, in its fanciful extravagance, surpassed the creations of romantic fiction. These schemes were vague and visionary all—abstractions—rich in quaint conceits and philosophy, reared on a glowing but impracticable model. They conjure up a government surrounded with illusory magnificence, exhibiting an oriental splendor, and a mathematical precision, but needing one thing to complete it, that it should be formed of perfect men. But while the science of government has been rendered thus successful in theory by the speculations of philosophers, very different results have attended its practical development. For thousands of years the various communities of earth have struggled on through turbulence, vicissitude and change, now crushed by the tyranny of despots, now frantic with the license of the multitude, vexed with continuous collisions between the rulers and the ruled, wading oftentimes through slaughter to the triumphs of ambition or the overthrow of the oppressor, and merging into barbarism at the last, or lapsing into utter ruin and distinction. And thus, while every form of government has essayed and tested by severe experiment, from the extreme of Absolutism to the dead level of a pure Democracy; none of these forms, save ours, has borne that test unscathed, or escaped universal wreck. The giant spirits that laid the foundations of our government, approved themselves no less sagacious in the cabinet than invincible in the field. They were bold and original in thought as in action. They repudiated all existing systems. They derived little aid from the schemes of philosophers, old or modern. They established Republicanism, but not the Republicanism of any former era. They realized that philosophy must be the corner-stone of every good government, but yet that the government itself must be practically adapted to the nature of man, alike capable of sustaining his personal rights and advancing his social interests. Adaptation and development are the characteristic and controlling features of the noble product of their genius.—*Jos. W. Winans.*

220. "ONE AND INSEPARABLE."—As I take my leave of a subject upon which I have detained you too long (speech on State of the Country, in U. S. Senate, Jan. 3, 1861—EDITOR) I think in my mind whether I shall add anything, in my feeble way, to the hopes, the prayers, the aspirations that are going forth daily for the perpetuity of the Union of these States. I ask myself shall I add anything to that volume of invocation which is everywhere rising up to high heaven, "Spare us from the madness of disunion and civil war!" Standing in this chamber and speaking upon this subject, I cannot forget that I am standing in a place once occupied by one far, far mightier than I, the lachet of whose

shoe I am unworthy to unloose. It was upon this subject of secession, of disunion, of discord, of civil war, that Webster uttered those immortal sentiments, clothed in immortal words, married to the noblest expressions that ever fell from human lips, which alone would have made him memorable and remembered forever. I cannot improve upon those expressions. They were uttered nearly thirty years ago, in the face of what was imagined to be a great danger, then happily dissipated. They were uttered in the fullness of his genius, from the fullness of his heart. They have echoed since in millions of homes and in foreign lands. They have been a text-book in schools. They have been an inspiration to public hope and to public liberty. As I close, I repeat them, I adopt them. If in their presence I were to attempt to give utterance to any words of my own, I should feel that I ought to say,

>"And shall the lyre, so long divine,
>Degenerate into hands like mine?"

I adopt the closing passages of that immortal speech; they are my sentiments; they are the sentiments of every man upon this side of the chamber. I would fain believe they are the sentiments of every man upon this floor. I would fain believe that they are an inspiration, and will become a power throughout the length and breadth of this broad confederacy; that again the aspirations and hopes and prayers for the Union, may rise like a perpetual hymn of hope and praise. But, however, this may be, these thoughts are mine; and as, reverently and findly, I utter them, I leave the discussion:

"When my eyes shall be turned to behold for the last time the sun in heaven, may I not see him shining on the broken and dishonored fragments of a once glorious Union; on States dissevered, discordant, belligerent; on a land rent with civil feuds, or drenched it may be in fraternal blood! Let their last feeble and lingering glance rather behold the gorgeous ensign of the Republic, now known and honored throughout the earth, still full high advanced, its arms and trophies streaming in their original luster, not a stripe erased or polluted, nor a single star obscured; bearing for its motto no such miserable interrogatory as 'What is all this worth?' nor those other words of delusion and folly, 'Liberty first, and Union afterwards,' but everywhere, spread all over in characters of living light, blazing on all its ample folds as they float over the sea and over the land and in every wind under the whole heavens, that other sentiment, dear to every true American heart, 'Liberty *and* Union, now and forever, one and inseparable.'"—*Gen. E. D. Baker.*

HOW A GREAT PEOPLE PERISHED.

221. In all the history of the past there is but one nation with which the great nation now growing up on this continent can be compared; but one people which has occupied the position and exercised the influence, which for good or evil, the American people must occupy and exert. A nation which has left a deeper impress upon the life of the race than any other nation that ever existed; whose sway was co-extensive with the known world; whose heroes and poets, and sages and orators, are still familiar names to us; whose literature and art still furnish us models; whose language has enriched every modern tongue, and though long dead, is still the language of science and of religion, and whose jurisprudence is the great mine from which our modern systems are wrought. That a nation so powerful in arms, so advanced in the arts, should perish as Rome perished: that a civilization so widely diffused, should be buried as was the Roman civilization, is the greatest marvel which history presents. To the Roman citizen of the time of Augustus or the Antonines, it would have appeared as incredible, as utterly impossible that Rome could be overwhelmed by barbarians, as to the American citizen of to-day it would appear impossible that the great American Republic could be conquered by the Apaches, or the Chinooks, our arts forgotten, and our civilization lost.

How did this once incredible thing happen? What were the hidden causes that sapped the strength and eat out the heart of this world-conquering power, so that it crumbled to pieces before the shock of barbarian hoards? A Roman historian himself has told us: "Great estates ruined Italy!" In the land policy of Rome may be traced the secret of her rise, the cause of her fall.

"To every citizen as much land as he himself may use; he is an enemy of the State who desires any more," was the spirit of the land policy which enabled Rome to assimilate so quickly the peoples that she conquered; that gave her a body of citizens whose arms were a bulwark against every assault, and who carried her standards in triumph in every direction. At first, a single acre constituted the patrimony of a Roman; afterwards the amount was increased to three acres and a half. These were the heroic days of the Republic, when every citizen seemed animated by a public spirit and a public virtue which made the Roman name as famous as it made the Roman arms invincible; when Cincinnatus left his two-acre farm to become Dictator, and after the danger was over and the State was safe, returned to his plow; when Regulus, at the head of a conquering army in Africa, asked to be relieved, because his single slave had died, and there was no one to cultivate his little farm for his family.

But, as wealth poured in from foreign conquests, and lust for riches grew, the old policy was set aside. The Senate granted away the public domain in large tracts, just as our Senate is doing now; and the fusion of the little farms into large estates by purchase, by force, and by fraud, went on, until whole provinces were owned by two or three proprietors, and chained slaves had taken the place of the sturdy peasantry of Italy. The small farmers who had given their strength to Rome, were driven to the cities to swell the ranks of the proletarians, and become clients of the great families, or abroad to perish in the wars. There came to be but two classes—the enormously rich, and their dependents and slaves. Society thus constituted bred its destroying monsters; the old virtues vanished, population declined, art sank, the old conquering race actually died out, and

Rome perished, as a modern historian puts it, from the very failure of the crop of *men*. Centuries ago this happened, but the laws of the universe are to-day what they were then.—*Henry George.*

CENTENNIAL ORATION.

(JULY 4, 1876.)

222. The great movements of mankind upon our globe, since it became the theatre of human life and human events, can never cease to be the subject of profoundest interest and loftiest contemplation. There is a spirit in man, urging him on with the strong momentum of eternal law, to a destiny that ever allures him with mystic wonder and fascination. The earthly horizon of that destiny, ever retreating, invites him to the full and complete dominion of a world not yet subdued to intellectual and moral being. Generations, races and nations, inspired by impulse greater and mightier than themselves, move forward in grand consentaneous procession, and history unfurls her banners, the symbols of eternal purpose.

One of the most sublime conceptions of which the mind is capable, is the contemplation of the periods of time during which the earth was being prepared to be a fit habitation of man. Compared with those periods, the lifetime of the human race is but a moment, or a thought flashed by electric touch from city to city. The introduction of man upon the earth is a modern event, modern as the morning of to-day! The Egyptian civilization is but of yesterday, compared with the formation of the delta of the Mississippi; and the alluvial plains of the Euphrates, the first abodes of human society, were the work of cycles and æons of unrecorded time. These periods of time and preparation, in the contemplation of which the mind is oppressed with the vague sense of infinity, suggest, with striking intellectual and moral force, the importance of man's place in the scale of created things, and the rank he holds in the order of being. The last term in an ascending series, involved in all that goes before, crown and summit of creation, end and fulfilment of primal intent and purpose. Science unfolds the order of nature and reveals her method and law, but man, his fortunes, his deeds, his nature and his destiny, are the noblest objects of thought and study. He is superior to nature, in that he recognizes the law of nature and the law of his own being. He discovers truth, good and evil, and is haunted by the thought that not death, but increasing life is his goal. Progressive reason achieves new conquests in every age, and can never rest until it is established upon the throne of the world, and the sublime affirmation is realized, "Thou hast put all things under his feet." Man, society, nationality, government, give intellectual and moral import to a material universe, and the progress of history is the elevation of the moral character of mankind.

The American Continent, earliest in geologic time of all the lands of the globe, was reserved to these later days to be the theatre of a new cycle of human culture, and a new display of the power of human society.

The ancient oriental civilizations had flourished for thousands and tens of thousands of years, and sent forth those great migrations that founded the succession of Asiatic Empires, reared the fair forms of Grecian culture and the strength of Roman arms, made Europe the nursery of nations, and England the foster-mother of the modern world. Christianity, that religion which more than any other seems adapted to universal man, had kindled its holy signals on the hills of Judea nearly fifteen centuries before the Pilot of Genoa was born. Rome expired a thousand years before. During all these vast movements of mankind, and through these historic ages, when the soil of the world was being prepared to receive the seed of the Modern age, the American Continent lay concealed behind the horizon. The Ptolemaic system held the universe in the thraldom of the senses, and religion, not yet allied to reason, enforced the thrall. The mind was enveloped in sense, and the sight of the eye, and the hearing of the ear, interpreted the world. The sun rose and set, and the earth was an extended plain. Imagination, strong angel of truth, had not looked with undazzled eye upon that inaccessible glory which the senses cannot touch. The outward manifestations of power filled the mind with vague wonder and fear, while reason had not yet discovered their law. It was the seed-time of history, the germinating period of human thought.

It is now four hundred years since the European world began to feel those premonitory pains that go before the births of time.

How the great ideas, that now govern the world as the common thought of men, first dawned upon the solitudes of genius, is beyond the power of man to tell. It is common to account for it in the intellectual law of suggestion or association. Accordingly, we are told that the apple falling from the tree in Newton's garden suggested the law of gravitation. But this is a mistake. The conception is in the mind; the apple does not convey it. It comes as the morning comes; it comes as the ripening of the grain; it comes as the flush of the vintage, distilled in mystery and silence— but behold, a new heavens and a new earth, without noise or fear! The round world, as it lay in the serene imagination of Columbus, is one of the most striking illustrations of the power of an idea that history records. His heroism to obey the idea, and, contrary to the opinions of his age, to follow it across the trackless deep, gives him an undisputed rank in the hierarchy of faith, and an immovable pedestal in the temple of earthly fame. Those masterly achievements of fidelity to a a thought that characterized the discovery of the New World were fit precursors of the fortunes of that New World, destined as it was to be the field of new principles, in which the majority of mankind did not believe. The birth of navigation may be said to have been simultaneous with the discoveries of the fifteenth century. Among the conquests that man has made over the obstacles that the barriers of the world offer to his progress, navigation must take first rank. It spans the awful abysses of the sea, makes the communication of nations and races possible, supplements human wants by the exchange of the products of the earth and of human skill, and tends by its mighty processes of intercourse and communication to establish the equilibrium of the condition of mankind. Navigation was the beginning of that system of communication upon the earth which is the striking feature of our own day, and makes man at home in the world.

A true theory of the solar and planetary worlds had vaguely emerged from chaos, in the devout reason of Copernicus; and the steady lights of the upper deep became the faithful guides of the trustful mariner, as he ploughed the dark longitudes from land to land. Copernicus did not announce and defend his theory, for fear of the Church, but his mind was the seed-plot of the idea of modern astronomy, and was one of the powerful causes that contributed to the intellectual conquest of the material world at that period. When lying on his death-bed, and near his end, he united the expression of his devout faith and inspired intelligence in sentiments such as the sacred lyrist has embodied in his verse:

>   Ye golden lamps of heaven! farewell!
>   With all your feeble light,
>   Farewell, thou ever changing moon—
>   Pale empress of the night.
>   And thou, refulgent orb of day!
>   In brighter flames arrayed—
>   My soul, which springs beyond thy sphere,
>   No more demands thine aid.

The two ideas, one of a round world, as it lay in the brooding mind of Columbus; the other of the solar system, as it dawned in the intelligence of Copernicus, were the sovereigns of that time.

But there was a nobler moment yet. It may be summed up in that general and somewhat vague expression, the Reformation. In all the complex causes and relations which conspired in that event, the pith and quick of it was that it centered in man himself, and concerned his rights, his duties, his nature, and his destiny. The Reformation was to man himself what the round world and the solar system were to his conception of the material universe. It was the free activity of the individual mind in fealty to eternal, moral law. It brought order into the moral world, by making the individual a centre of power. It abolished authorities imposed from without, and instated the perceptions of reason and conscience within. It appealed from the few to the many; from the priest to the people; from the traditions of the elders to the mind and heart of man. It was not the revival of an old life, but the inspiration of a new; the transfer of civilization to a new center of development. The old system had completed its orbit; but that orbit was not the complete cycle of human progress, ever widening its range and rising higher. Men are the conscious instruments of powers, principles and ideas which they do not fully comprehend. They are the exponents of a period, but they do not originate its principles. It is a mistake to suppose that Martin Luther originated the Reformation, or that he was the father of it in any sense. The

Reformation would have come if Luther had not been, and the moral grandeur of his figure in history is derived from his ability to discover the signs of the times, to read the horoscope of the period and confess the era of God. If you inquire for those mighty thoughts and sublime impulses, which are the seeds of human history, you ascend to those heights where genius o'ertops intelligence and insight becomes inspiration. The settlement of this continent by a strong and powerful race, who planted on these shores the seed of a new historic period, was the result of the Reformation. It was a movement that had its origin in the noblest moods of the human mind. Let no cheap animosities between Catholic and Protestant dim the clear, calm, historic vision; let no jealousies of the provincialisms of human feeling intrude themselves into that august presence.

Among the men who contributed by force of moral genius to reduce the chaotic elements of that period to order and form, thus supplying the practical working materials of progress, there is one whose name and whose principles have been singularly associated with the life of American institutions—I mean the lawyer, theologian, statesman of Geneva, John Calvin. It was he who gathered up the scattered moral powers of the Reformation, condensed them in definite, dogmatic, popular forms, and administered the affairs of religion in a republican spirit, thus making his *horribile decretum fateor* the seed-plot of Republican liberty. If his doctrine was cruel, it was the offspring of a cruel age. It was not Protestant or Catholic that was cruel; it was the condition of the human mind. That terrible doctrine, which now is like a nest of a former year from which the brood· has flown, pervaded Christendom, and sent forth a mighty race that fought against tyranny everywhere, always sided with the people, gave victory to the plebeian Roundhead over the lordly Cavalier and sent forth a new Israel to take possession of this promised land of mankind and liberty. Calvinism was dispersed throughout Europe, and probably influenced more minds than any other system of doctrine or polity devised by man. Scotland was imbued with it, and through her philosophy it tinged the thought of the intellectual world. The Huguenot stock of South Carolina inherited it. William Penn was taught by a famous Calvinist. The early Dutch colonists of New York were of that lineage, and the settlers of Plymouth were of that athletic race.

The system of free schools was devised by Calvin's brain and heart, and beyond the boundaries of sect, his hand, unconscious of its power, scattered the seeds of Republican liberty. As our American Idealist has wove it into verse that shall vibrate on all the chords of time, he

> "Wrought in a sad sincerity;
> Himself from God he could not free;
> He builded better than he knew—
> The conscious stone to beauty grew."

In the hard and thorny husk of a cruel system were hid the seeds of a new life among the nations, and a new era for mankind.

Thus the life of American institutions had its root in the old world. The health of the scion attests the vigor of the native stock. Whatever may have been the exploits of former races on this continent, whatever power or glory their civilization displayed, they acted no part in the drama of the new era, and contributed nothing to the life of the new age. The traces of the mound-builders are a melancholy record of a race that we may gratefully believe fulfilled its destiny, and had no reason longer to be upon the earth. The native Indian—humble child of the forest, weak and passionate—dashes himself against the walls of the world, or dissolves like ice flowing into tropic seas. American civilization is of European and English origin. It is a new center of human culture, from a seed matured in the highest and best experience of mankind.

It must be confessed, humanly speaking, that the union of the American Colonies, first against foreign encroachment and then under a constitutional government, was a happy accident. But history distils wisdom and honor and power from human folly. The mad councils of George III lost him his colonies, but created a new nation. Had a better spirit prevailed, England might have been the mother of the Republic, or two Englands might have ruled the world. The independence of the American Colonies was brought about by those mixed causes, which, to the superficial observer, seem to be an inexplicable jumble of stupid blunder, blind folly and mad self-will. But to the philosophic historian, they are that apparent chaos of human events and human things over which the spirit of order ever broods, bringing forth the true, the beautiful and good. Evil is never unmixed, and the truth enveloped in error, falling upon the furrows of the world, expands, bursts its environments, and buds and blooms.

Doubtless there is much vague declamation and would-be philosophic gravity in talking about the "idea" of our government, or the "idea" of our institutions. There is probably no proper sense in which it can be said that government has any idea or theory at all. Certainly the science of government, if there is such a science, is not an exact science, and its principles are continually applied to new facts and new conditions, in a new method. The unfolding of a principle is a growth, not a mechanic law. Thus, in all enterprise of man's affairs, in all administration of human things, the grand question is: Is it only a dead fact, or a living law? Admitting fully all the limitations that practice sets to theory, still theory goes before practice, and includes practice. But the only theory, or idea, which a free government can have, is the growth and development of the principle on which it rests. This is the difference between constitutional liberty and absolute monarchy. The one is the arbitrary application of a rule; the other is the unfolding of a principle. The one is a wooden fact, the other is an inspired truth. And thus in respect of ourselves and our historic origin as a people and a nation, the question is: What was there at the bottom of this display of social order, that has so gone on where man nor angel never dreamed? The early settlers of the continent had no conception of it. They brought with them the mature fruit of human experience, the latest that hung upon the branches of the tree of life. That fruit was the conviction, nay, more, transcending all reasoning process, the insight of inspired moral genius, that man's nature prefigures his liberty, and that he is and must be free to act of himself under moral law! That conviction, that insight, was new. The men themselves did not know what it meant nor where it would lead. And why should they? A man can not tell even what his house will cost beforehand, and why should they understand the vision of truth that had never been applied to the guidance and government of men? The world had been governed by force, invading even the recesses of thought. Exclusive powers and privileges were held and exercised by the few, and the idea of man as man had no place on earth. Even the Almighty Maker and Ruler had his favorites, and no long-minded eternities of beneficent power brooded over the destinies of mankind. One of the most influential races that has ever lived on the face of the earth, inhabiting a little country on the borders of the Levant, that the modern traveller can "do" in the saddle in five or seven days, made even religion aristocratic, claimed that God was their God, and that they were His people to the exclusion of everybody else. I am not indifferent to the historic development of opinion, nor to the influence of Hebrew Theism upon the destiny of the human world ; but it furnishes a striking illustration of the exclusiveness of human thought, associated as it commonly is, with the monopoly of God and contempt for man.

But truth mingled with error tends to work itself clear.

When we talk about the theory of free government, we mean, if we mean anything, that the bottom of it is the principle of liberty, as it is elementary and fundamental in human nature. And like other principles, if it is a principle, it is to be followed, and not to be led. If it is based upon the equality of men—that is, the equality of human nature—it is the affirmation that man everywhere is man—made of the same powers, passions and affections; that he has the same origin and the same destiny. The senses are the same in all; intelligence is the same in all; affection is the same in all; reason is the same in all; conscience is the same in all; faith is the same in all. These may be developed in different degrees, and expressed in different terms, but they have their root in the same soil—of the same common nature. As I was riding, the other day in the suburbs of the city, among the sand hills, that form so striking and bold contrast with the cultivated and powerful portions of the town, I met two children, who by their habit and manner, showed that they belonged to the worthy, respectable poor. Their frugal, tidy dress, their unstockinged feet, their modesty in presence of a stranger, flushed the very sand with loveliness; and in their little sun-burnt hands they held loosely a few flowers, such as Nature gives in her bounty to relieve her desert places; and they were comparing the colors, as the sunlight poured down its golden rays and filled the urns of beauty. I said to myself, Behold the identity of human nature! The same love of the beautiful that fascinates the soul of a

Titian or a Tintoretto! This is what we mean by the equality of men, the identity of human nature. This is the seed of human progress, and the promise of man's destiny. Our Republican Democracy is founded on that. It has always encountered suspicion and jealousy and evil foreboding from those who are not imbued with it; for if there are those who are too ignorant and wretched and benighted to be free, there are those, also, who are intelligent, yet who lack the moral genius to discern that they belong to the human race.

The history of the country for the hundred years on whose summit we now stand, has been little else than the development of this principle. On these mighty waters the nation sails, and the horizon forever recedes and earth and sky never meet. Our principles, so far from being exhausted, are only beginning to be unfolded, and we may justly expect that they are to play a leading part in the fortunes and destiny of mankind. If human progress means anything, it means the enjoyment of the highest privileges and immunities of existence by all; it means a fair field for every man to pursue that line of thought and action which his own individuality directs, and which, to him, is the purpose of his being. All truth is expansive, and greater than men think when they first adopt it. The smallest seed of liberty when it is sown becomes a tree, and struggling human aspirations take refuge in its branches, or refresh themselves under its shadow for new resistance against ancient and venerable wrong. He who would confine the influence of free institutions to this theater of our display, would make a great mistake. The winds are its messengers, the lightnings do its biddings, the ocean is its mediator. The heart of man, source of restless imaginations and never satisfied longings, aspires to it from afar.

It would be impossible, on an occasion like the present, to recount the events, the deeds, the persons of this century of republican liberty. That is the office of the historian, the philosopher and the poet. It is enough for us to-day to take counsel of our principles and reaffirm them as the profound conviction of our minds, attested by the experience of a century. It was announced a hundred years ago by the founders of the government that all men are free and equal. We have read it to-day from the famous Declaration, and it will be read by those who shall come after us down the rolling tide of centuries to the latest recorded syllable of time. It is no contrivance of extemporaneous device; it is no rule for the exigency of the moment, cheap subterfuge of tyrants. It is in the eternal nature of truth, and things, and man and God. Neither is it any vagary or "glittering generality" in our minds but of clear, decided import and energy. It is as old as the heavens, and as new as to-day, and we claim for it that immortality that belongs to essential truth.

We affirm and declare to-day, as the fathers did in 1776, that all men are free! And we mean by it that fundamental fact of human nature by virtue of which man is man, endowed by heaven with the power to choose between good and evil, and to direct his course towards those ends that seem to him best! We mean that the office of Government is to protect that freedom, and not to encroach upon it; to throw around it the environments of law, that under law it may be liberty indeed!

We affirm and declare to-day, as the fathers did in 1776, that all men are equal! Hear it, O Heaven! and give ear unto it, O Earth! We mean by it the identity of that nature whose inspirations of reason and conscience are the same in their eternal quality and divine essence! We mean that reason is reason, that conscience is conscience, that imagination is imagination, and that the progress of mankind is grounded in this common nature of man. On this we base our hope of human progress, and our faith in human destiny. Does experience give any ground for that hope and faith?

Human society on this continent for a hundred years, has been led forth under the power of the principles which we affirm and declare to-day. A continent has been subdued to culture. A degree of external human comfort has been attained and enjoyed, that probably has not been surpassed in any portion of the earth, or in any period of history. Let us cheerfully accord whatever is due to the cheapness and fertility of the soil, but let us also be just to human energies. The results of scientific research have been applied to the arts of life, and whatever pertains to man's conquest over the material world has been made as complete here as in any other country. The area of the country has been extended by peace and by war until its borders are laved by both oceans through twenty degrees of latitude. The country to-day presents a theatre of world-grandeur for the display of free Constitutional Government.

The affairs of the Government have been administered by those whom the people have chosen. Universal suffrage makes revolution unnecessary, by giving every man the right to appeal to the ballot as the final remedy of all public wrong. We have never had under this plan a wicked or dissolute President, and if we ever had a weak one, the people have been steady enough to endure his weakness, conscious of their strength. We have never had a corrupt or mercenary Judge, and the judicial mind and ethic of the country, I speak firmly without boasting, compare favorably with the judicial mind and ethic of Christendom. The bad inheritance of slavery, bequeathed to us from the ancient estate, we esteem no longer a portion of the nation's wealth, and have absolved ourselves from its obligations by the blood of the sons of men. We have received from the nations of the earth and the islands of the sea, more than five millions of men, welcoming them to fairer opportunities. We have entrusted religion to the religious sentiments of human nature, without the interference or support of the State, and the free contributions of men surpass the tribute of regal splendors.

We have laid the foundation of a system of education for all in making the public school free, and in making it secular. Its benefits are only beginning to be felt, but the mind of the country is awake, and we may expect the best results of a system that has an ideal excellence beyond any present practice. We live in obedience to order and law, without violence; and good feeling and good manners shed their invisible, mighty protection over all. American society has never required a standing army to enforce order upon the people. We feel that the Government is steady, because its base is broad—reaching to the freedom and equal rights of every man—and that, in the long run, the laws which the people make themselves they will respect.

One hundred years ago the foundations of this city (San Francisco) were laid by the ancient monarchy of Spain. If the principles which I have rehearsed are true; if the attainments that have been made under them are a just expression of their wisdom and power, we may take pride and gratitude in our citizenship, and renew our vow to the freedom and equality of men. Let mighty salvos proclaim it! Let banners wave in proud homage and triumphant joy! Let the sea roar, and the fullness thereof! Let us bid the future generations hail! Hail ye happy races yet unborn that shall receive such an inheritance! Let the people lift up their voice: Yea, let the people lift up their voice: *Te Deum Laudamus.—Rev. Horatio Stebbins.*

VII.

FRATERNAL SOCIETIES.

PART VII.

FRATERNAL SOCIETIES

FREEMASONRY.

223. THE TEMPLE OF SOLOMON must stand as it was built. It could not enlarge itself. It could not bud with smaller temples, and then take them in under a widening roof or a swelling dome. Neither, when some of its pillars decayed, could it restore its own decrease, as the living cedars of Lebanon repair their wastes and renew their leaves. But our conscious temple does all this, and noiselessly. It fills in its losses; it enlarges its sweep and sway; it does it through men of all conditions and classes and races; and still it stands in its old proportions, though in greater amplitude—symmetrical, mysterious, sublime.—*Thos. Starr King.*

224. EVERYWHERE, order is the great interest. What humanity needs is the fulfillment of the indications of nature; freedom with order; a proper consciousness of worth in every breast. A recognition by each man of the worth and claims of every other; and an acknowledgement by all of a common and controlling law. This idea of order, fulfilled in the architecture of nature, is committed as a trust to our fraternity, and the proper reverence for it is poured out continually through the influence of our hallowed bonds.—*Thomas Starr King.*

225. THIS IS the most remarkable social organization in the world. None on the globe, with half so many elements in its composition, is so old. We are told that excavations made under modern Jerusalem disclose remnants of the old city in various periods of its history. Portions of the massive masonry of the time of Solomon are uncovered. Above these appear fragments of the work of Zerubbabel. On a higher historic stratum are specimens of workmanship from the age of Herod the Great; and still above these, but below the level of the present city, are remains of the constructive toil ordered by Justinian. We delight to feel that the past, measured by as many ages, is under us; but it is not beneath us in a broken symmetry and a dead grandeur, as under Jerusalem. It is rather beneath us as the roots are beneath a tree, and as the central rings are hidden in the trunk. They give power and pith to the structure still. They are part of its present majesty, sources of its living vigor, prophecies of its future strength.—*Thomas Starr King.*

226. NO EDIFICE which our ancient brethren reared was equal to the living structure of which they and we are portions. How often we read or hear with pride, that in the building of the first temple, the stones were made ready before they were brought together;

so that there was neither hammer, nor ax, nor any tool of iron heard in the house while it was building. What is that to the growth of our Order itself? How quiet the process, yet how constant! Who hears the noise of it? Who sees or knows when the sound timber and the approved stones are brought together, and fitted and lifted to their place, amidst the roar and strife, and selfishness of the world? Yet, in thousands of towns and cities—in every zone—in almost all communities and tongues of men, this work, in substantial sameness of method and pledge, is going on.—*Thos. Starr King.*

227. Do WE ever get tired of the toils and tax of charity? Suppose the sun did! What does he receive in homage or obedience from the orbs that swing round him, in comparison with what he gives—all his light, all his heat, all his vitality, for the blessing of four-score worlds? Shall we complain of the demand upon our treasuries, or our private purses, for the sacred funds of the Masonic Board of Relief? What if the sea grumbled at the assessment which the mighty sun—the Most Worshipful Grand Master of the System—levies on its substance! Every day the sun touches its stores with its wand of light, and says *Give, give.* And it obeys. Evaporation is its tax, constantly demanded, constantly given. Remember, brethren, that every cloud you see, whether stretched in a beautiful bar across the east at sunrise, or hanging in pomp over the gorgeous pavilion of the retiring day, is part of the contribution for the general relief of nature, assessed by the lordly sun. The water which the ocean *keeps* is salt. Pour a bucket

in war thou hast kept the noiseless tenor of thy way.
Thy benevolent spirit has sought the couch of the sick,
the bier of the dead, and the place of the widow and orphan;
it has made a home for the stranger in a foreign
land, and has sent a friend to the prisoner in his cell.
Mysterious union of mingled excellencies! thy foundation
is laid in the profoundest wisdom, and thy corner
stone rests on immortal principles. We thank thee that
thou hast afforded us so clear a proof that it is in the
power of man to found a union of brothers that defies
alike the spirit of change and the vicissitudes of time!
—*Samuel M. Wilson.*

230. WHEREVER WE may go, upon whatever land
our feet may rest, there, among thinking men, we shall
find a language which speaks of faith, hope and charity.
Those are the three links in the golden cord which
binds men together in every part of the civilized world.
Even now, while I speak, (May 15, 1861) in the metropolis
of Great Britain a convocation of our brethren
from all parts of the earth are assembled. Around
their festive table will be found the representatives of
all races—men from all climes—the Caucasian, the
Mongolian, and Ethiopian. When the Grand Master
of that convocation, whether he is a noble, or of the
humbler walks of life, rises at the head of the table and
says, "Together, brethren," he speaks a language which
thrills every breast in the assembly. It is the same
language which says, "Our country, our whole country,
and nothing but our country."—*Milton S. Latham.*

231. FREEMASONRY, quietly, unostentatiously, un-

obtrusively, marches hand in hand with civilization. When the first flag of our country was reared upon the Pacific Coast, our own banner floated in a mystic union with it, and patriots and masons struck hands together in the good work of perpetuating human liberty, and alleviating human suffering. I thank God—and I say it with all the reverence due from the creature to the Creator—that there is one spot upon this green earth where we can all meet and all kneel around the same altar to offer up our devotions to the same ever-living God. There no envy, no strife, no discord, is ever permitted to enter. The humblest citizen in the land, if he be honest, true and faithful, and meet the requirements of our order, stands upon the same level with the chief magistrate of the commonwealth—aye, or a king with a crown upon his brow. No tests of nationality are known among us; but, one band of brothers, our mission is that of peace and good-will, and, though the sections of our common country should be arrayed against each other, bayonets bristle, military commands resound, swords gleam in the sunlight, and every patriot stand appalled, yet even the awful aspect of these things could not turn the heart of one brother mason against another.—*N. Greene Curtis.*

232. I WEAR my badge of masonry with pride and exultation. I know, as I pass along the streets, that men unknown to me, look kindly upon me because I am one of them. I know that I have no need of a long acquaintance before my brother trusts in me, confides his dearest interests and his most intimate secrets

to me. I know that the sunlight, as it is reflected from my masonic symbol, carries back with it a ray of sympathy and mutual understanding to the hearts of thousands; and it is for that I value and love it. But if this badge stands merely by itself, a piece of lettered gold; if there is no great meaning symbolized by it; if the fundamental law of masonry ceases to exist, whereby the doctrine of love to man and confidence in the goodness of his character, is inculcated as a precept; or if that becomes a dead letter—if it is not carried out in our lives and in the habits of our minds—what care I for the bauble? I wear it now, and feel myself stronger and better because I am permitted to do so. Strip it of its idea, and I can only wear it from mere vanity.—*John B. Felton.*

233. No MAN can ever be a mason at heart, unless he worships God, and loves his neighbor. No charlatan, no hypocrite, no drunkard, no spendthrift, no glutton, no adulterer, no miser, no man who does not aspire and labor to obey the moral law, can ever become a mason through any process of admission. Perfection in this life we cannot attain, but we can reach towards it with faithful hearts and steady eyes. Be it our task, amidst the teeming vitality of the Pacific Coast, among the race to which we belong, under the institutions by which we are protected in the spheres of labor to which we are respectively called, not merely on holy days but every day, by the cheerfulness and persistence of our industry, by the modesty of our pretensions, by the promptness and punctuality with which we keep our engagements, by the general probity of our conduct,

by our firmness and patience under afflictions, by our unaffected sympathy and charity, by our strong control over appetite and passion, and by our temperate enjoyment of pleasure, to spread the light and warmth of Masonry.—*Henry E. Highton.*

234. OUR BROTHERHOOD operating in lodges of labor, and extending through all lands, builded many of the noblest structures of the middle ages. Freemasonry was in those days of violence the ally of religion, and assisted the Church to represent in forms of enduring beauty and grandeur the sublime hopes of the soul aspiring to God and immortal life. Freemasonry, however, achieved its grandest triumph when, organized and directed by the wisdom of Israel's King, it erected the first temple on the sacred mount. No discordant sound of metal was heard in its walls; towers and pinnacles arose into the air like an embodied dream of loveliness. During seven years the work continued beneath the cloudless skies of Palestine. When at length the purple glories of departing day were reflected from its dome, he who beheld that vision might well exclaim:

> "A star is trembling on the horizon's verge;
> That star shall glow and broaden on the night
> Until it hangs divine and beautiful
> In the proud zenith."

Our Fraternity has ceased to be an operative institution. The implements of the craft are no longer employed in actual labor. They have become symbols of speculative truth, and speak to the mind of laws and duties the observance of which will render our lives pure and harmonious, and our characters firm and symmetrical. We may not regret the change. It was a modification demanded by the progress of civilization and the improved conditions of society. Throughout the world Masonry is to-day doing a nobler work than when its Ancient Craftsmen builded their stateliest columns. The Masonic institution itself is more wonderful than any edifice which it ever constructed from the perishable materials of earth. It has an unspoken language older than any living language of Christendom. It has survived wars and revolutions, and is now silently ascending to loftier planes of usefulness. It looks to the heavens for its model, and in its work imitates the Divine plan of nature. The Sun draws in vapory tributes the moisture from the ocean; the invisible winds carry it in clouds over the globe and distribute in refreshing showers the liquid treasures of the skies. In like manner Masonry draws its strength and resources from the deep sea of human sympathies, and employs them to redress the wrongs and relieve the sorrows of humanity.—*Frank Tilford.*

235. A LOVE OF TRUTH, with the practice of it in every relation of life, is the supreme virtue of Masonry. At each stage of his advancement the neophyte is reminded that "the first creature of God, in the works of the days, was the light of the senses; the last was the light of reason; and his Sabbath work ever since then is the illumination of his spirit." He learns that the oracles of truth are the inspiration of the Deity,

and in their very nature eternal and immutable. He sees the glowing fancies of youth dissolve in the clear light of experience, the passions expire in the flames they excite, and the strength of manhood vanish amid the infirmities of age, while truth alone defies the power of time and decay. Allied to the noblest of virtues, are the discipline of the mind, the subjection of the emotions to the dominion of reason, and the attainment of knowledge. The character of the period in which we live unites with the precepts of the Order, and invites us to enter the wide, the boundless fields of science.

The nineteenth century has been styled an age of transition. It deserves the appellation. Since its commencement waves of thought have rolled over the nations with a volume ever increasing, and in tides that never recede. The resistless movement carries society each revolving year further from ancient landmarks and systems of philosophy fast sinking into oblivion. In the application of scientific principles to natural forces; in discoveries and inventions which have wrought important changes in all the relations of the civilized world, and in the emancipation of the human reason from a thraldom which forbade any inquiry except in conformity to certain prescribed theories, the nineteenth century claims its splendid and enduring triumphs. In the lifetime of the present generation, science has launched the steamship on the trackless ocean, and impelled it forward against warring billows and opposing winds; has painted with the sunbeam, and made the subtle currents of electricity,—invisible yet unerring

—carriers of thought. It has descended into the dark chambers of the earth and exhumed treasures of gold and silver, surpassing in value all that men had gathered during previous centuries of civilization. Leaving the peaceful vocations of industry, and devoting its resources to the work of destroying life, science has forged engines of death more potent than the wildest dreams of imagination ever before conceived. It has swept with sublime confidence down the abyss of time, and, traversing the countless ages of the past, presents to the vision no uncertain pictures of the world from creation's dawn to the present hour. It exhibits the earth as a vast sepulchre in which are burried the forms of life that have perished. As one generation was about to expire, the creative energy of nature evolved from it another and higher class of existence. Thus, through successive epochs, we behold a series of phenomena, governed by harmonious laws, and evincing a complete unity of design. Science ascends with its torch to the skies, surveys the celestial worlds, defines their appointed courses, and discovers the very elements of which they are composed. It points to Alcyone in the constellation of the Pleiades, and demonstrates that it is a grand central sun, encircled by the universe of stars, forming our astral system. Around that resplendent orb, our sun, with his satellites, revolves in an orbit so vast that eighteen million two hundred thousand years must elapse before one revolution is completed.

Thus it is evident that no association, however ancient or benevolent, can exert an appreciable influence unless it calls to its aid educated intellect and the resources of knowledge. It becomes the duty, as it is manifestly the interest, of the Masonic Fraternity, to revive in its lodges that devotion to the liberal arts and sciences which constituted, in the medieval centuries in Europe, the attraction of Masonry. Chief among the instrumentalities needed to accomplish this noble object are Masonic libraries. Every lodge should have a collection of literary and scientific works; lectures should be encouraged, and members incited to prosecute with order studies appropriate to their tastes and pursuits in life. After contemplating what the genius and learning of man have accomplished, the mind naturally seeks the immortal source of all intelligence. A cardinal tenet of Masonry is a belief in the existence of a Supreme Ruler of the universe, and, as a corollary to that sublime truth, faith in the immortality of the soul. It teaches us that the ineffable spirit of wisdom and love animates and permeates all time and space. The soul discerns His presence in every form of being and every manifestation of nature; in the morning and the evening; in the Spring, with its refreshing showers, and the Autumn, with its rich sheaves and golden harvests; in the forest, with their infinite variety of flower and foliage; in the mountains that lift their hoary heads above the clouds; in the rivulets that sparkle in the sunlight; and in the seas that mirror the glory of the skies. Atheism may spread far and wide, shutting out from the soul the hope of immortality, but while the Masonic Order continues a power on earth, faith will find a sanctuary in its temples.

Masonry is a recognition of the equality of man, and of the fraternal obligations which bind all men together. It is the highest expression of the sentiment of universal brotherhood. Within its portals there is no distinction of lineage or caste. The hereditary ruler of an empire ; the scholar whose researches extend over all the realms of thought; the soldier, bearing on his person the glittering trophies of a hundred victories; the owner of untold riches, and the laboring man, whose ill-requited toil earns for himself a meagre livelihood, are all alike—brethren all.

While rank and wealth divide society into classes; while political and religious differences create animosities, Masonry speaks a universal language which all men understand, and occupies a platform broad enough and firm enough for all the world. It violates no law. It wars with no sect, party or State. It obeys literally the divine admonition: "Let not thy left hand know what thy right hand doeth," and performs in secret the holy offices of charity. Wherever sin and wrong have cast their dark shadow, *there* is Masonry, to reclaim the erring and lead the repentant again to paths of peace. Wherever are sickness and sorrow, there is Masonry, to watch and soothe; wherever is death, there is Masonry, to commit, with solemn rites, the lifeless form to the silence of the grave.

There is no eternity to matter. No work of man can resist the ruthless hand of violence or the unsparing scythe of time. Even the temple which our ancient Craftsmen erected on the sacred mountain, that marvelous structure of consummate beauty, has not escaped the universal doom. Note the changes wrought on our planet since the era of authentic history.

Science reveals to us the unchangeable decree of the Infinite that the time must arrive, in the grand procession of the ages, when all life shall cease upon our globe. The atmosphere, with its gorgeous hues and banners of clouds, will pass away; the rivers and oceans will disappear; the myriad voices of nature will no longer arise to the heavens in songs of rejoicing, and the mighty monuments of the past will remain, tombs of generations that have died amid the awful solitudes of a dead world; but the principles of Masonry cannot die. They must survive. They are rays from the eternal light, drops from the river of everlasting life, and, like their deathless original, they too possess the attribute of immortality.

Oh, Masonry! with origin vested in mystery, yet whose pathway is luminous with the love of humanity; whose life is the spirit of ever-working benevolence; whose mission is the divinest charity; may thy standards advance, thy temples rise, until Truth, Justice, Faith, Charity, and Fraternal Love encompass with their holy influences all tribes and nations.—*Frank Tilford.*

ODD FELLOWSHIP.

236. With the weaving force of the material messengers of man, latest brought under his dominion, we may name again a more certain agent in cementing the

ties of common nationality—the correspondence, the contact, and the council of conversation, of brethren in the Order of Odd Fellowship throughout the United States of America.

In a beautiful city at the head of a magnificent bay there stands a monument to the Father of our Country. It is a companion shaft for the granite column that marks the spot where the first real battle of the revolution was fought—on the hights of Bunker Hill. Every intelligent American who is a visitor in the city of Baltimore, feels it to be the duty of a grateful citizen—as well as a privilege of pride—to ascend the Washington column, and take the inspiration of patriotism anew from its lofty summit. In that same metropolis there is a far more humble monument, reared by the Order of Odd Fellowship a few short years ago. And while the spirit of reverential memory is glowing within us, we turn from the towering obelisk to the simple pile of granite, and feel that we do no injustice to the mightier shades when we give an hour of affectionate recollection and homage before the tablets which speak of Wildey's fame. We read of a great, honest sympathy, and a zeal according to knowledge in the imparting and adapting of fraternal rules for the alleviation of human suffering and the promotion of heathful social enjoyments. Who is he that has contributed most in all this land for the superadding of friendship's glorious bonds to the responsive claim of citizenship? We take nothing from other and more intellectual and more demonstrative captains of the age, when from immediate communication with their record we pass with a full consciousness of equal if not more deserving worth to the central altar of Thomas Wildey. And when we purchase from the bare-footed flower boy, a bouquet of ever-greens and roses, and lay it upon the foundation blocks of his modest but elegant monument, we think we have paid no vain tribute to the memory of a mortal man, but by the simplest token have recognized a service whose beneficence we have felt a thousand times; and which shall not be stayed in its rising wave until the tears and woes of this world are submerged in the healing tide which shall flow from the fountain of benevolence and peace. One sprig of the tenacious cypress that is bound in a votive cluster we detach with trembling hand, and lay between the leaves of a pocket manual of our Order. We will take that with us across the great continent; and in another great city, in the same latitude, by the side of another ocean, we will place the frail fragment upon the sod beside another monument,—which stands above the grave of SAMUEL PARKER.—*Charles A. Sumner.*

237. ODD FELLOWSHIP disregards the factitious distinctions in society which wealth and station have created, and requires personal worth and moral character as the only passport to its privileges and protection. It goes beyond the mere physical wants of man and proposes an expansion of the human sympathies. It ignores the tottering, palsied steps of superannuated antiquity, and grapples, with all the ardor of youth, the pressing duties of life and the realities of modern progress. It seeks to enlighten and educate the mind of man and enlarge the sphere of his affection.—*George R. Moore.*

238. Our order represents, perhaps in a greater degree than any other institution, the principle of mutual assistance, by which society can be reclaimed. The rich man would not seek it to increase his riches, the learned man his learning, or the great man his power; it commends itself to that great body of common men who bear life's burthens and responsibilities, and who sometimes grow weary with the load. It commands its disciples to counsel each other in health, to assist each other in difficulty, to defend each other in danger, to relieve each other in sickness, and when one falls in the ranks, to watch over and protect the objects of his love, whom he leaves helpless behind him. But these ministrations are only a tithe of its virtues. It seeks to improve and elevate the character of man, to enlighten his mind, to enlarge the sphere of his affection. Associated together, we can have schools, libraries and cabinets. In the charmed circle where we meet want must never come—the fear of it must be banished. Here must be diffused around all the healthful atmosphere of conscious independence. Meeting together frequently in our lodges, mind shall shape mind, intellect strengthen intellect. Surrounded by emblems and symbols, and listening to the teachings of the good, we can keep alive in our hearts the sense of the beautiful and love of the true. Our institution is a model State, whose laws are founded upon justice, administered in love, and whose only sanction is honor. We will earnestly but peacefully strive to inaugurate the era of social democracy, wherein labor will be endowed with the privileges it establishes and enriched with the blessings it creates.—*Newton Booth.*

239. I SHOULD deem that I chased shadows were I to recur to the forgotten slanders of the past, or dwell upon the feeble objections that a few yet present against Odd Fellowship. The world of to-day is too enlightened to embark in or encourage a crusade against a body of men against whom no evil can be proven— whose professed principles are pure, and whose acts, so far as they are open to scrutiny, are uniformly characterized by earnest and self-sacrificing benevolence. We stand not now upon the defensive. Our enemies have retired before our advancing hosts, their weapons of assault broken, their champions in the dust, and we are no longer molested in the great and glorious work of uplifting the city and temple of Odd Fellowship. May the work, so nobly begun, and so successfully prosecuted, go on, until its foundations encircle the earth, till its lofty spires reach the heavens, catching the first rays of the rising sun, and flashing back its beams till the last moment of time. May the millions of the future be numbered in its brotherhood, catch the inspiration of its free spirit, and forever transmit in their integrity the cardinal tenets of Friendship, Love and Truth.—*A. A. Sargent.*

240. ODD FELLOWSHIP, in its practical application to its own membership, is human fellowship. Ignoring in

this fellowship all political and ecclesiastical distinctions, all the caste classifications of human society, this Order plants itself distinctly upon the brotherhood of man and the fatherhood of God. Its organization is designed for efficiency—designed to give efficiency to its charitable purposes. It is not founded upon any Utopian theory of what may be at some remote period in the future, but upon the every-day character of man at the present time. Its government is neither a democracy, republic nor aristocracy, but has enough of each to prevent central despotism or popular insubordination. Its mission is one of charity. It aims to cultivate the holy principles of friendship, love and truth, yet it tolerates neither insubordination nor trifling on the part of its membership. Its present government did not spring forth perfect by one elastic bound, as Minerva from the head of Jupiter, but is the product of long and trying experience. Its trials have been numerous, often threatening its authority, and sometimes its very existence; but these have imparted to it strength, and fitted it for its great mission. Before its altars the rich and poor alike, the learned and the unlearned, the high and the low, stand upon a common platform. All contribute alike to swell its common treasury, and in sickness, all, rich or poor, draw alike from the same general fountain, not as a charity, but as a right, growing out of membership. The Lodge is a school-room for moral and intellectual training—for keeping the mind clear and active, and the spirit polished, that it may the more easily slide in fraternal grooves. Is it of no advantage to the growth of the human soul to have the wants of the sick and the claims of the dying, the necessities of the widow and orphan weekly, daily, hourly, brought before it? Odd Fellowship is now deeply rooted in American soil. Its beneficial influence cannot be confined within the circle of the Order—it permeates the entire social state. With its own elevation it lifts up society.—*Gen. John A. Collins.*

241. WHEN WE look around to see what occupies and interests the nation, we find political parties, with their various schemes of internal improvement, banks and tariffs, public schools, colleges, asylums, railroad corporations, steamship companies, Masonry, Odd Fellowship and the church. These constitute the nation's life, and upon them are expended its best energies; but they are not all equally lasting. The institution we strove the hardest to maintain, the party we deemed most essential to the prosperity of our country, has vanished. Where is the old Whig party of Webster and Clay? Where is the Democracy of Jefferson and Jackson? Shivered like glass. The Republic itself has shaken from foundation to dome. While we look, the object is gone. While the warm words of the orator ring in our ears, the institution he praised has flitted away; but there is always something left. Not all of the supposed pillars of the nation at any one time fall, and our aim is to learn which of the institutions of a given age are things of a night, to float like a dream on the surface of society, and which, with their cornerstones on the bedrock of national life, are destined to live.

The true test of the permanence of any institution is this: "Does it rest upon the great law that man is the child of God and the brother of man?" In proportion as it recognizes and enforces this law, in that proportion is it one of those great institutions which give life and power to a nation—swallowing up all lesser measures and reforms, or moulding them into shape, and imparting to them whatever of vitality they possess; flourishing when they decay, and living green when they are covered thick with the moss of the tomb. When, therefore, we commit ourselves to parties, or sects, or institutions, let us remember that some are to go out like a taper, or, at most, to live for a generation. On these let us not waste our time or substance, for their very name shall be blotted out ere the sod has settled on your grave. Oh! man, Oh! woman, take care lest the shrine at which you worship be a whited sepulchre, full of dead men's bones!

Assuming that the test of the real virtue of institutions is the degree in which they recognize the truth that there is one God, and He our Father, and that all men are brothers, how shall it be decided whether a particular institution does recognize this truth, and hence whether Odd Fellowship stands the test! One of the most difficult problems to solve is whether a given institution, potent in its sway over the age, be in fact built upon that eternal law, written upon the heavens and earth, that God rules and that all men are brothers. * * * Odd Fellowship has no other origin than the big hearts of the mass of men. To cheer each other in the toils of life, to aid each other in sickness and distress, and to bury the dead, were the objects of its founders. Gradually the sphere of the institution became so enlarged as to embrace the widow, and the orphan; and finally it assumed its present noble proportions, not only to aid in distress, but to enlighten the mind and expand the heart. Its fundamental idea being that man is the brother of man, and hence his equal, its constant tendency is to take man's thoughts from self and direct them to his fellow men, and thus to bring within the scope of his daily meditations millions of human beings instead of one * * Friend, brother! the man who rises from such meditations rises a nobler man. What a noble principle! Implant it in the heart of every man in the State, and you have a whole people animated by one great thought—the learned sharing their knowledge with the unlearned—the rich spreading out an open purse to the poor—each breathing into the other's ear his struggles, his hopes, and his fears. A State so constituted would be a glory in peace, a terror in war.

America boasts that she is a watch-tower of liberty—that here the portals of freedom's temple ever swing wide open. Odd Fellowship stands around republican institutions a wall of fire against their enemies; and if ever the stately columns of this republic crumble and go down amid the billows, and the darkness of despotism settles upon the land—then, if there be any hope—if there be a single gleam of light,—the sentinels of Odd Fellowship will be there upon the outer wall as in the olden time, and to the anxious question, " Watchman, what of the night?" will cry out, "The morning cometh."—*John B. Harmon.*

242. THE ADMIRERS OF ANTIQUITY have toiled to discover the land-marks of Odd Fellowship far back amid the mysterious realms of the past. Impressed with the beauty and simplicity of its morals and philosophy, they would teach us to believe it has been garnished and enriched by the noblest intellects of all time. Through the dim vista of cycles lost, amid the mouldering monuments of ancient empires, they trace its fabulous history, ever struggling to embellish and perfect its fair proportions, by shedding around it the light and lustre of primeval grandeur and greatness. In the Roman legends, and following their victorious legions over the plains of Andalusia, or amid the Druidical oaks of Britain, on the fields of Palestine, where followers of cross and crescent met in deadly conflict, in the brilliant age of Pericles, amid the flickering lamps and solemn mummeries of scholastic cells, they point us to the doubtful evidence of its existence.

I choose to reject the fable of its ante-feudal birth, and hail the truth that the dust of antiquity has never tinged its vestments. No ancient records tell the story of its praise or shame; it holds no key to unlock the mysteries of another age. No Pagan monarch in purple has known it, no holy prophet in the dim old wilderness, no chosen high priest of the Infinite has lifted up his incensed hand to consecrate its forms. But the weary and the fatherless, the distressed and desolate of our own land, and age, have enshrined it in their hearts and blessed it with prayers and tears. I choose to find its origin in the development of that modern English civilization which has been ever foremost in all that tends to ameliorate the condition of society, and improve and perfect the character of man. Reason and philosophy indeed would never bid you seek its presence beyond that period. An institution like this, founded on the most ennobling truths of modern religion, proclaiming and vindicating the fraternity of man, with the last and grandest of the commandments, "Love ye one another," as the summary of its faith, would not in the nature of things rise and flourish while the social distinctions of the Middle Ages prevailed. While science, art, literature and learning were confined to the monastic cell; while the pall of barbarism enshrouded the world, and the glory of man was estimated by the thousands he had slaughtered rather than by the good he had accomplished; the earth presented but a barren field for the cultivation of the virtues which Odd Fellowship inculcates. It required another and a vastly different condition of society. When the social distinctions of the Middle Ages had been partially broken down—crown and coronet trampled in the dust—and prince and peasant taught to weep and pray together; when the plebeian dared assert that flowers bloomed for him as well as for the prince, and that the natural elements of life and impulses of humanity belonged no less to him than to his imperial master; when the mariner's compass had revealed a new continent, and the telescope new worlds; when the two great engines of civilization—war and commerce—had made man better acquainted with his fellow man; and the art of printing had stepped in to disseminate truth and intelligence; when the church, at last mindful of her peaceful mission, was proclaiming the idea of one vast brotherhood in the practice of virtue and enjoyment of fraternal love; when in brief all antiquated forms and systems were dissolving in the light of increased knowledge; and charity, benevolence, and kindred virtues were supplanting the selfish vices of our ancestors —Odd Fellowship sprang into existence. It was the legitimate fruit of that great social and moral transition—the child of progress, the ward of civilization.

It has strengthened the cause of good government, by teaching obedience to law and respect for superiors, in the administration of its own internal polity.

It has built up a system of jurisprudence, the counterpart of the law of the land, and by a rigid enforcement of its sanctions, taught at once the law, and the process and necessity of its observance.

It has frowned on turbulence and strife, and diminished the chances of insurrection and rebellion, by promptly punishing in every instance insubordination in its own ranks.

It has built up the altars of religion everywhere, by teaching with a force and beauty rarely attained in other schools, the lessons of immortality and dependence on Almighty God.

It has added new charms to the volume of inspiration, by presenting it as the fountain head of its own beautiful teachings, and adopting its precepts as part of its own ritual and lectures.

It has made religion more inviting, by making it more practical—by compelling its votaries to *do* that which religion was satisfied to teach them they *ought* to do.

It has taught man the true fraternal relation, by impressing upon his mind that God is the Common Father of All.

It has promoted temperance and truth, by keeping their innate charms ever before the mind in the most attractive form, and promptly punishing every departure from their principles, or violation of their requirements.

It has established a new bond of unity among men, and by its agency settled and adjusted peacefully the thousand difficulties, which otherwise violence and strife would have made perpetual.

It has made man more just and upright, by making him more confident of the justice and integrity of his fellow-man.

It has gilded Charity with additional charms; and, rearing her altars at every fireside, has widened the field of her ministrations, and multiplied her servants.

It has broken down the artificial distinctions of society, which mere wealth had reared, by compelling its followers to meet on the same level and recognize merit as the only passport to preferment.

It has infused the masses with a common sympathy and aspiration, by bringing them together in interchange of thought and wish, and uniting their efforts for the accomplishment of a common purpose.

It has made man better, by compelling him to be a perpetual witness to its deeds of kindness and good will, and laying on his heart the thanks and benedictions of those who have experienced his friendly offices.

It has stifled resentments and stayed the passion of revenge, by pointing, with unerring certainty, to a speedy remedy for every wrong, a voluntary atonement for every injury and insult.

It has cheered the poor and unfortunate, kept from the heart the demon of despair, from the brain madness, and stricken down the suicidal hand by providing that timely aid which could be supplied from no other source, and pointing to a future full of hope and joy.

It has promoted the cause of education, by founding schools and libraries, to which the friendless orphan gains as ready admission as the son of luxury and wealth.

It has conserved morality, by banishing the hard necessities which drive men into crime—by keeping out from thousands of homes the spectre of famine, and casting around its altars the allurements which lead the young and giddy up from the play-house and saloon to the more refined and virtuous enjoyments of the lodge room.

It has fitted young men for the struggles of life, by familiarizing them with the forms of business and debate, and sending them out on missions at once most arduous and delicate.

It has made them independent, self-reliant and self-respectful, and developed them into earlier manhood, by charging them with grave responsibilities and the consideration and decision of the most serious and complex propositions.

It has made man more thoughtful of the future, more attentive to his present duties, more considerate towards his fellow-men, and more solicitous for his own ultimate destiny, by requiring him, as often as the grim messenger invades the Lodge, to join the funeral procession to the Silent City, and there contemplate the solemn lessons of mortality.—*Leonidas E. Pratt.*

THE IMPROVED ORDER OF RED MEN.

243. The Improved Order of Red Men is the offspring of love of country, of fortitude, and of self-sacrifice. It is the child of patriotism, and, as may be readily conjectured, it is peculiarly and entirely an American order. Not American in that narrow sense which questions a man's birthplace, or inquires into his theological or anti-theological opinions; but American in a broader and more comprehensive definition. American as Niagara is an American cataract, and the Columbia an American river. There are tribes of our order whose council fires are kindled near the icy glint of lakes which lie far beyond the northern confines of the Republic. There may be wigwams shadowed by the forests which circle the base of Orizaba. The order invites to its membership all worthy pale faces, whether aliens or citizens, wherever born or of whatever faith. It is American only in the sense that its spirit is the spirit of the mountains, the forests, the prairies, the cataracts, the white-lipped lightning, and the thunder's voice. It gathers its traditions from the lost races who have passed away and who left in some places the imprints of a strange civilization, and in others the mementos of a cruel barbarism—races which like those of England, seem to have had an age of stone and an age of bronze, but, unlike those of Europe, never an age of iron; races which have left behind them the *casas grandes* of New Mexico, the ancient fortifications of the Mississippi Valley, the sculptured monoliths of Copan, the aqueducts and cities of Arizona, and the pyramids of Northern Mexico; races whose carvings in stone, and whose ornaments in pottery and metal, and shells, and obsidian, and porphyry, are often unearthed all the way from Lake Superior to the Belize; races whose temples are crumbled, whose gods are vanished, and whose records exist only in the undecipherable hieroglyphics of a language lost and gone.

Our wigwams we dedicate to the use of an order whose chief object is brotherhood and charity; an order which hopes to accomplish its benign purposes through the love that comes from knowledge of each other, and the strength that is born of association and cohesion.

Perhaps there is not, in the whole vast vocabulary of human speech, syllables more articulate with honorable emotion than that one word—"dedicate." In the beginning, when the morning stars sang together, the first grand dedication was made, and I wonder that painters of the pre-Raphaelite school did not choose this subject of all others for their master efforts. A new and swinging world, plucked out of the stilly and starless unknown, her brooks filtrated from the mists of chaotic wastes, her fields unblown, her first born forests yet succulent with nature's milk, her airs warm with wooing motion, and her freshly-tinted skies painting the crest of creation upon new-made lake and river. Suns unshorn of a virgin beam, and moons propelled along unplowed paths, and stars yet untaught in sentinel duty, over all this songless world shone ever. What though but a dew-drop hanging from the finger of the Great Author! It was a world set apart for the uses of mortal man, and dedicated in the presence of angels to the universal brotherhood.

No dedication ever brought evil to mankind. It is an observation of history, that the temple and the tabernacle, whether dedicated to the Oracle, to the Unknown God, or the One Supreme, or to Love and Charity, still retain the master idea of ages old, still rear their proportions, a perpetual rebuke to tyranny, and always a stronghold of rectitude and justice, catching glints (even through the quagmires of the superstitions of heathen nations, or the jungles of obscure faiths) of that celestial light which must endure forever.

The walls of our wigwams shall never echo a sentiment that is not kindly, and their doors shall never open for a deed of injury to any human being. When we have been gathered to the hunting grounds of the summer land our wigwams will look upon a field of labor and supply larger than we know. A million souls shall dwell on 'the peninsula of San Francisco; temples of art and industry, and science and religion, and benevolence, shall send a thousand spires to the skies. The out-reaching arms of an iron-Briareus will bring to our doors the trophies of a conquest which commerce shall achieve over forty degrees of latitude. And still, even as Yosemite, in the presence of awe-struck tourists, tosses her soft white lace of falling waters to the air, as simply and as purely as in the days when she was alone with the forests and the meadows, so will the maxims and the deeds and the life of this Order bear themselves serene amid the din of human industry and the selfishness of human struggle.—*Thomas Fitch.*

ANCIENT ORDER OF UNITED WORKMEN.

244. It builds no palatial offices for its managers, it accumulates no hoard to tempt its treasurer. It has ten thousand trustees in California alone. Every man holds a dollar of the funds, which he lays at the desolated fireside of the stricken. When the humblest member of the Order of this State dies, its Governor contributes to the fund for his widow. It brings a man into good company, and makes the most out of him. It teaches the hand of velvet to rest with confidence within the hand of iron. The banker and the baker are one for an hour of need. The weary farmer rests his head upon his pillow with the assurance that, if he fails to greet the morning light, the faith of ten thousand men is pledged to lift that nightmare of a mortgage. It commends sobriety, exalts labor, and enjoins virtue. It shadows the land like a fleecy cloud, ready, when the thunder rolls, to drop showers of blessings in barren places.

It gathers money quietly, with little effort here and there, as the sun drinks dew from the open hearts of a thousand flowers, and returns it when and where most needed. It is instinct with the truest, broadest humanity; it teaches men to help themselves, and "do as they would be done by." It has not aroused jealousy in other benevolent and fraternal organizations. They recognize that it supplies a want, and extend it their support. It is a grand experiment. Other Orders are true through life; some do relieve to a certain extent the widows and children; this assures them of a right, almost a competence. It is the severest test yet made of the fraternal spirit. It is the flower of the ages, a culminating blossom on the aloe that requires thousands of years to develop a bloom.—*Philip M. Fisher.*

FRATERNAL INSURANCE SOCIETIES.

245. The establishment of fraternal insurance associations upon a practical and permanent basis is among the chief triumphs of the human mind—in the line of moral invention. That this grand consummation, or it may be called discovery, should be reserved for our day, must excite at once our pride and our wonder. At once simple in its operation and grand in its results, we are amazed that its blessings were not enjoyed by our remote ancestry as they will be by our remote prosterity. If, as the great poet of humanity tells us, "all the world's a stage, and all the men and women merely players," proud, indeed, may we be, and proud, indeed, we are, that we are actors in this new drama of brotherly love; surprised, indeed, may we be, and surprised indeed we are, that this drama was not put on the stage of human action until the Star of Empire had gilded the remotest West, and more than eighteen centuries after the Star of Bethlehem first illumined the Eastern world. It is given us now, in the fullness of time—a living fact, a beautiful reality.

This great work of fraternal insurance is now being prosecuted on a broad basis, and is the mission of several powerful organizations, chief among which are The Ancient Order of United Workmen, The Knights of Honor, The American Legion of Honor, The Knights of Pythias, and The Order of Chosen Friends.

The great truth that one can rarely help many, but many can often help one, has never been so generally exemplified as now, in the lives and conduct of men. Closely allied to it, and entitled to a like recognition, is that other great truth, which Odd Fellowship has done so much to impress upon the minds and hearts of men, that all men are brothers, having a common origin and a common father. As upon two certain commandments in Holy Writ "hang all the law and the prophets," so upon these two golden truths rest the stately edifices of these Orders whose names I cluster here. The work and mission of these fraternities are worthy to engage the noblest mind, the most eloquent tongue, the amplest study, the closest scrutiny, the broadest criticism. They present no abstraction, no abstruse proposition, no occult science, no perplexing theory, no knotty problem. They unfold a new system of organized benevolence, a new plan of co-operative effort for mutual security against want and distress.

No zealous member of either of these societies can fail to cherish an abiding love for the Ancient Order of United Workmen. That fraternity first opened up the broad highway that leads to perfect security in life insurance. To the beauties and charms of Freemasonry and Odd Fellowship it adds a more substantial feature. It has found a way whereby men may help their fellows without making the recipients of their bounty objects of charity. Throwing its fraternal arms around each brother in life, it watches over him in sickness and death, gives him to the grave with tenderness and tears, then goes to his widow and orphan and empties into their laps its purse of gold.

And this it does, not as *charity* but as a *right*. It simply executes a sacred trust. It merely turns over to loved ones left behind, that which has been honorably won for them, and which is legally their due. All this it does, and in all this it finds a noble rival in each of the other orders whose names I have lovingly entwined with its own.

We who belong to these fraternal bands, are mindful of the compensations of Nature which make life such a thrilling drama. We need no skeleton transfixed upon our walls to remind us of our end. It was the mighty fact of Death that called us into being. A serene consciousness of our mortality binds us together, and will abide with us on the mountain's top and in the meadow's lap—when the frost is biting and when the flowers are blooming—not pursuing us like an avenging fury—not lowering over us like a black shadow to blight the landscape of our life; but as the fiat of a just God, to purge us of our dross, to stimulate our noblest faculties, to strengthen our manhood, and to enable us to confront with serenity and hope, "the great mystery of the grave."

Verily, beloved Orders! As ye multiply in numbers, ye shall remain but one in essence. Ye differ from each other only as one star differs from another star in glory. Rooted in the hearts, and devoted to the wants of men, ye will never pause or tire until some more powerful organization, with a greater capacity for good, and more adapted to the spirit of the remote age that gives it birth, shall take the sceptre from your hands. Engaged in a common cause, pursue your beneficent mission with unfaltering step. While cherishing a spirit of generous rivalry, may ye ever feel the impulse of a common purpose, and move onward, hand in hand, to the fulfillment of your destiny.

But yesterday ye were an enigma to the multitude. Now ye are known and read of all men. The world sees your work. Humanity applauds it. And the marvelous story of your birth will be written by more than mortal fingers, to be preserved in the Archives of Eternity.

And when the bound volumes of centuries shall have been laid away on the broad shelf of time, and coming generations shall look back to this era as to the infancy of the earth, these Orders will continue to be recognized as the strongest ties among men, and the widow and the orphan will point to them with gratitude and exultation.

To Thee, great Author of the Book of Life, who teacheth to men the lessons of humility and interdependence—who knoweth wherefore death came into the world, and all our woe—who hath endowed with more than mortal powers that offshoot of Thy mind, the mind of man—whose comprehensive love doth wrap all souls, all worlds, all things that space can hold or thought can reach—in whose grand plan the tiniest atoms find recognition—God of the Storm, at whose command the warring elements lay down their arms and fold their hands in peace! God of the storm-rocked soul! whose power is revealed not more terribly in the external world than in that fiercer realm, the human breast—to Thee, unfailing source of life and hope, we address our perpetual appeal!

O, Spirit of Brotherly Love! Ever poised on healing wings above the smitten heart, sending thy unfaltering ministers into every home of desolation: we offer thee the incense of our grateful salutation! Thou art a spirit of love indeed! Thou art a harbinger of mercy! Thou art clothed with light as with a garment! Thy voice is like the melody of the brook, thy smile like the golden dawn of day! Thou art brightest in the presence of gloom, thou art bravest in crises of want and misery! No human anguish can turn thee aside, no conflict of arms can put thee to flight, no plague or pestilence can beat thee back! Thy destiny is interwoven with that of the race whose wayward steps thou watchest, and whose woes thou dost assuage! There have been Dark Ages, because thou hast hid thy face; but through the eons of coming time, thou wilt ever live among men and go with them from the cradle to the grave.—*Oscar T. Shuck.*

VIII.

DISTINGUISHED MEN.

PART VIII.

DISTINGUISHED MEN.

246. To the Infinite Eye, the qualities that are housed in character only, have weight. Indeed, even with us, they are not reckoned out, when we weigh men. We say an eloquent man has weight on the platform, as naturally as that the fat man has weight on Fairbanks' scales. I greatly admire the philosophy wrapped up in the Hoosier's answer to the Yankee, when asked how much he weighed: "I weigh 180 pounds as you see me, but when I'm mad I weigh a ton." Almost the first question we ask concerning the newly-arrived man on our planet, is "How much does he weigh?" And it is wonderful how much weight is increased by the proper gymnastic training of our spirits. Wellington, at the start, weighed ten pounds; before he died he weighed Great Britain and the balance of Europe. Jefferson was tossed easily in his nurse's arms at first; but later he lifted America. Newton hung very lightly on the steel-yards, when first known; but afterwards he hung all the planets on the steel-yards that he suspended.

—*Thomas Starr King.*

LOUIS AGASSIZ.

(DIED DECEMBER 14TH, 1873.)

247.—
Open your gates, O grave!
Make broad your passage way!
The form, for which we ask a place,
Is not of common clay.
The fertile brain, the silver tongue,
The genial voice which we
Rejoiced to hear, are still. We bring
The dust of Agassiz.

Chant in the pines, ye winds,
Murmur, ye waters deep;
The searcher of your heights and depths
Lies in his last calm sleep.
The seeker after truth and light,
The reader of the past,
The leader in incessant work,
Has found his rest at last.

Ye rustling autumn leaves,
Drop gently o'er his tomb!
Ye creatures whom, in life, he loved,
In reverent silence come!
Pupils that by his earnest life
And burning words were led,
Gather around his quiet grave
In tribute to the dead!

Earth, in thy bosom sweet,
And soft brown mantle, fold

The ashes of the sage, who taught
That truth is more than gold.
Leave to the warlike chieftains
The vaunted laurel crown!
Be lilies, white, and violets,
Upon *this* grave, laid down.
—*W. H. Dall.*

GEN. E. D. BAKER.

248. One there was whose noble form was in our midst, it seems, but yesterday—gifted with power to touch the chords of every heart, endowed with magic to open the fountains of laughter or of tears—whose words could soothe the malignity of foes, and lift the mind to regions of serenest thought; to whom eloquence was but the out-breathing of his soul—gone now, swept down in the fierce tide of battle! That wondrous brain, at one moment the home of strange fancies, the next, insensate clay! No more shall his glorious words kindle the enthusiasm of our hearts, no more his eagle eye flash with the hidden fires of the soul.—*Newton Booth.*

249.—

Leap up, My country! not alone the sword
Is swift and strong;
The eloquent and soul-inspiring word,
The earnest flow of song—

All these may in a whelming force be poured
'Gainst citadels of wrong.

No one unto himself is solely lent;
Each human soul
Must with the surging tides of life be blent.
The stars that roll
In shining orbits through the firmament
Are parts of one great whole.

A star! *He* was a star! whose radiance here
Thro' the dark night of war,
Lit up our hearts with tenderest beams of cheer
None may restore;
And thus we mourn him stricken from our sphere
To shine on us no more.

Lay him all gently on his mother Earth!
While tears, like rain,
Bedew his grave from nation and from hearth
There rests no stain
Upon his sword, no tarnish on his worth—
So dust to dust, again.

—*Mrs. James Neale.*

280. IT WAS something more than the fierce thirst for glory that carried the Senator to the field of sacrifice. Hero blood is patriot blood. It was in the spirit of the patriot hero that the gallant soldier, the grave Senator, the white-haired man of counsel, yet full of youth as full of years, gave answer as does the war-horse to the trumpet's sound. The wisdom of his conduct was questioned. Many thought that he should remain

for counsel in the Senate-hall. The propriety of a Senator taking upon himself the duties of a soldier, depends, like many other things, on circumstances; certainly such conduct has the sanction of the example of great names. Socrates, who was not of the councils of Athens simply because he deemed his office of a teacher of wisdom a higher and nobler one, did not think it unworthy of himself to serve as a common soldier in battle. In the days when Greece was free, when Rome was free, when Venice was free, who but their great statesmen, counsellors and senators, led their armies to victorious battle? In the best days of all the great and free States, civil place and distinction were never held inconsistent with military authority and conduct. So far from it, all history teaches the fact that those who have proved themselves most competent to direct and administer the affairs of government in times of peace, were not only trusted, but were best trusted with the conduct of armies in times of war.—*Gen. Jas. A. McDougall.*

251. HIS CAREER from the time he came to California, is depicted in characters such as checker the earth when the morning sun, coming from the chambers of the east, illumines with a glory only its own, every mountain top, and every city, and every hamlet spire, and every ascending slope, and every aspiring ridge on which he turns, leaving behind them the long dark shadows of the still lingering night. Gradually, as he rose to the zenith, those shadows, one by one, in couples, in multitudes, fled away, until there lay none

upon the scene save the few dark lines that fell on the frozen North. These were the icy souls that no heat of genius, no light of intellect, no fire of patriotism, could dispel.

To the untutored eye he presented nothing remarkable; but to the educated vision he presented a rare spectacle of beauty. No frame was more admirably developed, no limbs were more admirably poised in their setting. Every fibre of his face was a line of intellect, sagacity and nobility; his entire head was a combination of the type Roman and the type Greek —Cæsar and Socrates in one. There was not a rigid place, not a waste spot, not a lacking place about him; everywhere throughout, in mind and body, he was one of the most supple, elastic, well-developed of men. Whatever untutored eye might overlook in him on the crowded highways of life, yet when he stood upon feet, delivering his eloquent utterances to his countrymen, he was the most graceful and polished of men. Not Pericles, not Cicero, not Webster, the grandest of them all, in all the personnel of the speaker, was a purer, more classic person and orator than Baker. When it is considered that his oratory grew and was schooled in the wild west, we know of no higher proof of the overmastering genius of the man, who, from so rough a workshop, could produce what takes rank with the master models of all time.

In the Courts, those cases that most deeply stir the passions of the soul were his to press or to defend, by common consent. In the lyceum, in the lecture room, in the learned assembly, no man aspired to be his peer.

On the stump, it seems to me—I speak it deliberately, as the calm conviction of my judgment—he never had a rival here, nor yet anywhere, nor at any time. I have heard the most celebrated stump orators. There was always an effort, a reaching forth for the *outre*, and the fantastic trickery of humor, to please the crowd—a general letting down to the vulgarities of the multitude. No one of them seemed to be able to hold the mixed mass without resorts to the craft that wheedles or that makes them stand agape with laughter or with wonder. In one word, the orator had to descend to the level of the lowest of his hearers. Not so with Baker. He lifted the multitude—the red-shirted and the gray; the blue-minded, the sour-minded, the envious, the jealous, the ignorant, and the wise; the ruffian and the gentleman, the low and high, all—the great multitude—he lifted them up to himself, face to face, and there, like a sage, with an eloquence classic as unapproachable, he inspired them, the meanest of them, until they thought that in them lay sublime power.

We have been in the habit of looking upon Baker more in the light of an eloquent orator than in any other aspect of his character. All will be surprised when I state that this was not his forte. I have his own word for it.

During an exciting political campaign, I had the rare privilege of accompanying him, and being in close intimacy with him day and night. He said to me once, alone in our room, after the fatigues of the day, "You admire my eloquence, for which I am really grateful, but you do not know me; this is not my forte." "What can it be, then?" I exclaimed in astonishment. "If you can beat yourself as an orator, in another direction, you are certainly an extraordinary man." "Well, think what you may," he replied, "my real forte is my power to command, rule and lead men. I feel that I can lead men anywhere."

How well he proved his claim to this great power—a quality that has no superior among human endowments.

The axiom of the ancients that the orator should be a man of universal learning, was fulfilled in Baker. Upon all the leading sciences and arts, he had mastered exhaustless stores of information. With what beauty could he group his learned possessions! Who but Baker could satisfy the excited heart of a great people on the laying of the Atlantic Cable, with a speech in which every line was equal to the promise of that sensitive chord itself, as it lay under the ceaseless throb of the mighty deep? (See Part X—EDITOR.)

Not seldom have I stood with him before works of art—of the artist and the artisan—when his rare ability of appreciative criticism would have instructed the masters of the works themselves. His acquaintance with all the range of literature was as nearly complete as falls to the lot of any man, and no human being ever knew the use of books more excellently well than he. In public speaking, no man ever reached higher, and trod those altitudes with a statelier step, or poised himself above them with a steadier wing, and all the way down to the valley of every day life, a strange charm hung about him.—*Samuel B. Bell.*

JOSEPH G. BALDWIN.

252. My friendship for Mr. Baldwin commenced long before he came to the bench, and it afterward warmed into the attachment of a brother. He had a great and generous heart; there was no virtue of which he did not possess a goodly portion. He was always brim full of humor, throwing off his jokes, which sparkled without burning, like the flashes of a rocket. There was no sting in his wit. You felt as full of merriment at one of his witticisms, made at your expense, as when it was played upon another. Yet he was a profound lawyer, and some of his opinions are models of style and reasoning. The opinion of the Supreme Court of California in Hart *vs.* Burnett, prepared by Mr. Justice Baldwin, is without precedent for the exhaustive learning and research it exhibits upon the points discussed. (The report of this case—Hart *vs.* Burnett—covers 100 pages of the 15th volume of California Reports, of which 79 pages, octavo, are devoted to Justice Baldwin's decision—THE EDITOR.)

—*Judge Stephen J. Field.*

DAVID C. BRODERICK.

253. He had a scorn of falsehood and prevarication which it exceeds the power of language to express. He had a love of truth, a directness of purpose, a simplicity of manner, impressing conviction on all ingenuous minds, and confounding the craft of his opponents. He had a bold, outspoken frankness, a tenacity of purpose, an indomitable will, and an unflinching bravery, which commanded admiration and often conquered success, even when they did not win conviction. He was quick of perception, ready in resource, faithful in friendship, true to his pledges, consistent in principle. Withal, he was placid in demeanor; his smile was winning, and the natural tones of his voice in conversation often as gentle as those of a woman. In morals he was pure, far beyond the common standard of public men. But if he had great merits he had great defects also. He was often too open and free of expression, sometimes employing unmeasured denunciation, when silent contempt would have been equally or even more effective. He was often too bold, too fond of effecting by sheer force of will what might have been as well accomplished with more moderation. His openness prevented him at times from a cautious withholding of his plans until they were sufficiently ripe, and made them liable to surprise and counter-plot. He was too magnanimous; he could not believe that the same generosity which would conquer himself would not subdue others. He was too often deceived by those who came to him with professions of friendship or repentance; when he forgave an offense, he seemed to forget that it had ever been committed, although the injury might have involved treachery to himself or a betrayal of his confidence. He was sometimes imperious, even beyond the privilege of a party leader; he often offended, and sometimes estranged, those who thought that even in the emergency of an unexpected crisis, they ought to be consulted. This last, however, was not owing to a defect of temper, but to a principle which Broderick assumed, that to be a party leader, one must be acknowledged as qualified to *lead*, and that in a sudden crisis, he becomes a dictator so far as regards the tactics of his party. He sometimes made great mistakes, but they were errors of policy and tactics; they never involved consistency of purpose or of principle. These were his greatest faults, but even these were the faults of a great, generous nature. It was doubtless fortunate for his country, although a source of melancholy to him, that Broderick became isolated, with no kindred to participate in his fortune and his success—that he had no wife or children to share in his affections, or to distract his purposes. The man lost in domestic enjoyment, but the public gained in the efforts of his undivided patriotism and singleness of purpose. Simple of tastes, with no expensive habits, and disbursing more for purposes of religion and charity than was demanded for all the other outlays of his life, whether personal, political, literary or æsthetic, he was above corruption, because he was superior to avarice, and to the lust or necessity of gain; and the only temptations to which he was subject as a public man were the stimulus of a patriotic ambition and the cravings for an honest fame.

I do not wonder that the people of the prehistoric ages deified many of their great men who were cut off in the prime of their powers. If we read the obscure lessons of history aright, I do not doubt that the demigods of antiquity were but the historic memories of great men whose mission had been interrupted by death—a catastrophe to which the wants and hopes of their contemporaries could not be reconciled. Could so much power, so much potential goodness *die?* Would they not return again to earth, where so much remained for their accomplishment, so much for them to *do?*

Hope awaited their new advent until "hope waited against hope," and finally deified the attribute whose return to earth had ceased to be expected. "They will no more contend *beside* us in our earthly conflicts, but *for us* with the fates above."

When we see the aged Adams expiring in the Capitol, we are ready to exclaim with him, "This is the *last* of life." When the great soul of Clay sends up its last aspiration in the legislative city where his life had been spent, we ejaculate a reverential "Amen!" When the wearied spirit of Calhoun, in its intense intellectual activity, wears away the last thin film which binds it to corporeal life, we joyfully chant at once the "Requiescat" and the "Resurgam." When the great intellect of Webster seeks a death-bed in the retreats of his "Sabine farm," we tune our throats to the *Non omnis moriar* of Horace, and the more sublime, "I still live!" of the Puritan patriot. But when one goes forth like Broderick, in the maturity of his manhood, in the fullness of his powers, in the ripeness of his intellect, in the perfection of his moral discipline, hoping so much himself, and of whom so much was hoped—when such a one lies down forever upon his bloody couch we are as unreconciled as the husband over the grave of his first love; as inconsolable as the mother over the corpse of her first born. With swelling hearts and tearful eyes, we vainly protest against the irreversible decree, and are almost tempted to exclaim: "It cannot, must not, shall not be!" But alas, while we struggle in the closing coils of a great grief, the departing spirit passes onward, solemn, silent, and majestic, towards the spirit land, ever expanding its colossal proportions as it recedes, until it is swallowed up by the still more gigantic darkness. And while we still gaze, with longing, eager, straining eyes, as if the rending veil of night would again reveal his returning form, comes to us upon the moaning wind from the great Walhalla of the dead: "He will not turn back again, he will return to earth no more."

God speed thee, then, true son of the masses, most appreciated when forever lost! Brave type of manhood! Bright example of self-reliance and self-culture! Noble illustration of free institutions! Firm patriot and true man, friend dearly loved and truly mourned, . farewell, farewell!—*John W. Dwinelle.*

254. The politician and the ambitious man of the world, as he appeared to most people, was the worst side of his character. His intellect was of the quickest and most comprehensive order, and his will was so powerful as to enable him to concentrate his whole mind on any given subject. Hence, in the midst of the most exciting political contest, he could at will withdraw his mind from it, and give the closest attention to whatever he was reading. His active intellect com-

pelled him to read, for he had little relish for vulgar amusements, and his tastes always inclined him to be very much alone. He was almost an ascetic in his life and habits. His passions and appetites were completely subject to his will. Accordingly, he read immensely. Of classic English literature he had read everything; and what he read, he analyzed, weighed, and considered. His nights were spent over the works of the grand old masters. No one who did not know him intimately would have supposed on meeting him in the street, that he had spent half of the night previous in reading the most abstruse poetry. Yet very likely such was the fact. The works of all the great poets were as familiar to him as houshold words. His tastes led him to admire the weird-like, subtle, and mysterious. Of all English poets, he especially admired the mystic, spiritual Shelley. Tennyson, too, was a great favorite of his; so was Wordsworth. But how few of those who supposed they knew him well, had any idea of his rich stores of classic knowledge. He had such an aversion to anything looking like pedantry or affectation, that only very few, and those his most intimate and trusted friends, were aware how extensive was his reading, and how general his knowledge of books and men. He also felt his want of early education, and distrusted himself very much when books and literature were under discussion. Yet as he grew older and came more in contact with men, he more fully appreciated his own powers. During a long personal intimacy, I can recollect no act of his unworthy of a man. I have walked the streets for hours with him when the world was wrapped in slumber, and conversed on every conceivable subject, but never knew him to give expression to a low or ignoble thought. I was his friend, and, knowing him so well, shall cherish with pride his memory to the last.—*Frank Soule.*

ROBERT BURNS.

255. Burns caught his inspiration in the walks of daily life, amongst his own class, and from the nature in which he lived and had his being. The wings on which he soared, were love and humor. His flights were through the free air, and were guided by a fine moral sense. He was not sublime; but beyond any poet, he comes home to the heart, he leads us into the quiet sunlight. The sweet smell of nature salutes us, and the fresh dew hangs trembling on his leaves and flowers. By the rippling streams, on banks and braes and heathery knolls, in the green dell and along the moorland edge, he takes us. Sometimes his spirit apostrophises the storm, as it sways the lofty pine, and sweeps through the forest with a mighty sigh; but generally, it bathes in its tender light something that we can love. * * * Thy voice is heard as a sweet tenor!—scarce heard, indeed, when the swell of mighty notes prevails, when Milton's superb bass rolls out, as from unseen spheres; when again, the martial recitative of Scott, or Byron's sonorous baritone peals forth; but ever and anon stealing in the ear with a quiet melody, clear, simple, and true, which searches and plays amongst the tendrils of our nature, stirring the fountains of tenderness within us, until the unbidden tears come forth, and our touched hearts acknowledge a Master's power! A nation's tongues take up thy strains! They go, wandering in pathos and power, through the valleys and amongst the hills of thy native land, waking her echoes and sinking into the hearts of her people, softening them and making them brave— prolonged beyond her narrow bounds, and carried wherever her sons wander, till they encircle the earth, and from every clime ascends a spontaneous thank-offering to the Great Source of all poetry, in gratitude that He woke thy glowing minstrelsy.—*George Gordon.*

AARON BURR.

266. With many qualities which go to make up greatness, Burr was not a great man in the highest sense of that exalted character. He was not great because the moral element was absent, for which no daring deeds or brilliant faculties can compensate. Not vulgarly selfish in small things, he *was* selfish as to everything which he proposed to himself as an object worthy of achievement or acquisition. Self was the center to which and from which everything else flowed and radiated. His country, his party, his friends, were only prized or regarded as so many instruments of self-aggrandizement, to be cherished or laid aside as they were, or were not, useful to his purpose. His sense of honor was little more than an intense personal

pride, and he was bound loosely, or scarcely at all, by the ties of justice or of social or moral obligation. He had no enlarged love of country or of race. He was not so much an unprincipled man as a bad-principled man. He acted from system, but it was a false system. His character, so robust and manly in some of its attributes, was deformed by a love of intrigue, which deceived himself at the same time that it betrayed an utter destitution of sincerity and truth. He was one of the few brave men who preferred to prevail by cunning rather than by strength or boldness. His intellect was more remarkable for cultivation, finish and perfection, for the number and activity of its alert faculties, than for its scope, or comprehension. He was, indeed, fitted for the highest excellence in some executive posts; but these were not the highest positions, and did not require the highest genius—and even in these offices it was not safe to trust him. In the depth and amplitude of his understanding, and in profound and varied learning, he was not the equal of Hamilton. He never could have written the numbers of the *Federalist*, or have debated with Jefferson on the Funding Bill or the Bank of the United States. He left no favorable opinion of his genius, or sense of his character, upon the country. Burr must be assigned no higher position than that of a brilliant and unscrupulous adventurer, with the good and bad qualities which have distinguished such characters in all times—in the Crusades, as hireling soldiers of fortune, called Knights of the Temple, as the Companions of the Norman Conqueror, as among the DeBracys, the Brian de Bois

Gilberts, the Dalgettys of fiction, and the Murats, the
Junots, and the Massenas of modern history. He was
not guilty of treason—he was only a filibuster—the
pioneer of filibusters. As a man of intellect, he was
not comparable with Hamilton, Marshall, Jay, Jefferson
or Madison. We know less of him as a statesman than
of any man of his time. He neither established any
principles of government, nor prominently advocated
any; he proposed no measure of importance; he left no
new views of civil polity, nor had he any distinctive
scheme of administration. He was a politician rather
than a statesman; a lawyer rather than a jurist; more
anxious for personal success than the triumph of a
party; solicitous of the elevation of particular men to
office, especially of himself, more than the ascendancy
of any determinate principles. As a partisan politician,
and as a partisan soldier, he was eminent. All of his
faculties were employed to advance the immediate purpose before him; but he was too restless and too intent
upon the present, to be wise or provident for the future.
He was a hand-to-mouth politician; he left the future
to take care of itself; and his whole failure in life is to
be attributed to this eagerness, impatience and improvi-
dence * * At an advanced aged he was stricken
down by paralysis, a helpless bed-ridden old man over
whom the darkest shadows of penury and desertion
gloomed in the bleak winter of an unprosperous life,
another Lear in his afflictions, but bearing up against
them with a buoyancy of spirit which was denied to
the smitten king whose calamitous fortunes he represented. He was at the close of his career the same

man in all the characteristics which distinguished him, that he was in his summer prime. He turned upon the misfortunes of his latter days, and upon the death that was to consummate or to end them, the same gaze of unquailing courage and of cheerful composure, which he had turned in earlier years upon his mortal enemies. He died at the age of eighty, in the full possession of his faculties, without a groan or a murmur. We are reminded of the memorable picture Scott has drawn of the combat between Bothwell and Balfour of Burley; when the bold royalist had fallen, his sword-arm broken, and his dagger lost; and the fierce covenanter, having passed his blade through his body, and putting his foot upon his neck, exclaimed: " Die as thou hast lived— hoping nothing—believing nothing," "and," said Bothwell, collecting his whole strength for his last respiration, *"Fearing Nothing."*—*Judge Joseph G. Baldwin.*

CLAY, WEBSTER AND CALHOUN.

257. Clay, as in death he went between his compeers, so in his life he was a medium between their vast diversity; but Webster and Calhoun were perfect opposites in mind and thought and habit. The one based all his reasoning upon fundamental principles of right and wrong, and these were of divine original. The other drew his criterion of argument and duty from the obligations of the human law. While one asked, "Is it right?" it was the sole inquiry of the other "Is it

legal?" The discourse of Webster is pervaded and illuminated by a living faith; the speech of Calhoun is cold, and stern, and rayless. Taking for its first principles the fundamental compact among men, it argues up to this with unerring accuracy and iron logic. Yet, by a seeming paradox, though Webster, in his private life, did frequent violence to the faith he professed, Calhoun, on the contrary, practiced the habit of severest virtue. He, of Massachusetts, gave a liberal indulgence to his appetites and passions, while the Carolinian lived in asceticism the most rigid, a recluse from all indulgence. Here ends the parallel: In powers of mind the most exalted, in patriotism the most inflexible, and in devotion to the service of their country which endured unto the last, these master spirits stand in strong resemblance, and to each the dying hour was bright with the radiance of immortal hope.—*Joseph W. Winans.*

DICKENS IN CAMP.

258.—
Above the pines the moon was slowly drifting,
    The river sang below;
The dim Sierras far beyond uplifting
    Their minarets of snow.

The roaring camp-fire, with rude humor, painted
    The ruddy tints of health
On haggard face and form that dooped and fainted
    In the fierce race for wealth.

Till one arose, and from his pack's scant treasure,
    A hoarded volume drew,
And cards were dropped from hands of listless leisure,
    To hear the tale anew;

And then, while round them shadows gathered faster,
    And as the firelight fell,
He read aloud the book wherein the master
    Had writ of "Little Nell."

Perhaps 'twas boyish fancy—for the reader
    Was youngest of them all—
But as he read, from clustering pine and cedar,
    A silence seemed to fall;

The fir-trees, gathering closer in the shadows,
    Listened in every spray,
While the whole camp with "Nell" on English meadows
    Wandered, and lost their way.

And so in mountain solitudes—o'ertaken
    As by some spell divine—
Their cares drop from them like the needles shaken
    From out the gusty pine.

Lost is that camp, and wasted all its fire!
    And he who wrought that spell?
Ah, towering pine and stately Kentish spire,
    Ye have one tale to tell!

Lost is that camp! but let its fragrant story
    Blend with the breath that thrills
With hop-vine's incense all the pensive glory
    That fills the Kentish hills.

And on that grave where English oak and holly
 And laurel leaves entwine,
Deem it not all a too-presumptuous folly—
 This spray of Western pine!

—*F. Bret Harte.*

HENRY DURANT.

(FOUNDER OF THE UNIVERSITY OF CALIFORNIA, AND WHO SELECTED THE SITE OF BERKELEY.—EDITOR.)

289. So simple and unpretending was this man, so unobtrusive and so modest, that it will astonish many when I predict for him a longer and greater future than for any man who has yet come to our shores. It seems to me that when men who living, have attracted much more attention than he, are forgotten, as if they had never lived his memory will grow fresher and greener with every succeding year; that, like the wine of California, which is said to lose its earthy taste when transported from its native soil, he will lose whatever gave to him mortal appearance in the long lapse of years.

To his cultured mind everything that man had thought, everything that man is thinking now, was full of interest. There was in him none of that spirit which would throw a Galileo into prison, or clip the wings of a Newton to prevent his flight among the stars. He delighted to sit with Plato at the feet of Socrates. He delighted to let his imagination roam with the old poets, and with them see a god in every hill and a nymph in every tree. He was glad that the learned men who are now living are giving their lives to bold, unfettered thought, and he believed that the result of their deep and reverential meditation would eventually be to show that revelation and profoundest philosophy were but different roads to the same great truths. He knew, for his studies had taught him, that the argument, apparently the most unanswerable, might hide a fallacy which would take ages of profound thought to disclose; and when any system of philosophy denied, or even led up to a doubt of the great religious truths which he learned in childhood, he waited patiently to discover the error.

In the freedom of thought which he allowed himself and which he considered right, I have no doubt that there were times when his mind was agitated—when doubts, spite of himself, would creep in—when the argument so ingeniously put would leave him for the moment without an answer. But still he remained steadfast to his early faith. Like one of those stately ships in our harbor, tossing and straining, yet riding securely on the waves; so he, though the winds shook him, and the seas dashed over him, still rode securely, and the anchor of his faith and hope never dragged!

Standing on the heights of Berkeley, he heard the distant generations hail, and saw them arise, "demanding life, impatient for the skies," from what were then fresh, unbounded wildernesses—from the shore of the great tranquil sea. He welcomed them to the treasures of science and the delights of learning, to the immeasurable good of rational existence, the immortal hopes of Christianity, the lights of everlasting truth!

And so, hero and sage, the memory of whose friendship raises me in my own esteem, I love to think of thee! I love to think of thee thus standing on the hights of Berkeley, with strong emotion lighting thy features, and the cry, "Eureka!" on thy lips, as thy gaze goes through the Golden Gate to the broad Pacific Ocean beyond. And I love to think of thee when, in other and sadder times, I have seen thee stand on the hights of thine own self-raised character, pointing through the Golden Gate of Death to the Pacific Ocean of Eternity dimly seen beyond it.—*John B. Felton.*

260. HE WAS pre-eminently a scholar. And this means, first, that he was a lover of all learning. He welcomed truth wherever found. His attitude toward it was not passive, but active. He went after it; he sought it eagerly, on beaten highways and shaded byways, in every nook and hiding-place. He sought it on the side of man and on the side of nature, not forgetting the relations of both to the God above both. He was never afraid of the truth.

And so he became an adept in learning—in language —that is, in the expression of man's thought, and God's also, in revelation. He had stores of philosophical learning. He had powers of curious combination, rare felicity of expression; this, both in interpretation and in origination. There were terms of expression that threw unexpected light on a point in question. He used words with meanings hitherto unrecognized; but so apt that the world seemed dull in not having discovered them.

He was an adept in thought, which is what language is good for. Any man that is fond of Plato may be called a lover of thought. Durant made Plato a special, life-long study.

He was an adept in science. He had an open eye, quick to read the outer as well as the inner world. He was an adept in oratory; he sometimes spoke in such fashion as to enchant and thrill. He was almost an adept in authorship. Alas! for the "almost." I know of generous, far-reaching plans in that direction, which he never fulfilled. He was too busy with other work. Multitudinous cares and the very wealth of his aspirations combined to thwart his plans—and we are so much the poorer. We know how much Horace Bushnell, the classmate and intimate acquaintance of Durant, has accomplished as an author; and I doubt if his mind was more suggestive, more fertile in ideas, than Durant's. He had more concentration of purpose, more fortunate surroundings. But who shall say that even he has done a nobler life-work? Durant had power, not only as a scholar and a benefactor, but as an example. He was so lofty in his aims; so unworldly, while yet not unpracticed; so modest, so pure, so noble, altogether so grand a pattern of a man. When the students saw one, so advanced in life, so scholarly in habit, go into the rugged Winter of Esmeralda, and share the hardships of the poorest miner, not to make money for himself, but to make money for his darling College, they could not but catch something of his spirit of self-denial, of devotion to a noble cause.

To some his memory will remain as an inspiration

to all things whatsoever that are true and lovely and of good report. And when this generation has passed quite away; when colleagues and co-workers, pupils and admirers, have all followed him to the grave, his *work* will remain. It will remain in the institutions of high culture, for which he toiled to prepare a foundation; in the loftiness of purpose which shall ennoble some of the best leaders of the "good time coming;" in the blended beauty and strength of character to which *he* contributed in the forming period of California's higher and better life.—*Prof. Martin Kellogg.*

STEPHEN J. FIELD.

261. Like most men who have risen to distinction in the United States, Judge Field commenced his career without the advantages of wealth, and he prosecuted it without the factitious aids of family influence or patronage. He had the advantage, however—which served him better than wealth or family influence—of an accomplished education, and careful study and mental discipline. He brought to the practice of his profession a mind stored with professional learning, and embellished with rare scholarly attainments. He was distinguished at the bar for his fidelity to his clients, for untiring industry, great care and accuracy in the preparation of his cases, uncommon legal acumen, and extraordinary solidity of judgment. As an adviser, no man had more the confidence of his clients, for he trusted nothing to chance or accident

when certainty could be attained, and felt his way cautiously to his conclusions, which, once reached, rested upon sure foundations, and to which he clung with remarkable pertinacity. Judges soon learned to repose confidence in his opinions, and he always gave them the strongest proofs of the weight justly due to his conclusions.

When he came to the bench, from various unavoidable causes the calendar was crowded with cases involving immense interests, the most important questions, and various and peculiar litigation. California was then, as now, in the development of her multiform physical resources. The judges were as much pioneers of law as the people of settlement. To be sure something had been done, but much had yet to be accomplished; and something, too, had to be undone of that which had been done in the feverish and anomalous period that had preceded. It is safe to say that, even in the experience of new countries hastily settled by heterogeneous crowds of strangers from all countries, no such example of legal or judicial difficulties was ever before presented as has been illustrated in the history of California. There was no general or common source of jurisprudence. Law was to be administered almost without a standard. There was the civil law, as adulterated or modified by Mexican provincialism, usages, and habitudes, for a great part of the litigation; and there was the common law for another part, but *what that was* was to be decided from the conflicting decisions of any number of courts in America and England, and the various and diverse considerations of policy arising from local and other facts. And then, contracts made elsewhere, and some of them in semi-civilized countries, had to be interpreted here. Besides all which may be added that large and important interests peculiar to the State existed—mines, ditches, etc.—for which the courts were compelled to frame the law, and make a system out of what was little better than chaos.

When, in addition, it is considered that an unprecedented number of contracts, and an amount of business without parallel, had been made and done in hot haste, with the utmost carelessness; that legislation was accomplished in the same way, and presented the crudest and most incongruous materials for construction; that the whole scheme and organization of the government, and the relation of the departments to each other, had to be adjusted by judicial construction—it may well be conceived what task even the ablest jurist would take upon himself when he assumed this office. It is no small compliment to say that Judge Field entered upon the duties of this great trust with his usual zeal and energy, and that he left the office not only with greatly increased reputation, but that he raised the character of the jurisprudence of the State. He has more than any other man given tone, consistency, and system to our judicature, and laid broad and deep the fountain of our civil and criminal law. The land titles of the State—the most important and permanent of the interests of a great commonwealth—have received from his hand their permanent protection, and this alone should entitle him to the lasting gratitude of the bar and the people.

His opinions, whether for their learning, logic, or diction, will compare favorably, in the judgment of some of our best lawyers, with those of any judge upon the Supreme Bench of the Union. It is true what he has accomplished has been done with labor; but this is so much more to his praise, for such work was not to be hastily done, and it was proper that the time spent in perfecting the work should bear some little proportion to the time it should last. We know it has been said of Judge Field that he is too much of a 'case lawyer,' and not sufficiently broad and comprehensive in his views. This criticism is not just. It is true he is reverent of authority, and likes to be sustained by precedent; but an examination of his opinions will show that, so far from being a timid copyist, or the passive slave of authority, his rulings rest upon clearly defined principles and strong common sense.—*Judge Joseph G. Baldwin.*

HENRY H. HAIGHT.

262. In this age, when scepticism, if not fashionable, is certainly not wholly unfashionable, and when often the sceptic thinks warranted in becoming a scoffer, there is something refreshing in the spectacle of a man of acknowledged integrity, high cultivation and intelligence, who publicly avows that in respect of the relations of man to his God he has attained to the condi-

tion of an absolute belief, and that he is ready and willing to carry this belief out—not only in theory, but in action—to its remotest results. Governor Haight had attained to this condition. He early adopted the faith of a Calvinistic Presbyterian, never wavered from it, and was at the time of his death an ordained elder of that church. He accepted that belief with all its duties; he was faithful to it, not only in his family, but also in all the forms into which it ramified itself; in the church, the bible class, the Sunday-school, and in every collateral organization and enterprise. He was not obtrusively demonstrative in his profession of faith, and yet his conduct left no one in doubt what it was. If challenged, the answer was sharp and ringing. It is pleasing to hear his religious associates speak with deep affection of the reliance they placed on him for judicious counsel, for support in crises of difficulty, for ready material relief in times of great exigency. His was a faith so anchor-bound to the idea of duty, that in other times he might have emulated some of the early Christian martyrs, and have accepted, with equal readiness, the mitre of an archbishop, or death at the stake as a missionary to the Iroquois.

He did not possess merely a few good and exalted qualities, nor was his character marred by great defects, but it was well rounded. He possessed many good qualities in a great degree of excellence, and if any defects existed in his character, they were so few and so small that they were not apparent to the general observer. And when we have said that his character was excellent, we have said all that is claimed for that of

Washington himself. He was good; he was sympathetic; he was kind; he was learned; he was perspicacious; he was honest; he was trustworthy; he was religious; he was faithful. From the many public tributes which have been offered to his memory, there comes up the audible and distinct utterance of one word which embodies the greatest encomium which could be passed upon his character; and if a monument were erected to him, and upon its base were inscribed that one word, it would suggest the greatest eulogy we could pronounce upon him as a man, a professor of religion, a lawyer, and the Governor of our State—FIDELITY.

—*John W. Dwinelle.*

OLIVER WENDELL HOLMES.

263. In the choir of American poets, distinguished in many respects above the rest—in limpidity of tone and variety of expression beyond rivalry—stands Oliver Wendell Holmes. In him the freshness and variety of nature unite with the brilliance and finish of consummate art. From youth to age, breathing an atmosphere of literary taste and achievement, he has shown how little real incompatibility there is between the pursuits of the scientist and the artist. For more than thirty years, professor of anatomy and physiology, in the leading American college—a position demanding in the occupant the keen scrutiny, the profound thought, and rigid deductions of the scientist—he has yet found and improved opportunities for frequent

excursions into the realms of imagination and philosophy. As poet, novelist, essayist, critic, *causeur*, he is familiarly known to many who are oblivious of his life-long studies, labors, and achievements in the fields of science. In poetry or prose,—whether touching the lightest themes of the hour, or discussing the awful problems of man's origin and destiny,—drawing a satiric sketch of New England life and character, or limning in never-fading colors the traits of universal humanity—he is ever master of his subject. There is no crudity of idea or of phrase. Beauty of conception shines through his clear-cut, diamond-pointed sentences, every one of which is a refutation of the famous saying attributed to Talleyrand respecting the use of language. Of him, as of his great Irish name-sake, the author of "The Vicar of Wakefield," and "The Deserted Village," "She Stoops to Conquer," and "The Citizen of the World," it may be said, *Nihil tetigit quod non ornavit*. An attempt to deepen the impression or heighten the admiration felt by the student of American literature for him—the highest type of New England "Brahminism"—would too much resemble the proverbial folly of painting the lily or gilding refined gold. To characterize, with discriminating judgment and accuracy of phrase, a genius so unique and so versatile, were a task requiring an acuteness of insight and apprehension, a cultivation of taste, and a pen possessing a grace, kindred to his own. A literary critic like Sainte-Beuve, and a literary artist like Théophile Gautier, uniting their talents and special gifts, alone could give just estimate and fitting expression of Holmes' character and genius. Sentiment, the deepest and the most delicate; wit, the most brilliant; insight into the human mind and heart, the most subtile; modes of expression the happiest and most graceful, find brightest illustrations in the pages of this nineteenth century literary magician. Admirable as he is in the commoner walks of life and letters, it is as a poet that he will live forever in the history of literature. When obscurity and profundity shall cease to be regarded as synonymous, when quality rather than quantity of work shall determine an author's rank, the brightness and brevity of Holmes' verse will be in some measure appreciated; and then fully by those choice spirits only, who, in exalted moods, look through

"Charm'd magic casements, opening on the foam
Of perilous seas, on faery lands forlorn."

—*Henry H. Reid.*

EDWARD JENNER.

264. Medicine has canonized him—benevolence claims him as essentially her own. Run back through all the pages of history, back further yet, until the bright light of history, growing indistinct, is gradually merged in the sombre twilight of fable; ransack the records of philanthropy, dive deeply in the musty tomes or more modern volumes that commemorate the lives and deeds of those who loved their fellow men, and made that love in all respects practical, and you will see high above them all, shining in solitary splendor,

burning, blazing in immortal light, the mighty name of
Jenner; and the century in which he was born, teeming
with great events as it undoubtedly was, can show none
that can compare with his discovery. There were dreadful wars and frightful revolutions, the demolition of
monarchies and the establishment of empires; colonial
rebellion, struggles for freedom and the acquisition of
liberty, all of which involved the destruction of human
life; and just when the century was closing, came his
discovery, a bloodless, glorious triumph, a deathless
victory, redeeming, in some measure, the past—its sole
object the salvation of the human family. The most
terrible scourge that has ever afflicted mankind, which
in one century, in Europe alone, destroyed 45,000,000
of lives, a distemper in itself and surroundings horrible, drying up the wells of sympathy, overwhelming
the maternal instinct—so hard to weaken, almost impossible to destroy—driving the mother from her
stricken child; this is the pestilence that the genius of
Jenner has robbed of all its terrors; and medicine today, in the exhibition of all her marvellous possessions,
cannot show any prophylactic measures against the invasion of a serious malady to be at all compared with
vaccination. So much can be said of Jenner's discovery; it has given science complete, absolute mastery
over one most disastrous plague—others remain, bidding defiance to the science and the art of medicine,
darkening the world wherever and whenever their
frightful presence is made manifest. Vaccination is indeed the Sacrament of medicine, omnipotent to save,
and the dreadful rumors of variolous visitations here

and there over the world weaken not our reverence and love for Jenner, or our faith in his discovery; they only serve to demonstrate the criminal blindness, the culpable stupidity and inexplicable negligence of mankind. Jenner idolized his discovery. In his persecutions and imminent martyrdom the reflection of what untold benefit it was ultimately to be to the human family, upheld and consoled him; he predicted, as the final result of his discovery, the entire annihilation of small-pox, and did man respond with a zeal commensurate with the importance of the measure to the necessity of faithfully following the precepts of its great author, we might all see the prediction realized and this most loathsome disease swept from the face of God's fair earth forever.

—*Dr. J. Campbell Shorb.*

THOMAS STARR KING.

("RELIEVING GUARD—MARCH 4TH, 1864.")

265.—

Came the Relief. "What, Sentry, ho!
How passed the night through thy long waking?"
"Cold, cheerless, dark,—as may be fit
The hour before the dawn is breaking."

"No sight, no sound?" "No; nothing save
The plover from the marshes calling;
And in yon Western sky, about
An hour ago, a Star was falling."

"A star? There's nothing strange in that."
"No, nothing; but, above the thicket,
Somehow it seemed to me that God
Somewhere had just relieved a picket!"
—*Frank Bret Harte.*

266.—

CHASTE AS the fleecy pillow of a star,
And purely pale as angel watchers are,
Shines the clear porcelain of your magic bowl
Till red bright wine is poured into its soul.
Then lo! a luxury of vines and flowers,
Of wildwood wreaths and foliage-tangled bowers,
A blest profusion of enchanted things,
Gladden its side in fairy pencilings.
So, when the wine of genius and of life—
Its taste with sweets, its breath with fragrance rife—
Filled up the measure of thy years on earth,
And Manhood's crown had followed Childhood's mirth,
All we that gazed upon that life complete,
Found glorious Beauty there the soul to greet—
Found Truth and Sweetness, Nobleness and Grace;
Found Love of Country and the Human Race.
The bowl is broken, and the wine is poured;
Stricken the wing that to the sun blaze soared;
And Genius mourns her gentlest, brightest son,
And Eloquence her grand and peerless one.
Whilst she, Columbia, only calms her woe,
To rouse our drooping hearts with patriot glow:
"O ye, my children, faster by my side
Stand ye henceforth, since he is gone, my pride!"
—*Charles Russell Clarke.*

ON A PEN OF THOMAS STARR KING.

267.—

This is the reed the dead musician dropped,
With tuneful magic in its sheath still hidden;
The prompt allegro of its music stopped,
Its melodies unbidden.

But who shall finish the unfinished strain,
Or wake the instrument to awe and wonder,
And bid the slender barrel breathe again,—
An organ-pipe of thunder?

His pen! What humbler memories cling about
Its golden curves! What shapes and laughing graces
Slipped from its point, when his full heart went out
In smiles and courtly phrases!

The truth, half-jesting, half in earnest flung;
The word of cheer, with recognition in it;
The note of alms, whose golden speech outrung
The golden gift within it.

But all in vain the enchanter's wand we wave:
No stroke of ours recalls his magic vision;
The incantation that its power gave
Sleeps with the dead magician.

—*J. Bret Harte.*

LAFAYETTE.

268. Animated by the same feeling that prompts the maiden to lay aside, in her vows to religion and charity, the shining locks her fond mother tended, her vain girlhood prized, and the voice of affection praised, Lafayette, a boy of nineteen, sacrificed upon the stern altar of freedom the brilliant gifts with which propitious fortune adorned his birth. To love one's own country is but obeying the instinct of the heart—it is sweet to die for our fatherland. The blood quickens, the eye illumines, and the arms grow strong, when the ruthless hand of enmity would pluck one honor from the flag of one's country, or rob her children of one right of their inheritance. But how much more exalted is that spirit that weeps over the wrongs of the great heart of humanity without regard to place or clime? Lafayette worshipped the Genius of Freedom, and defended her votaries wherever the sun of a beneficent Creator shone. Born to titles of nobility, to claims on kings and great men, to wealth, to honor, to opportunities of distinction, to domestic happiness and precocious talent, he laid these things of earth in the dust, and scorned them as little worth, when compared with an enthusiastic love and sacred veneration for the rights of humanity and the equalities of life. Who among us, with all the gifts of fortune and power, the smiles of beauty, the happiness of home, would sacrifice them while life was vigorous, and the stream of youth bedewed the freshly springing flowers along its course, to struggle for the supremacy of a cause affecting a people with whom his own had nothing in common but hereditary wrongs. To do so is to attain the highest point of human greatness. It is to join the vanguard in the march of human things. From the humble avocations of life, the workshop, the forge, the laborer's bench, oftentimes spring such souls as these, covered with the heat and dust of want, galled by actual necessity, and smarting under the hand of wrong, and who force through the restraints of lowliness, spurn the iron heel of dependence, and from the envious crowd rise up erect, calm, self-possessed, and great in lofty determination of purpose. Another order, and more praiseworthy because they have more to lose by failure, are those endowed by auspicious fortune with all the attributes and blessings of power and greatness; who, without a stimulus for their energies other than the noble seed sown in their blood by their ancestors, become forerunners in the advancement and elevation of their species. To this latter class belonged Lafayette, fulfilling by his illustrious life, Socrates' description of a great man: "In childhood modest, in youth temperate, in manhood just, in old age prudent."—*Milton S. Latham.*

MAXIMILIAN.

269. I do not envy him, whatever his political feelings, who has read without tears the last scene of the tragedy which closed with the death of Maximilian. Gallantly, with heroic mien, the young Prince steps forward to his fate. The executioners stand trembling before the undaunted victim. He is in the presence of that great Democrat, Death, who laughs at human distinctions. His place is in the center. His two friends are one on each hand. With a gesture he stays the executioners. He is still monarch, and his hand has the right to confer honor, though on the brink of the tomb. "I belong to a race," he said, "from which

come only the leaders of a people, or their martyrs. A sovereign has the right to recompense services, and you, Miramon, my friend, who have stood by me through life so faithfully, take in death from my hand the last honor I can bestow. Take the place assigned to your monarch to die in, and let me die in the place allotted to you." And Miramon, with a pride exultant even in that dread moment, bowed gratefully to the monarch, whom death was powerless to dethrone. Whence came this sublime self-respect, asserted in defiance of death itself? The pride of Maria Theresa, caught from a hundred Hungarian nobles as they shouted "We will die for our king," was running through his veins; the old traditions of a family that felt itself humiliated when Napoleon became one of its members, had cradled him. Well he knew that at that moment, when the executioners were pointing their guns with horrible aim at his heart, far away, in the land of his birth, thousands of guns were presented in honor of his brother, as the iron crown of St. Stephen was descending on his annointed head. He belonged to an order accustomed to read in the faces of men, as they passed, the awe and respect which it inspired, and he revered himself because he belonged to it.—*John B. Felton.*

THOMAS MOORE.

270. The brilliancy of the warrior, the gleam of beauty, and the triumphs of the statesman are forgotten; their names perish and their monuments fall to decay; but the memory and works of the great National Poet last forever. The influence of poetry upon the dim and shadowy outlines of the past is unequalled. When imagination first plumed its half-fledged wing, and passion kindled its flame within the heart of man, the undying power of this offspring of sentiment and feeling began, and will continue among men until the eternal sunset shall fling its reddening light upon the fragments of the dissolving world.

In the mists of antiquity Ireland alone among nations, was known as the "Island of song." Literature, music and poetry were state institutions. The people carefully fostered these aids to civilization. The thread of poetry was woven into all the occupations of the race. Their bards constituted one of the most honored classes of the land. They were its lawyers, its musicians, its historians, and its genealogists. Their harp is to-day the national emblem. In peace they sung of love and deeds of valor; in war, accompanying their kings, they incited armies to heroic achievements. When their country was enslaved, they clung to her, and animated her children to remain true to faith and fatherland. When the nobles fled, the bards remained, scaled their devotion to their native land with their blood, and, with dying lips, crystalized the object of their existence in the words, "Erin forever."

It was the mission of Thomas Moore, to revive the poetry and music of Ireland. He found, preserved in the unwritten songs of his countrymen, the character of the people, their legends, their traditions, their superstitions, their love for the past, their sorrows in the present, and their lofty aspirations for a great and glorious future. Love, loyalty, religion, constancy and unswerving devotion for the fatherland were contained in these almost forgotten Celtic airs, which roused the spirit and chivalry of Erin's greatest bard to those displays of word-painting and harmonious numbers that have made his name synonymous with that of the Lyric muse.

What is poetry? Poetry is the mirror of nature, and the blossoming of the soul. The elements that enter into its composition are invention, memory of the past, brilliant imagination, sensitiveness, judgment and the power of expression, evidenced by rich language and musical feeling. The mind of a poet must be a lyre that continually vibrates to the joys of innocence, the pangs of misery, and the love and hate of men. It should be at one moment like the bright sky; at another like the fleecy cloud, when, under the influence of the sun, it sheds its brilliantly tinted tears. His duty it is to call on men to behold the infinite and indefinable character of Omniscience. In a word, the intellect of a true poet should be composed of all that is great, noble, learned and heroic; and his thoughts, moreover, should be resplendent with the emeralds and sapphires of a gorgeous fancy glowing upon the white bosom of truth and justice. The real and unreal, under his magic prism, in assuming varied forms, should display all the hues of the rainbow.

If these tests are applied to the poetical works of Moore, they will be found possessed of all the necessary qualifications in an eminent degree. His name should therefore shine forever as one of the trinity of poetical luminaries with Byron and Scott.

Contented for a short period with the lyric laurel, he offered his Lalla Rookh on the altar of Fame. Then criticism placed its author with the immortals. Without possessing that great degree of sublimity, passion and nervousness which characterizes Byron, and wanting to its full extent the exciting, descriptive, spear-clashing narrative of Scott, he excelled them both in play of fancy, warmth of feeling, honied flow of verse and splendor of imagery. What reader of English poetry has not been charmed with the rise and fall of the words in Lalla Rookh! Does not the rhythm of the verse remind him of the dip of the oar in the blue and placid waters of some quiet bay? Byron's strength resembles the crash of the Atlantic wave as it strikes the shore; Moore's the sustained tide of the noble Shannon, as it booms along its banks.

In no other poem of the language are such dazzling similies and images found united with such Tasso-like tenderness. The critical eye may range in vain through English literature for such exquisite ideas as float along the melodious stream of this glorious production. The author dipped his brush in the most brilliant tints of imagination, without sacrificing his love for truth. The fame of this work is circumscribed only by the globe. It is read in all languages. The Persian lover claims it as his own, when, in the soft twilight hour, under the curtained balcony, he recites its burning lines to his enchanted mistress. The Pole, fascinated by its glowing thoughts, believes that they are applicable to his historic but ill-fated land. Oh! Bard of the Green Isle, these are thy triumphs!—*Francis J. Sullivan.*

271.—

ALL HAIL to thee, where'er thy home be now,
All hail to thee, thou soaring soul of song!
Before thy shrine let me a moment bow,
Thy most devoted followers among.
To fame's eternal galaxy belong
The glorious offspring of thy teeming brain,
Which on the mind in happy tumult throng.
Lo! Nature opened not her broad domain
In panoramic splendor to thine eye, in vain.

Like gems that quicken with perennial blaze,
Thy fancies flash along each burning line—
Truth, virtue, valor, love, devotion, praise,
Mantling upon each page, resplendent shine,
While music breathes through all her soul divine.
Music, inspiring and inspired power!
The heart's intensest ectasies are thine.
Heaven claims thee as its best and brightest dower,
And where thy smile doth gleam, no angry cloud can lower.

Poetic impulse never yet was given
In swifter volume or in sweeter flow.
Than unto thee, whose muse at founts of heaven
Caught drops to charm the cup of mortal woe.
Grief, at the solace which thy notes bestow,
Trembles with hope, and lifts her tear-washed eyes;

While faith, inflamed, with visage all aglow,
And pinions burnished with celestial dyes,
Beholds, in rapt delight, thy fragrant incense rise!
O, for a spark of that immortal fire
Which fed thy soul and nerved thy plastic hand,
That I might feebly wake the lofty lyre
Which glowed with symphony at thy command!
But motionless, in silent awe I stand,
In hushed communion with its breathing strings.
They seem to woo me to a fairy land,
And whisper soft, Earth hath no mortal stings
For the aspiring soul that soars on lyric wings!
—*Oscar T. Shuck.*

NAPOLEON BONAPARTE.

272. Who that has ever lived had a more individual peculiar power than the great Napoleon? What colossal figure in history stands out in more bold relief? Yet it was as a member of a class that he respected himself, and achieved his power. It was to that class that he looked for his reward. Members of that class from all ages fired his ambition. On the Alps, Hannibal was by his side, spurring him on; the rivalry of Cæsar and Charlemagne invited him to unite the glory of a law-giver and orator with that of the great captain; and when mankind had paid him the greatest compliment he ever received—that of shutting him up in the stifling cave of St. Helena, as the only means of repressing his terrible energy—when his great soul was about to escape—"I am going," he said, to "re-join Kleber, Desaix, Lannes, Massena, Bessieres, Duroc, Ney; they will come to meet me; they will feel again the intoxication of human glory; we will talk of what we have done; we will commune about our professions with Frederic, Turenne, Conde, Cæsar, Hannibal." Then, interrupting himself, he added with a singular smile, "unless, indeed above, as here on earth, they are afraid of seeing so many soldiers together." Was this last remark simply in irony at the fears of those who had thus surrounded a single man with chains and soldiers, on the solitude of a rock in mid ocean? Or was that audacious mind dwelling, as death approached, on the possibility of some new eternal theater for his boundless ambition—some Titanic enterprise which would again enable him to hurl the combined thunder of his terrible order?—*John B. Felton.*

PLATO.

273. Plato, on the Immortality of the Soul, will be read, consulted, and revered by millions yet unborn, when legions of Christian authors on the same theme will have passed away forever from the recollection of man. No matter what his ideas were in reference to the nature of the Deity, or the lesser deities of his theology, who clustered around the throne of the Supreme Good; no matter what his conceptions were in relation to the creation of the material world, the origin of ideas, and the pre-existent state of the soul, its immortality discovered in him a champion whose strength, like the momentum of a falling planet, and whose eloquence, sweet as the honey of Hymeltus, struck widely and deeply in the heart of Paganism, giving to faith a longevity not disturbed by death, giving to hope amplest assurance of celestial satisfaction, recreating that sublime philosophy amid the trials and vicissitudes of life, that splendid indifference to death, not born of brutish insensibility, which characterized the conduct of Cato the Younger when at Utica he believed that with the fall of Pompey the liberties of Rome were crushed forever. The gates of Plato's heaven opening before his enraptured vision, with a majesty of reliance which no terror could shake or doubt disturb, he passed calmly into that undiscovered country from whose bourne no traveler returns. Such was the influence of Plato's almost Christian philosophy upon a noble heart— Pagan in all respects save in its faith in the soul's immortality. His influence was not ignored by grateful Athens, who saw her children inspired by it, grow virtuous in conduct, wise in life, and brave in death; and who erected to the memory of her first philosopher mighty even in death, a temple, statues and altars; and cut in gems defying time, which even to this day are found near the scene of his great labors and splendid triumphs, the features of his divine face, the cynosure of the Athenian eye two thousand years ago. His philosophy was not for his day and generation alone, not for to-day or to-morrow, but for humanity to the end of time and the beginning of eternity. Would to

God that in this cycle of irreligion, infidelity and crime, some such master spirit could arise, even from the ashes of Paganism, to meet and vanguish the legions of impious and blasphemous teachers who cumber the earth, destructive to man and offensive to God.—*Dr. J. Campbell Shorb.*

PRESCOTT AND MACAULAY.

274. When one passes from a chapter of Macaulay to Prescott, he perceives an unpleasant thinness, a watery paleness. The opulence of language, the affluence, the Rubens hues of Macaulay make him feel that Prescott used a very limited dictionary. But when a volume of each has been read, he sees how vastly superior to Macaulay is the thin-worded Prescott in opening a vista through the tangled wilderness of the politics of strange lands. In the arrangement of backgrounds, in the ability to secure large space, unity and repose, Prescott was as much superior to Macaulay as he seems to be inferior when you look only at the foreground.—*Thomas Starr King.*

EDWARD NORTON.

275. Edward Norton was the exemplar of a Judge of a subordinate Court. He was learned, patient, industrious, and conscientious; but he was not adapted for an appellate tribunal. He had no confidence in his

own unaided judgment. He wanted some one upon whom to lean. Oftentimes he would show me the decision of a tribunal of no reputation, with apparent delight, if it corresponded with his own views, or with a shrug of painful doubt if it conflicted with them. He would look at me in amazement if I told him that the decision was not worth a fig; and would appear utterly bewildered at my waywardness when, as was sometimes the case, I refused to look at it after hearing by what Court it was pronounced.—*Judge Stephen J. Field.*

WILLIAM C. RALSTON.

276. A moneyed king has fallen from his throne of gold prostrate in the dust. A more dreadful fall has ushered him into the portals of the everlasting world. The loss is a general one, a great indescribable calamity to the State. Had I the power I would hang California in the blackest crape, from Siskiyou to San Diego, for he has left us who made California a synonym for princely hospitality and generosity to the uttermost bounds of the morning. Whatever may have been his defects, his many virtues, his tragic death, have hidden them from mortal sight and criticism forever. His most fitting, touching and eloquent eulogium was pronounced in the question asked in every street of San Francisco, "Who shall take his place?" His heart was as large as the mountain; he was noble, generous and true; his friendship unswerving. Honor, unfading honor, to his memory! Peace, everlasting peace, to his soul.—*Dr. J. Campbell Shorb.*

277. WHAT PARTS of human speech can eulogize him? What brush of artist, what pen of dramatist, what voice of speaker can depict the benefaction of his generous life and the tragedy of his death? His deeds may be heard in tones that sound like the blare of trumpets. His monuments rise from every rod of ground in San Francisco. His eulogy is written on ten thousand hearts. Commerce commemorates his deeds with her whitening sails and her laden wharves. Philanthropy sings the chimes of all public charities, in attestation of his munificence. Patriotism sings pæns for him who, in the hour of the nation's struggle, sent the ringing gold of mercy to chime with the flashing steel of valor. Unnumbered deeds of private generosity attest his secret munificence. Sorrow has found solace in his deeds. Despair has been lifted into hope by his voice. There are churches whose heaven-kissing spires chronicle his donations; schools claim him as their patron; hospitals own him as their benefactor. He was the supporter of art; science leaned on him while her vision swept infinity. The footsteps of progress have been sandaled with his silver. He has upheld invention while she wrestled with the forces of nature. He was the life-blood of enterprise; he was the vigor of all progress; he was the epitome and representative of all that was broadening and expansive, and uplifting in the life of California.—*Thomas Fitch.*

OSCAR L. SHAFTER.

278. To walk in justice, mercy and humility before God, saves the soul. Judge Shafter believed this. To say that some special belief or mystical experience must be added, he held as the cant of a technical faith. He was a devoted worshiper of God. As his writings abundantly showed, he was what the church would call a man of prayer. At every piece of good news or instance of unusual prosperity there is an expression of heartfelt thankfulness to the Divine source of blessing. When sad tidings came or calamity befel, he turned to his closet, his bible and his God, for thought and comfort. And no puritan with his catechism was more diligent in the family than he, in inculcating the great truths of religion, reverence towards God, and love to man. This never ceased until disease broke his strength. The world may have given him little credit for his religion. He did not wear it on the outside, for show. It was in the heart, in the honest doing of the work given him to do, and in quiet deeds of goodness to men. The church sometimes called him an infidel. His piety did not run in the channel of her ceremonies or bear the stamp of her dogmas. Will God reject pure love for that reason? The churches must make room for such a man, or that grand day of broader light that hastens on will have no room for her. Educate a people till they love the truth as well and can see as broadly as Judge Shafter did, and they will not go into our churches *as they are.* Germany is saying this to us to-day; Oxford is saying it; Cambridge is saying it;

Yale is saying it. Every center of learning and superior intelligence in Christendom is saying it. The guild of scientific men all over the world are saying it, with an approach to unanimity that ought to be alarming to one who really loves the church, and sees its importance. It is a question of life and death with the church. Her teachers may shut themselves up in their little circle of thoughts, and deny that there is any broader flow from the Fountain of Eternal Truth, but the mightier minds of the world that sweep through their lines and out into the ocean that rolls all around them, will never, never strike back towards the center of darkness and ignorance for the sake of sailing in their company.—*Rev. L. Hamilton.*

SHAKESPEARE.

279. More than two centuries have elapsed since Shakespeare's Works were first published, and still the ages, rolling onward, add greener leaves to the eternal amaranth of his fame. The circle of his influence, widening and expanding, has extended to lands undiscovered in his day, and embraces all the empires of the civilized earth. Within the cloistered walls of Westminster Abbey, arises a pale forest of monumental marble above the ashes of England's illustrious dead. Even in that grand mausoleum, no monument erected to sovereign, hero, philosopher or statesman, appeals to the heart and imagination of the world like the tomb which, on the banks of the beautiful Avon, bears the immortal name of Shakespeare.—*Frank Tilford.*

PERCY BYSSHE SHELLEY.

280. In Shelley's works we have a sufficient basis for fruitful study both of the man and of his place in literary history. Especially is this basis for study an important one, if we wish to consider Shelley with reference to the great political and intellectual movement of his age and ours, the movement to which may be applied the one name, the Revolution. As is true in case of every individual man, and especially in case of any great man, so of Shelley it is true, that wonderful as the personal qualities of the poet are, they do not so much deserve study as do the works and words whereby the man influences his Age, embodies its thought, and plays a part in its conflicts.

Human consciousness, both theoretical and practical, has in it, two elements, one of ceaseless change, the other of permanence. In so far as all conscious thoughts and deeds are in time, each moment is in some measure independent of all others, and so human ideas, and acts, and purposes, are in reality recreated, made afresh, from moment to moment. Ceaseless activity, in some sense creative activity, is the universal rule of conscious life. Hence simple, passive, submission to tradition is in itself not possible. Even the oldest tradition must be over and over again restated, and so in a measure reformed, reconstructed from moment to moment, and so subject to alteration, yet this tendency to alteration, resulting from the fact that doctrines and customs do not live on from age to age as continuous existences, but have to be reborn for every generation, this law of change is modified by the other law, the law whereby in each new effort to formulate doctrine or to readjust custom, appeal is made to the past, and conscious effort to imitate the past is always to be found. The rebirth of old traditions from moment to moment, from age to age, in human consciousness, is not a rebirth or remaking at random, but a deliberate attempt to produce something that is like the past. And this second tendency, the tendency towards permanence, only gives place to the former tendency altogether when new experiences, new problems, in short a new environment, make impossible or intolerable a conscious imitation of past traditions. Then we have the phenomenon called revolution. The extent and character of the revolution depends in any case on the nature of the new experiences, on the character of the old traditions, and on the activity of the minds concerned. Very common in revolution is the effort to appeal from a tradition of an age immediately past to the tradition of a long past time, or from a complex tradition to a simple one. In other words, the tendency towards change is never pure and unmixed, but we always find a union, or, better, a conflict, between the tendency to permanence and the tendency to new constructions. Absolutely conservative and absolutely revolutionary movements do not exist. The conservative is a revolutionary spirit who has succeeded in his revolution and has brought his traditions into harmony with his experience. The lover of revolution is simply the seeker after a tradition in which he may rest; he is desirous of nothing so much as a good opportunity to become conservative.

—*Josiah Royce.*

SOCRATES.

281. A short time since, a lawyer in the Court of Athens moved that the sentence of Socrates be reversed on the record. It has already been reversed. The Judges took the poison in their verdict. To him the hemlock was a pledge of earthly immortality. Not a particle of his bodily frame is lost. Is that robust soul quenched? Is the Almighty so penurious of matter and so careless of mind, that he saves every ounce of man's poor body, yet permits a gill of poison utterly to extinguish his spirit?—*Thomas Starr King.*

282. HE WAS a mystic, a fellow with Quakers and Swedenborgians, a seer, a saint. He *believed* truth intuitively—he did not *investigate* it. He believed he had a call to his work, that he was empowered by the Deity to perform his calling. He had faith in oracles and dreams, in supernatural influences and divinations. He experienced divine warnings, had spirit-rappings in his bosom. He carried a flaming heart hidden under his philosophic ice. He would hold a thought and inspect it as a mineralogist holds a mineral. He would strip off layer after layer of logic as one peels off the plates of mica from a specimen. He was a Jeremy Bentham and a George Fox welded into one.—*Thomas Starr King.*

GEN. JOHN A. SUTTER.

283. He was the architect whose hand laid the foundation of this commonwealth; the patriarch whose voice encouraged those who built its stately fabric. It rarely happens that an individual gives form and character unto an epoch; yet the life of John Augustus Sutter, and the events of his career, exemplify the civilization of nearly half a century; that civilization which began with the colonial enterprise of a resolute explorer and expanded into the formation of a mighty State. As Napoleon was the King of the Kings of Europe, so this man was the Pioneer of the Pioneers of California. In him were manifested all the hardihood, the energy, and the courage which distinguished those illustrious pioneers of an earlier day, whose achievements have become historic. Insensible to peril or privation, he and his scanty band of followers forsook the busy haunts of men to penetrate into the remotest regions of the West, where nature still held solitary sway. He brought the light of culture and refinement into a wilderness whose only tenants were the wild beast and the savage. As a bulwark against their attacks, whether insidious or open, he constructed a rude fort upon the very spot where afterward, before his eyes had closed in death, a populous city reared its solid structures, and massed its teeming life. Impelled by a spirit of enterprise, untiring and resistless, he extended his operations over a wide expanse of territory, until accident revealed the startling fact that the soil he cultivated concealed a harvest in its bosom, not such alone as responded to the customary course of tillage, but a harvest *literally golden*. In the land he had chosen for his heritage he had realized the Ophir of tradition.—*Joseph W. Winans.*

284. IN THE histories of past ages and nations, there are names that will live in enduring remembrance while freedom exists on earth. The virtues and patriotism of Epaminondas perpetuate his name as the brightest that adorns the history of Theban Independence. The courage of Hannibal, whose conquering legions traversed the Alps, and overswept the classic plains of Italy, is indelibly associated with the unforgotten glory of Carthage. With Athens is identified a galaxy of her brilliant sons, and clusters of constellated names adorn the coronal of Roman fame. But in the cycle of coming years, when the pen of the historian shall trace the origin and settlement of this occidental commonwealth, shall depict the virtues, the sufferings, privations, fortitude and intrepidity at the basis of the achievement, shall describe the mighty impulse it has given to the progress of free government and extension of free principles, and shall glisten the truthful page with the names of the heroic founders of its fame, there is none that will gem the record with a purer or more enduring lustre than the name of the immortal SUTTER—the illustrious ORIGINAL of CALIFORNIA PIONEERS.—*Col. E. J. C. Kewen.*

WASHINGTON.

285. Washington was the chief builder of our temple of freedom. His principles were liberty and the constitution. He fought for liberty, not for itself alone, but that we might have a Union to protect us.

The Union, in his view, was not only a blessing, it was the store-house of all the blessings which a free government could dispense to man, and by means of which any individual man could rise up to take his place among the princes of the earth. Men of the North and of the South, Washington was your countryman. No sectional feeling animated his breast when he drew his sword for liberty on northern soil, or when followed by northern soldiers, he tracked the foe through the land. He was of the Union and fought for the Union.
—*Edward Stanly.*

286. OF ALL men who ever lived, I think the judgment of his cotemporaries and of posterity is, as it will be the judgment of all history, that he never in his life yielded to one ignoble or merely sectional thought. He yielded the whole of his glorious life, the whole of his great heart, the whole of his self-denying, wise and majestic nature, to the whole people, of the whole country, in all the States, in all the sections, without distinction of creed, or race, or party, or locality, for his own time, and for all time.—*Eugene Casserly.*

287. THE GENERALITY of men do not properly appreciate the character of Washington. Many feel that his talents were not above mediocrity, that his greatness consisted in his goodness, his freedom from ambition, his punctuality and method, his admirable balance of faculties—that, in short, destitute of all brilliancy and genius, his qualities were akin to those of an "an old fogy." This mistaken idea has perhaps

been brought about by the eulogies of mediocrity, dragging him down its own level; aided perhaps by the general dissemination of the engraved portrait by Stuart, in which the noble lines of the mouth are distorted and weakened by a set of false teeth. It is absurd and dangerous to paint for the popular eye show-pictures of stalwart soldiers, or on the other hand, portraits of old men. It would have raised the patriotism of the country thirty per cent. to have had as its ideal the Washington of 45, as Leutze painted him, crossing the Delaware, to make his eagles swoop on Trenton. The great eminence of Washington is attributable to the tremendous forces of spirit that in his character were nicely balanced and harmonized. Stuart, the painter, said that every feature of Washington was indicative of the strongest passions, and yet men have come to regard him as the type of serene benignity, simply a very judicious man. In 1799, at a dinner party, Washinton received the news of St. Clair's surprise by the Indians, and the bloody massacre which followed. He put the dispatches into his pocket and remained tranquil until the last guest had departed, and then burst forth in a torrent of indignation, which shook him like an inward tempest. Then, growing calm, he said in a low tone, "Nothing of this; Gen. St. Clair shall have justice. I will receive him without displeasure; I will hear him without prejudice; he shall have full justice." It is important that men should have these glimpses through refts into the depths of Washington's being, that he shall not seem a huge, moral wax statue. It is just as important to know that once, in a boat on the Hudson, he threw himself back in a paroxysm of glee, and on another occasion, actually rolled on the grass in uncontrollable laughter at a comical story. He once danced three hours with Mrs. Gen. Greene, without sitting down, and Gen. Greene, not at all jealous, spoke of it as "a pretty little frisk." Washington's nature was like that of a planet, with massive momentum, and his fits of passion were earthquakes, showing the flame pent within the planet's granite ribs.

His greatest service was not military, but civil—the work of organizing the Republic. He believed that God created this country to be one. The Creator placed no Mason and Dixon's line upon it; that was the work of foolish men. He marked no boundaries for rival civilizations in the immense basins of the West. The Mississippi, like a great national tree, has its root in the hot gulf, and spreads its top to the far, icy North —a glorious tree, with boughs in different latitudes, and branches binding the Rocky Mountains and the Lakes together, its great trunk the central artery of a national unity. And so Providence seems to have set Washington in the core of the national history, as he set the Mississippi in the core of the land, to be a perpetual force upon the affections of the nation in behalf of union. We should feel prouder to be of the Nation than of the State. Our feet may stand on local soil, but we should cherish the idea that our country is bounded on the East by the Atlantic; and on the West by the Pacific.—*Thos. Starr King.*

WASHINGTON AND GARIBALDI.

288. The life of the Washington of Italy, unlike that of the Washington of America, was not always on one grade of dignity. He relieved his heroic campaigns by candle making on Staten Island, and, when at the very flood of his career, was "Red Shirt the First." In writing the story of Washington, the only reliefs to the monotonous dignity of his life, of which the writer may legitimately avail himself, are the rare glimpses of the foremost of modern men on his farm and among the children. But the story of Garibaldi, told correctly, furnishes glory and shadow, in all desirable alternation, action and repose, lofty military bearing and candle-dipping—a charmingly varied display, looking on the canvas more like the master's composition than a copy from nature; a specimen of realism lived out after the programme of an idealist.—*Dr. Franklin Tuthill.*

IX.

CALIFORNIANA.

PART IX.

CALIFORNIANA.

289. BECAUSE COMMODORE SLOAT did not rush to the execution of the orders issued in anticipation of war, on the very first report of a collision between the United States and Mexico, the anxious Secretary of the Navy, dreading to lose the prize, hotly censured him in a letter which reached him after the event had broken the sting of its reproaches, and served only to assure him how well he had fulfilled the wishes of his government. The flag of the United States was no sooner flying, than the *Collingwood* entered the bay of Monterey. There had been a race between the *Collingwood* and the *Savannah*. What a moment was that for us, and for the world! What if the *Collingwood* had been the swifter sailer, and Sloat had found the English flag flying on the shore! What if we had been born on another planet! The cast was for England or the United States, and when the die turned for us, the interest was at an end.—*Edmund Randolph.*

290. CALIFORNIA in full possession of the white man and embraced within the mighty area of his civilization! We feel the sympathies of our race attract us. We see in our great movement hitherward in 1849 a likeness to the times when our ancestors, their wives and little ones, and all their stuff in wagons, and with attendant herds, poured forth by nations and in never-ending columns from the German forests, and went to seek new pastures and to found new kingdoms in the ruined provinces of the Roman Empire; or, when swayed by another inspiration, they cast their masses upon the Saracens, and sought to rescue the Sepulchre of Christ from the infidels. We recognize that we are but the foremost rank of the multitude which for centuries has held its unwavering course out of Europe upon America, in numbers still increasing; a vast, unnumbered host, self-marshaled, leaderless, and innumerable, moving onward forever, to possess and people another continent; separated but in space, divided but by the accidents of manners, of language and of laws—from Scandinavia to California—one blood and one people. Man of our race has crowned the earth with its glory! Knowledge is but the conservation of his thoughts, art but the embodiment of his conceptions, letters the record of his deeds. And still in the series of his works we have founded a State. May it be great and powerful whilst the ocean shall thunder against these shores. We have planted a people; may they be prosperous and happy whilst summers shall return to bless these fields with plenty. And may the name of the PIONEER be spoken in California forever!—*Edmund Randolph.*

291. It is wonderful how little of vulgar avarice, or even of the just and prudent intention to improve their fortunes, had to do with the earlier immigrants to California. Theirs was the antiquated Homeric spirit. It was their pride and boast—and the memory of their contemporaries and the enduring result proves the fact—that they were able to win the greatest of all triumphs, the victory over themselves; that they were able to preserve order without law; that they were able to maintain justice without tribunals; that their possession of absolute personal independence never degenerated into selfishness, nor the almost savage liberty of a country without law, into cruelty or oppression. Shall we, who, in conscious fulfilment of a great mission, brought method out of chaos, and cultivated the flowers of justice and safety in the soil of anarchy—yield to lesser dangers and baser temptations? Shall we soil the splendor of the past?—*Edward C. Marshall.*

A Girlish Cleopatra.

292. And what shall be California's effigy? Assuredly woman; that soft, round, poetic bundle of voluptuous sensibility, that bankrupted nature *in* the making. But what class and quality of that sweet gender? Not as a sovereign do we see her, howsoever enthroned between the Sierra and the sea, or howsoever sometime she shall queen it over West and East; not yet as fine lady, or peasant, or prudish spinster, or staid matron, even though she be mother of men. Not as Hippolyte, the war-god's daughter, shall we personate her, or other Amazonian breast-cutter; she is too virgin and amiable for fighting. Not as Sheba, to probe with hard questions any Solomon; wit and wisdom are not to be despised, but the chink of gold is more satisfying than any words, though accompanied by the music of the spheres. Not as Pandora, for though all-gifted, she never was created to bring misery upon men. If for California's fit representation we must have a goddess, perhaps Athene, who now graces her seal, is as proper a personage as any. Springing all armored into being, appearing at once as the protectress of men and of women, of arts and agriculture and government, with wisdom and power harmoniously blended, and more ethical in her character than any of the deities, she presents more perfectly the ideal of a healthful, vigorous minded, and progressive people.

Too perfectly, in fact. Minerva is a noble creation; but for California's incarnation I should choose flesh more wanton, more sensuous, less intellectual, less severely chaste, more artless. Indeed, I should not trouble the Olympian divinities at all for my prototype, but take from some lesser hill a creature nearer me in warm, palpitating humanity; not so lofty as to be lost in unreality, nor yet so prosaic that her simple presence should not act upon me like a medicine. She should be large, and supple-limbed; low browed, with a flood of golden hair veiling her exquisitely moulded form; deep blue eyes, whose dreamy languor a merry recklessness sadly should disturb; nose and chin Grecian; ripe, luxurious lips, parted by a breath of almost visible fragrance; while expression, voice, and attitude should all betoken an indolent, romantic nature, overflowing with high, exultant spirits. A thousand years hence, the patron goddess of Athens may be California's appropriate model; but to-day she is a girlish Cleopatra, rather than a full-fledged Minerva.—*Hubert H. Bancroft.*

293.—SUNRISE FROM THE SIERRAS.
The gentle lustre of the morning star;
The sweet submission in its fading rays;
The rising radiance of the golden bar,
The eastern sky in grayish fields displays:
The leaping up, from some great sea of fire,
Of mighty lances of resistless light,—
Betokening the Day-King's fierce desire
With martial pomp to slay the hosts of night.
—*Charles A. Sumner.*

294. OUR DUTY AND DESTINY.—Each age in the history of the world has received its enlightenment from some central point. Light first shone in the fabled regions of the East, and the birth-place of the race was the starting point of its intellectual illumination; thence through the mysterious schools and priestcrafts of Egypt; through the delicate philosophies of Greece; through the Pantheism, unbelief and brutal force of ancient Rome; through the martyrdoms, councils and hierarchies of modern Rome; through Germany, France and England—this light at last has reached to us. It has crossed four continents; it has traveled six thousand years, and returns now to greet us at the very portals of its starting point. This light is the light of civilization, of progress, of religion, of the arts and sciences, of all useful improvements, of all ameliorations in the conditions of men; it is the light of knowledge, humanity, love and power; it is the sum of all experiences; the epitome of all histories; the grand result of all that the human race has ever said, or thought, or done. We look across a narrow sea and behold in the forms of government, modeled upon the patriarchal, and assuming naturally the despotic, in the doctrines of the Brahmins and the moral teachings of Confucius, that state of society, morals and religion, almost without a change, which existed in the first ages, and which has been constantly modified, enlarged and illuminated in its western progress, until it has reached us such as we find it to-day. The sun does not go backwards. We stand at the outer verge of this course, midway between the East and the West—the interpreter between the old and the new, the living and the dead.

From us, and not back again over the weary course which it has traversed for six thousand years—from us must come the inspiration and the light which shall revivify and re-glorify the worn-out nations of "the land of the East, and the clime of the sun."

For this great destiny, I fondly hope that we are a peculiar and a chosen people. I hope still more fondly that California will be fitted and prepared to stamp upon the age impress of an influence no less happy than grand—the impress of a free and imperial race.

—Judge T. W. Freelon.

295. We cannot, if we would, separate our pride in our own State from our love of all the States. When, in mental contemplation, we behold our beloved California in the Pantheon of the Nations, her majestic form reclined upon her mountain couch of gold, and the rippling tide of a mighty ocean toying with her marble feet, we see her surrounded by the grand figures of her sisters—composing a group the admiration and delight of the peoples. Already we boast that we are citizens, not of a single State, but of a wondrous Empire, extending from the blue lakes, which part us from the British Dominion, to the great Gulf of the South; from the Atlantic-beaten cliffs of farthest Maine to where the surges of the Pacific lave the cleft mountains of our own beautiful Golden Gate. Soon may generous legislation and fraternal love produce their natural result—unending harmony within our borders. May all hearts, throughout the vast expanse of our territory, respond in sympathetic unison to the electric thrill of every living thought, every noble impulse, so that—old disputes ended, old quarrels healed—there shall be no rivalry between the citizens of our dear country, save the rivalry of self-denial, magnanimity and patriotism. Long years hence, when our children shall celebrate the returning anniversary of this day, the last of the Pioneers, with bent form and whitened locks, shall take the place of honor amongst them. And as he shall hear a speaker, more worthy of the theme and the occasion, rehearse the eventful story of his contemporaries, it will be the old man's proudest reminiscence that he, too, performed his part in extending the foundations of that great Temple of Liberty, whose base shall be a continent; beneath whose protecting shadow shall dwell, in peace and prosperity, a hundred millions of freemen; and the glory of whose summit shall illumine a world.

—*Judge E. W. McKinstry.*

296.—EL RIO SACRAMENTO.—

    Where ice-clad summits greet the morn,
    And where the beetling crags look down
    On dark blue lakes with sullen frown,
    This bantling of the clouds is born;
    Forth from its granite cradle creeps,
    At first in play it laughs and leaps,
    And then in dusky pools it sleeps.
    Down silent, sunless glens it glides,
    And under long sedge grasses hides,
    Where aspen leaves, like quivering wings,
    Quaver above its hidden springs.

    Anon, in silver-sheeted falls,
    It leaps the terraced mountain walls,
    And tumbles into rocky urns,
    Beflecked with foam and fringed with ferns.

    At last this half-grown infant, fed
    By melting snow and falling rain,
    Like bruin chafing with his chain,
    Growls hoarsely in its granite bed,
    And plows its pathway to the plain.
    Meanwhile, by some designing will,

Harnessed and schooled, it turns the mill,
And with its ponderous sledge unlocks
The concrete coffers of the rocks.

In middle summer, lank and lean,
It creeps, the shelving rocks between,
And then in spring and autumn tide,
Crimson with carnage, flushed with pride,
In serried ranks of gleaming pikes,
It dashes on the yielding dikes,
And breaks the ramparts, rushing down
Upon defenceless farm and town.

In tamer moods, content to hold
By croft and thorp, by field and fold,
Past orchard boughs and bending grain,
Past grazing herds and loaded train,
Past children laughing at their play,
The tedious tenor of its way.

In ceaseless, silent sweep, between
Low lying meadows, rank and green,
Along the marge of bastioned banks,
Its dimpled face reflects the ranks
Of graybeard oaks; its liquid kiss
Thrills all the river reeds with bliss.
The thirsty fibrils of the vine
Reach down to quaff its amber wine;
The grasses and the willows lave
Their tangled tresses in its wave.
The silver cord has grown to be
A mother avalanche set free—

Its paths the highway of the world,
Where sails of commerce are unfurled,
Emblem of Time's resistless tide.
On, and still on, its currents glide,
Until, at length, far, far below,
It weds the sea with stately flow.
—*Gen. L. H. Foote.*

297. SAN FRANCISCO.—Our modern civilization is a three-fold product. From Rome we get our concrete logic, and the theory and practice of our legislation. From Athens our modes of thought, and the taste for the beautiful and the true. From Judea our morals, and that idea of the equality of men in the sight of God, which has resulted in that political equality which we call democracy.

Rome had her Capitol. There were her archives; her Sibylline oracles, her treasury, her mint; the spoils she had taken in war; the Sabine wolf, the symbol of her origin; the temples of the Capitoline Jove, of Juno, and of Minerva.

Athens had her Acropolis. There were deposited her laws; her revenues; the busts of her founders; the portraits of her heroes; the images of her gods; the wonderful statue of her protectress, Minerva.

Jerusalem had her double hill, where were her temple; the altar of the unseen God, the Holy of Holies; the City of the King; the treasury; the citadel; and the Courts of Justice.

It may therefore be regarded as an instinct of civilization that every enlightened people should select some favored spot, and stamp it as the centre of its power, by the erection of monuments which symbolize at once its advancement, its institutions, its culture, its taste, and its hopes for the future. And such an event is a great one.

In such a presence I cannot turn back to the past and recount what we and our comrades have done. [Address at laying of the corner-stone of the New City Hall, San Francisco, February 22d, 1872—EDITOR.] I seem rather to be rapt into the presence of the great future. I am not unmindful of that great immigration, unprecedented in all history, which set down at once three hundred thousand men, with all the training, wants and aspirations of the highest civilization, in the desert wastes of California; we found ourselves a mere military colony, outside of the guaranties of the Federal Constitution, and our very laws written in a foreign tongue. We were in the midst of chaos, but we knew that the whirling forces were the elements of empire. We felt the spirit moving on the face of the waters, and were sure that the dry land of the continent would soon appear.

On this occasion we cast behind us all that we have achieved, all that we have suffered, during the past twenty-five years. The fires and floods, the paralysis of panic, the intestine struggles, in which the higher law of self-preservation was indicated by the temporary suspension of the law of routine—these are sufferings which live only in memory, and no longer in feeling, and whose recollections produce even a sad pleasure. Not so the thought that so many of our comrades have perished by the way. The very soil upon which we stand [the old cemetery, reclaimed from the dead and made the site of the beautiful New City Hall—EDITOR.] is sown with the bones of some of the noblest Pioneers that ever cast their lives in the balance to win the destiny of Empire; while we, not braver nor more worthy, stand in the presence of that future in which they, too, believed, and to which we, bending over their graves, now give a new date, and of which we thus make ourselves a part. So looked the great leader of Israel from his mountain hight upon the Promised Land. So looked Columbus, with earnest, straining gaze, upon the New World which he gave to civilization. So looked out Cortez and Pizarro upon the great Southern Sea.

But we have accomplished more than these men did. We are in possession of the Promised Land. We have found the way to India, which Columbus thought he had discovered, but which he never reached. We have made conquests in the Pacific Ocean of which Cortez and Pizarro never dreamed. Commerce is the queen of nations. Hers is the Universal Empire. It knows neither geographical nor political limits. To her, both civilization and barbarism bring their tributes. Throned upon the land, she wields her scepter over the most distant sea.

In 1850, we looked at the future of San Francisco with the same assured hope which we cherish to-day. And yet at that time we believed that the placers would be exhausted, as they have been; we had no hint of the precious veins in the rocky ribs of the Sierras;

nor did we hope that ours could ever be an agricultural State; but we looked at our glorious bay, mighty enough to receive the fleets of all nations; at the vast Pacific Coast, as yet virgin to systematic commerce; and at the great islands and continent of the Southern Sea, and boldly wrested from the oracles of destiny, a prediction of the future greatness of our city.

Not unto us be the glory; "The Lord hath built the house; the Lord hath kept the city." He hath given commerce as her sustenance and her strength. She is not great and powerful, nor will she be enduring in her strength because she is the metropolis of California, but because she is the metropolis of the whole Pacific Coast and of the Great Southern Sea. And because she is so great in this element of strength, she is, in this, greater than the State itself. She is more necessary to the State than the State is to her. She is the great entrepot of the Pacific Ocean, the great point of reception and distribution, and such she would still be, though she were built like Venice, on a few sandy islands; or like Petra, in a desert; or like Tyre, upon a rock.

Oh, People of California, cherish San Francisco! She is not merely one of your jewels, but she is the very crown of your glory, all gold and jewels. You cannot control her destiny, although you may impede her march. You may make of the State a cattle pasture, and give it a mock legislature which shall represent beasts and not men; you may tax her commerce and retard her development; but you cannot defeat her destiny. Or you may cherish her as your first and noblest born; you may people her outlying valleys with a happy and cultivated population, and plant with dwellings, school-houses and churches, the wastes which now resound only with the tread of cattle and the bellowing of brutes; you may give her a free port; and, above all, you may *let her alone*, with her limbs unswathed and strength unaided, to work out her high destiny. So shall she be for untold ages, the Queen City of the vast Southern Sea. Into her lap Commerce shall pour the treasures of the Pacific, while her heart responds to the electric pulsations of the great continents and empires washed by the boundless oceans of the West. Here to-day we have marked and consecrated the centre of her legislation; of her executive and financial administration; of her educational institutions; and of her administration of justice.

The day is auspicious. It is the anniversary of the birth of Washington, the only one who has given to history the patriot's name, without tarnish and without reproach; the serene sky spreads above us, mild and beneficent, the symbol of hope and peace; the eternal hills, in their varied beauty, seem to promise endurance to our work; the ever-moving sea presents an emblem of the unrest, the ceaseless activity, and the ultimate success of our commercial empire.

—*John W. Dwinelle.*

THE MODOC STRONG-HOLD.

298. The Lava Beds are of historical interest. As the scenes of Modoc triumphs they will ever claim the attention of the civilized world. Seventy warriors, encumbered with women and children to the number of two hundred, had defied the United States Government for months and months, killed and wounded soldiers equal to three times the number of their own fighting force, and again and again repulsed attacking parties consisting of several hundred regular soldiers. I recall to mind no instance in ancient or modern warfare surpassing in rude heroism the desperate defense made by the Modocs. Their success, of course, was largely due to the fact that the soldiers were not familiar with the ramifications and sinuosities of the beds. The Modoc Lava Beds (there are other lava beds in Oregon, Idaho and Arizona) are situated northeast from Yreka, Siskiyou County, California, about fifty-three miles in an air line. The distance is over eighty miles by road. The beds proper have a width of ten miles north and south, and run east and west fifteen miles. They are bounded on the north by Rhett Lake, half of which sheet of water is in Oregon. The old emigrant road, familiar to many who crossed the plains in early days, skirts the eastern side of the beds. To the south is a nameless range of mountains. The western boundary is a bluff which continues north along the western shore of the lake. It is a rocky bluff, its face nearly a sheer precipice, and from the level of the beds to its summit the distance is five hundred and eighty-six feet. The bluff is the coigne of vantage in viewing the beds. The entire lava country is compassed in a sweeping glance. Looking over the beds with the naked eyes, they appear to consist of an undulating plain. The sight is uninviting because of the general suggestion of desolation. A forsaken region is the impression left upon the mind. No trees are seen in the immediate foreground, and those in the distance are dwarfed into bushes. The counterpart of this apparent plain may be seen along the ocean shore of New England. Let grounded sea-weed represent the dark lines twisting through the bed, and the picture is complete. The gentle undulations, as they appear from a distance, the waving grass and bushes, the lights and shadows cast on the surface by passing clouds, are in strict keeping with a beach landscape. The white, pumice-strewn shore of Tule Lake makes the resemblance most complete. I know the beds of old. To me the dark lines are something more formidable than sea-weed. Every one of them recalls to memory adventures more or less disagreeable. Away in the east, distant three miles as the crow flies, is a long, dark, ragged line—Jack's famous strong-hold.

It is assumed that the beds were once occupied by an active volcano. Through a freak of nature the volcano sunk into the earth during an eruption, and left upon the surface a sea of seething lava. The lava fused the rock with which it came in contact, and, as a rule, caused a complete metamorphosis. The primary rocks were stratified in new and curious forms. The formations exposed are of trachyte and basalt. Every ledge, so far as I observed, was mineralized with iron. Rock from the ledges is heavy and very tenacious. The rim of the beds is from fifty to one hundred yards in width, and consists of chunks of lava and lava dust.

The lava in the rim is of a light brown color, occasionally bordering on white, and weighs little more than pumice stone. The tough lava of which the beds are mainly composed is black, or has a bluish shade, according to locality. The loose pieces of lava on the outskirts of the beds indicate that the coating, as before suggested, was once in a liquid state. The fragments are porous and curved. Each had its place in the huge bubbles of the lava sea. There are immense numbers of funnel-like outlets, in which steam has been generated below and gas exploded, the openings being small at the bottom and large at the top, with crevices around. Where the steam has not exploded strongly enough to blow the rocks entirely clear, and has left these funnels, it has upheaved the rocks and allowed them to fall back loosely, so as to form immense heaps.

The true character of the Lava Beds cannot be learned by inspection from afar. Nothing but close acquaintance will inform the visitor. Pass inside of the rim and you fail to find a level spot. Every rock stands on end, and exposes angular points. When the war began, the Indians were scattered along the western border. After several battles they suddenly vanished as by magic. It was supposed that they had fled to a distant locality. A reconnoissance developed them in what was aptly termed the back-bone of the beds, or Captain Jack's strong-hold. This bone consists of a nob of giant ledges in the northeastern portion of the lava section. These ledges crop out boldly and have no special course. The best defined ledge generally trends north and south. The lesser ledges run nearly parallel at times, and again cut in at right angles. The mean level of the beds is below that of the lake. As you draw near the stronghold it becomes necessary to descend into irregular chasms. Before you have time to study the topography of the place, ledges loom up fifty and sixty feet high, directly in front, and all but compel a halt. The savages, pressed by the troops, retired from ledge to ledge, and each retreat carried them to higher ground and gave them additional advantages. The strong-hold proper is about the summit of several of the boldest ledges. They radiate from a common center and are difficult of access. Along the top of each ledge is a natural channel three or four feet in depth, wherein the cunning savage can skulk and shoot and still remain unseen. The channels are complicated and labyrinthian. Modocs had dwelt here for ages, so said tradition, and yet the followers of Jack would not trust to memory as they moved about. They failed to feel securely familiar with this pile of rocks two hundred yards square, and had the different channels marked by bits of wood! The rocks are not adapted to cave formations. The caves mentioned in war telegrams are spacious basins occurring in the solid rock. Those in the strong-hold are one hundred or more feet in circumference, and have a depth of fifty feet. Overhanging rocks furnish a few of these caves with what might be termed incomplete roofing. Jack's band made a stand in the strong-hold, and played sad havoc with assailing parties. One night the water in the strong-hold gave out. The only convenient source of supply was the lake, distant one mile. Between the strong-hold and the lake was a line of soldiers. Before morning the Modocs fled from this rocky fastness to the southern end of the beds, where Hasbrouck finally gave them so much trouble.

Five miles south of Rhett Lake, and in the southeastern portion of the lava deposit, are two bold buttes, united by a narrow tongue of black lava, which are of pure scoria. Each of these buttes has a crater at its crest. Close at hand are a number of lava buttes, with craters. All of these buttes combined could not have made the overflow constituting the beds, albeit the lips of the craters have been cut by streams of lava which cooled in the shadowy past. The marvelous power of nature, as exemplified in the configuration of the rocks about these buttes, and the lines of demarkation between fusion complete and arrested, make a lasting impression upon the most superficial beholder. There is an appalling sublimity in the sight which one cannot shake off. The surface of the earth is in ruins here. Tree, plant and grass are absent. The lava is sombre black. There are bottomless fissures from one to two feet in width and miles in length. There are broad chasms over one hundred feet deep. There are perfect arches—keystone and all—suggesting remnants of a Roman temple. There are odd forms and profiles which would do credit to a gifted sculptor. The ledges often lie parallel, like so many dark, forbidding waves, each ledge dotted with circular, sharp-edged hollows. The striking characteristics of this wonderful home of the Modocs were outlined in my mind as I stood on the bluff that night. But darkness wrapped the beds in a pall, and I retired to a welcome couch on Mother Earth.—*Wm. M. Bunker.*

299. OUR DUTY AND DESTINY.—The poet's Golden Age is lost from sight in the mists of Fable, and hid by centuries of war and crime; but the Age of Ages, the Song of Songs, lies before us, brought nearer by each changeful year. The world, which began with a Garden of Eden, shall complete the cycle, and come once more to be a garden as fair as that lost, angel-guarded beauty. Nations, it may be, shall yet unite their wealth and energy to reclaim the historic deserts of Asia, to replant the treeless wastes, to revive the dead rivers and rebuild the fallen cities of the East. Here in California, we too, have deserts to plant with palms, and naked mountains to clothe with cypress and pine. There are swamps and malarial regions to be reclaimed with Eucalyptus, and red lands to be covered with orchards and vineyards. There is room for many more homes and industries. Our most fertile valleys must sustain a much greater population, and in the course of time become beautiful beyond expression. Wheat-culture will in a measure pass to newer States and virgin soil, and the sceptre of grain will leave our hands. Our large ranches will be divided and subdivided, and we shall enter upon a period of unclouded prosperity, founded on diversified interests and the highest development of horticulture in all its branches.

To this future, then, we look. Southern Europe is in many respects our type and example. Whatever Greece, Italy and Spain were in their noblest days, that we, also, hope to become, except that as our facilities are greater, so our mingling of the beauties of a world may be greater. A cosmopolitan people, not narrow or prejudiced, strong, earnest, truthful, original; state-builders, home-lovers, believers in education, full of nature's naturalness—this is that end to which we of a ruder, more fertile age must toil, setting our faces toward the morning. Our State is not a tent of the Saxon race, pitched hastily by this western ocean, but a temple rising in the sight of all men. It is not yet finished; the pioneers of '49 hewed monolithic stones, fit for a new Temple of the Sun. Here the great shall worship when, ages hence, the story we are now beginning shall be continued in the deeds of our children; when our ancestral oaks, now just planted, shall become hoary monarchs tottering to their fall; when the new walls of our young University shall be as gray and venerable as classic Oxford. Let us patiently do the work of to-day, so that our rude beginnings shall not be useless, but linked with past and future. These rivers and lakes, the beautiful bay of San Francisco, the lonely cliffs, the pallid snow-peaks, shall all be parts of a classic clime. It is man's labor and heroic deeds which put a new and more divine seal to Nature's fairest scenes. Mount Shasta, in its translucent majesty shall out-rival Mont Blanc; our Sierras shall awaken nobler poems than Alps or Appenines. So shall these western shores become lands of cultured groves and gardens, and horticultural triumphs, linked closely with Art, Literature, and the multiplied pursuits of a refined and powerful race.—*Charles H. Shinn.*

300. CALIFORNIA HUMORISTS.—California, during this quarter-century, has produced more humorists, and more of that literature which is essentially humorous, than all the rest of the country. It may be difficult to trace to any outward sources the inspiration of so much wit. Does it lie in the odd contrasts and strange situations which so often confront the observer here? Nor has this facetiousness depended at all for its development upon any degree of prosperity. In fact, the boldest and bravest challenge which has ever been given to adverse fortune here, has been by the gentle humorists who have suffered from her slings and arrows. It is said, "Cervantes smiled Spain's chivalry away." But these modern satirists made faces at bad fortune; they lampooned her and defied her to do her utmost. The more miserable they ought to have been, the happier they were. They found a grotesque and comic side to the most sober facts. They were facetious when there was small stock in the larder and smaller credit at the bankers. They smiled at the very grimness of evil fortune until she fled, and, in doing this, they half-unconsciously tickled the midriff of the world. A ripple of laughter ran over the surface of society. It sometimes made slow progress when it here and there met a mountain of obtuseness. But wit is wit; and what difference does it make if, failing to see the point, some people laugh next year instead of this? I will not be distressed because my friend does not, to this day, see how the immortal "Squibob" conquered his adversary at San Diego by falling underneath him and inserting his nose between his teeth. Nor does it

greatly concern me that he does not assent to the proposition that John Phoenix, having made a national reputation by editing the San Diego *Herald* for one week, was the greatest journalist of modern times. If reputation is the measure of greatness, Phoenix is to this day without a peer. He made the very desert sparkle with his wit. He was a humorous comet, shooting across the horizon of pioneer life. Men looked up and wondered whence it came and whither it had gone.

Possibly, there is something favorable to the play of humor in a greater freedom from conventional limitations. If one grows into this larger liberty, or is translated into it, a flavor of freshness comes to pervade all his intellectual life. A certain spontaneity of expression, a spring, a rioting song of gladness, are some of the signs of this more abounding life. In homely phrase, we say there is a flavor of the soil about it. It might, therefore, have been necessary, that Mark Twain should sleep on this soil, and should have a wide range of pioneer experience, before he could become the prince of grotesque humorists. He got up suddenly from the very soil which in its secret laboratory colors the olive and the orange, and began to make the world laugh. With a keen sense of the symmetry and harmony of things, he had a keener perception of all the shams and ridiculous aspects of life. His pungent gospel of humor is as sanitary as a gentle trade wind. He knew a better secret than the old alchemists. Every time he made the world laugh, he put a thousand ducats into his pocket. But never until he had slept in his blankets, had been robbed on the "Divide," and had learned the delicate cookery of a miner's cabin, could he do these things. But now he cannot even weep at the tomb of his ancestor, Adam, without moving the risibles of half the world. He has also a finer touch and flavor, not of the rankest soil, but of that which gives the aroma and delicate bouquet to the rarest mountain-side vintage. When this man had tried his wit on a California audience, and had won an approving nod, he had an endorsement that was good in any part of the English-speaking world.

Of a more subtile wit and a finer grain was Harte, who did his best work as a humorist in California. All his earlier triumphs were won here. His subsequent endorsement in a wider field was only an affirmation of this earlier public judgment. Sometimes in the thicket, one may come upon a wild mocking-bird which is running up the gamut of its riotous burlesque upon the song of every other bird, and the sound of every living thing in the forest. But when all this is done, that mocking-bird will sometimes give out a song which none other can match with its melody. As much as this, and more, lay within the range of this poet-satirist. His mocking had, however, a deep and salient meaning in it. When Truthful James rises to explain in what respect Ah Sin is peculiar, he has a higher purpose than merely to show the overreaching cunning of this bronzed heathen, "with the smile that was child-like and bland." When the supposed pliocene skull, found in Calaveras County, had developed a good deal of scientific quackery, Harte, in his "Geological Address," makes the skull declare that it belonged to Joe Bowers, of Missouri, who had fallen down a shaft. For six months thereafter no theorist was able to discuss the character of that fossil with a sober countenance. No Damascus blade ever cut with a keener stroke than did the blade of this satirist, even when it was hidden in a madrigal or concealed in some polished sentence of prose.

As a humorist, he appreciated humor in others. When Dickens died, not another man in all the length and breadth of the land contributed so tender and beautiful a tribute to his memory as did Harte in his poem of "Dickens in Camp." It was left to this shy man, who came forth from the very wastes of this far-off wilderness, to lay upon the bier of the dead humorist as fragrant an offering as any mortal fellowship could suggest. It was a song in a different key—as if one having entered into the very life of the great novelist, had also for a moment entered into his death.

Another humorist, radically the product of California, was Prentice Mulford. When it was found that he had a genuine vein of wit in him, recognized alike in the brilliant *salon* and the miner's camp, he was sent forth as another missionary to reclaim the world.

The wit and the poetry which ripen here are under the same sun which ripens the pomegranate and the citron. The grain and texture have always been better than that suggested by the coarser materialism without. It is little to him who is cutting his marble to the divinest form, that the whole city reeks with grime and smoke, and all its outlines are ugly and misshapen. It is little to poet or painter that sometimes the earth has only a single tint of gray, since he may also see in contrast what a transfigured glory there may be on mountain and on sea.

There are not at any time, in this dull world, so many genuine humorists as one may count on his fingers. For lack of some healthy laughter the world is going to the bad. It welcomes the gentle missionary of humor, and for lack of him it often accepts those dreary counterfeits who commit assault and battery on our mother tongue. As in olden times the prophets were sometimes stoned in their own country, so in modern times one cannot tell whether the poet-prophet, who comes up from the wilderness, will fare better or worse. Woe to him if the people cannot interpret him, or are piqued at his coming.

None of us would be comfortable with only some pungent sauce for dinner; but when a dreadful staleness overtakes the world, it is ready to cry out, "More sauce!" Whoever comes, therefore, bringing with him salt and seasoning, and whatever else gives a keener zest to life, never comes amiss. Sooner or later we shall know him. He will come very near to us in his books, and by that subtle law of communion which, through the brightest and noblest utterances, makes all the better world akin.

After we have seen the tricks of the magician, we do not care to know him any more; but the magician of wit works by an enchantment that we can never despise. His spell is wrought with such gifts as are only given from the very heavens to, here and there, one. It is not the mythical Puck who is to put a girdle round the world, but the man of genius, whose thought is luminous with the light of all ages. So Shakespeare clasps the world, and Dickens belts it, and the men of wit and genius furnish each a golden thread which girds it about. The book of humor is the heart's ease. In every library it is dog-eared, because it has in it some surcease for the secret ills of life. If a million souls have been made happier for an hour through the fictions of Sir Walter Scott, what is the sum of good thus wrought! What lesser good have they wrought who have come in later times to lighten the dead weight of our over-weighted lives?—*W. C. Bartlett.*

AUTHORSHIP IN CALIFORNIA.

801. The exacting conditions of pioneer life are not favorable to authorship. If, during this quarter of a century, not a book had been written in California, we might plead, in mitigation, the overshadowing materialism which, while coarsely wrestling for the gains of a day, finds no place for that repose which favors culture and is fruitful of books. But over the arid plains, in the heat and dust of the long summer, one may trace the belt of green which the mountain-stream carries sheer down to the sea. So there have been many thoughtful men and women who have freshened and somewhat redeemed these intellectual wastes. They

have written more books in this quarter of a century than have been written in all the other States west of the Mississippi River. The publication of some of these books has cost nearly their weight in gold. During the period of twenty-five years, more than ninety volumes have been written by persons living at the time in this State.

No one has sought to live here exclusively by authorship. It has only been the incidental occupation of those persons who have written out of the fullness of their own lives. If they heard no mysterious voice saying unto them: "Write!"—the great mountains encamped about like sleeping dromedaries, the valleys filled with the aroma of a royal fruitage, the serene sky, and the rhythm of the great sea—all make audible signs to write. They have written out of a fresh, new life.

It is this large acquaintance with Nature—this lying down with the mountains until one is taken into their confidence—that may give a new vitality and enlarge the horizon of intellectual life. Whence comes this man with his new poetry, which confounds the critics? And that man with his subtle wit, borrowed from no school? I pray you note that for many a day his carpet hath been the *spicula* of pine, and his atmosphere hath been perfumed by the fir tree. He has seen the mountain clad in beatific raiment of white, and their "sacristy set round with stars." He will never go so far that he will not come back to sing and talk of these his earliest and divinest loves. So Harte comes back

again to his miner's camp and to the larger liberty of the mountains. And there fell on Starr King a grander inspiration after he had seen the white banners of the snow-storm floating from the battlements of Yosemite.
—*W. C. Bartlett.*

X.

MISCELLANY.

PART X.

MISCELLANY.

THE ATLANTIC CABLE (A. D. 1858).

302. Thought has bridged the Atlantic, and cleaves its unfettered way across the deep, winged by the lightning and guarded by the billow. Though remote from the shores that first witnessed the deed, we feel the impulse and swell the pæan. As in the frame of man the nervous sensibility is greater at the extremity of the body, so we, distant dwellers on the Pacific feel yet more keenly than the communities which form the centers of civilization, the greatness of the present success and the splendor of the advancing future.

From the dark, unfathomed caves of ocean the pearl that heaves upon the breast of beauty is dragged to the glare of day. The unburied dead lie waiting for the resurrection morning, while above them the winds wail their perpetual requiem; there the lost treasures of India and Peru are forever buried; there the wrecks of the Armada and Trafalgar are forever whelmed. But amid these scattered relics of the buried past, over shell-formed shores and wave-worn crags, the gleaming Thought darts its way; amid the monsters of the deep, amid the sporting myriads and countless armies of the sea, the single link that unites two worlds, conveys the mandate of a king or the message of a lover. Of old, the Greek loved to believe that Neptune ruled the ocean and stretched his trident over the remotest surge. The fiction has become reality; but man has become the monarch of the wave, and his trident is a single wire! All creeds, all races, all languages are here; every vocation of civilized life mingles in the shout and welcomes the deed. The minister of religion sees the Bow of Promise reflected under the sea, which speaks of universal peace; the statesman perceives another lengthening avenue for the march of free principles; the magistrate can see here new guards to the rights of society and property, and a wide field for the spread of international law; the poet kindles at the dream of a great republic of letters tending toward a universal language; and the seer of science finds a pledge that individual enterprise may yet embody his discoveries in beneficent and world-wide action.

The spectacle which marked the moment when the cable was first dropped in the deep sea was one of absorbing interest. Two stately ships of different and once hostile nations, bore the precious freight. Meeting in mid-ocean, they exchanged the courtesies of their gallant profession—each bore the flag of St. George, each carried the flaming stripes and blazing stars—on each deck that martial band bowed reverently in prayer to the Great Ruler of the tempest; exact in order, perfect in discipline, they waited the auspicious moment to seek the distant shore. Well were those noble vessels named—the one, *Niagara*, with a force resistless as our own cataract, the other, *Agamemnon*, "King of Men," as constant in purpose, as resolute in trial, as the great leader of the Trojan war. Right well, oh, gallant crew, have you fulfilled your trust! Favoring were the gales and smooth the seas that bore you to the land! And if the wishes and prayers of the good and wise of all the earth may avail, your high and peaceful mission shall remain forever perfect, and those triumphant standards, so long shadowing the earth with their glory, shall wave in united folds as long as the Homeric story shall be remembered among men, or the thunders of Niagara reverberate above its arch of spray.

—*Gen. E. D. Baker.*

303. A REFLECTION, peculiarly beautiful and appropriate, is suggested by the first dispatch transmitted from Europe to America: "Glory to God in the highest, and on earth peace, good will to men." This salutation fell from angelic lips, addressed to the simple shepherds of Judea, as they watched their flocks upon the star-lit plains of Bethlehem, two thousand years ago. It breathed the spirit of thanksgiving, of peace and kindness. Since that period the world has undergone strange mutations. The star of empire has steadily held its course westward; commerce has changed its

seat; Palestine lives only in history; and Jerusalem, the pride of the East, has long since fallen from her high estate. The torch of war lit up her temple and her streets, and her gates yielded to the Saracen. Rome, the then mistress of the world, at whose shrine the learned and great of earth paid submissive homage, is now but a spectral shadow of her former self. Her orators are silent, her generals slain, her legions scattered, her sceptre broken. Britain was then a rude, barbarous island, scarcely regarded or known. Learning and religion had not blessed or instructed her, nor the light of science dawned upon her. To-day she is a great nation, occupying a place in the front rank of wealth and civilization, powerful on the land and supreme on the sea. America was then unknown to civilized men. The foot of the Caucasian had never pressed her soil, nor had her peaceful bosom been disturbed by the shock of barbarous war or political strife. She was just as God had made her—silent, beautiful, grand. Nineteen centuries have passed away, and more than fifty generations of men have gone down to their graves. The Church has endured bitter persecutions; Science has bled beneath the heel of military oppression; the lamps of learning have often been well-nigh extinguished; splendid libraries have been consumed; and yet the heaven-born salutation song to the Judean shepherds is still preserved. The lightnings of heaven catch the strain, and through the deep, resounding sea, along the watery thoroughfare of thought, beyond the explorations of curious man, amidst coral, rock, and drifting sands, among the graves of lost mariners, shut out from the light of day, the gaze of stars and the din of men, these words of peace are conveyed to expectant millions. How beautiful! how auspicious! how replete with signs and promises of peace!—*E. D. Wheeler.*

MATERIALISM.

304. Materialism is no new theory; materialists have disturbed the peace in the harmony of truth from time almost beyond record; but especially does the world remember the name of Spinoza; and his doctrine called Spinozism is little other than the materialism of to-day. The creative power, God, the Almighty, was not absolutely denied by Spinoza; but as in his doctrine of chances a geometrical forethought antecedent to the formation of an organism was impossible, God was only an early form of matter.

Spinoza, born in 1632, in Holland, was a learned Jew; but, for his heresies, was expelled from the Hebrew Church. In a spirit of charity and honor to his erudition, he was accepted into the Christian Church. Herein he proved equally obnoxious, and was summarily dismissed, or excommunicated. Nothing daunted, he published his reticent controversies, only to see them suppressed or burnt. But he worked an influence upon his age; bribery could not tempt him; menace he did not dread; and his influence will endure forever. Nor is he the first, nor the last learned man whose mind has failed to be inspired with the transcendent beauties of divine creation, or his moral emotions mellowed with the poetry and the harmonies of Nature.

Since the appearance of man on earth many of the great epochs of life, involving thousands of centuries, have transpired; but it is not so very many years since man discovered and reduced to order the simplest laws and conditions of physics; the first mechanical data of the principles which govern force and motion; the scientific combinations of architecture; the minute details of house carpentry; the incessant and so often ruinous influence of gravitation, on whose nice adjustments man's equilibrium, both in full action and repose, depends; the great demonstrations of geometry, with all their applications in the great areas of astronomy—all, all, are but recent, in comparison with the evolutions of organized beings, with man, their highest type on earth; and yet the work of every vitalized organism demonstrates that the antecedent conception by a superior intelligence was indispensable to their existence; and in their exquisite symmetries are proved the preknowledge of all the great physical laws.

The human body, in general terms, consists of a solid head, a movable trunk, supported by a flexible column and four limbs. These several members are united by joints or hinge-work. It represents a conical form, inverted with its apex, or, one might say, its two apices, resting on the ground without any further attachment than the soles of the feet and the attraction of gravity. Viewed as a mechanism, you perceive that this construction is very unfavorable for stability in its upright position, and would be very easily overturned.

Indeed, if unaided by a constant mutation of muscular forces kept in play by voluntary efforts, it could only maintain its upright position for a very short time. Through the centre of this cone a vertical line represents the line of gravitation. Now it is only by careful obedience, learned by long experience, to the laws of gravity, that this erect position can be continued; the various departures from and returns to which constitute all the movements—as walking, leaping, dancing, the art of equitation—which the body assumes. So thoroughly do all these motions become educated by the action of thought and will on the muscles and joints, that their voluntary motions come finally to appear involuntary; but in truth they are never so. So rapidly is the telegraphy of the brain conducted that we fail to register its time. As an illustration of its perfect ability, all the grace and rapid performance of a Fanny Elssler is but the music of the mind transmitted to and enacted by the feet, every quaver and semi-quaver of the one being converted into motion by the other.

This, then, is the converse of the mind with the great system of muscles it controls; and its perfection depends upon the trained application of the laws of gravitation and mechanism through the centre of the body, and the possible departures from it. See the exterior semblance of this grand mechanical combination, [pointing to a human statue divested of the skin] and yet how coarse and rude it all appears if compared with those unseen constructions of the eye, the ear, and the vocal apparatus. Is this mere chance? or is it the workmanship of a God?

Religion, assume what cast it may be, is only the tender poetic child of devotion, and devotion is that holy differentiation between godlike man and apelike animal; that impassioned sentiment, inwrought of a jealous Deity, whose love for His last and best creation, with the mother's for her feeble, willful infant, fearing and pre-knowing ingratitude, engrafted this profoundest of all emotions in its inmost nature, to secure its fidelity. This is the differentiation which Mr. Darwin, in constructing his chain of many links, has ignored or forgotten; but an all-wise Creator so planted it in every human bosom from creation's dawn, that it is as indispensable as life to existence—all nations feel it, all nations adore and worship. Riot over it as they may, the Creator ever attains His loving object; to their knees all races bend in trembling adoration at His shrine.—*Dr. A. B. Stout.*

THE SCIENCE OF MEDICINE.

305. The Science of Medicine in this age of the world is endowed with marvelous vitality and progress, it draws richest nourishment from all parts of the earth; and, fed at the hands of thousands of loving and earnest devotees, its growth and development are objects of immeasurable splendor. It leaps and bounds along the plane of the century—swift and bright as the sweep of a comet, exploding the errors of the past—dissipating present obscurities and illuminating the the future; untired by time, endowed with exhaustless energies, it knows no halting place save the last station

at which the finite must stop and the infinite begin. In the contemplation of this truth may be perceived the necessity for unceasing labor and study on the part of Professors and Students; on the part of all, in fact, who would keep pace with the progress and improvement of our science, or rise to distinction among the savans of the century.

If the "*ultima thule*" of our science were reached; if it were finished in all its fair proportions; the degree of labor necessary to attain this station of knowledge, language is indequate to describe; and once attained, the infirmities of memory are so great, that it must needs be constantly refreshed by study, or the accumulated learning of the past would insensibly disappear and finally be lost to the world forever.

In the prosecution then of the study of all unfinished sciences, the relations between the teacher and the taught, between professor and student, are not and can not be severely drawn; they stand more on equal footing, something like older and younger brothers, the former guiding, scarcely instructing the latter, for the way after a while is full of difficulty and obscurity to all, and under such circumstances every one is a student. No longer, then, are there professors and pupils; ignorance levels all such distinctions and there is in reality no difference between them.

A community of labor, an identity of interest and equality of position, should draw us very closely together, making of us a confraternity devoted to science and to each other, finding in each other sufficient reason for attachment, at least in this, that we have voluntarily and *con amore* given ourselves to a science which, unless we are altogether abandoned, must elevate the soul and chasten the heart, teaching us reverence for Him who has done all things wisely and well; teaching us charity for all men, sympathy for their misfortunes, patience for their transgressions; teaching us our own weakness and littleness, and the awful majesty of Omnipotence, making of us all better and wiser men, practical philanthropists, working to practical ends and aims, whose grand objective is the relief of all the ills that flesh is heir to, all the mental and physical infirmities of mankind.

It is in medicine, and in medicine alone, that benevolence finds a field for its fullest scope, wondrous foresight, exhaustless energies and most signal triumphs. Benevolence that leans not upon medicine nor invokes her aid in the consummation of its mission is indeed a most impotent virtue.

On the face of all nature are impressed, sometimes indistinctly, sometimes in frightful perspicuity, the characters of suffering, disease and death. Take from the mead, where an emerald waving sea of luxuriant freshness proclaims the perfection of life, a single blade of grass and examine carefully the structure. A minute perforation in one portion tells the story that a destructive worm has been there; in another portion a blight or mould announces that some mysterious chemical action or physical vicissitude has commenced a series of processes whose climax is death. The leaf that flutters from the tree and falls at your feet in your rambles through the forest, is a sermon in miniature on the decay and death which fasten themselves inevitably on all organized bodies. Death is indeed one of the conditions of life. Wherever we see life, no matter in how humble or exalted way it manifests its presence, death is the inseparable associate of its continuance. In the disintegration of the blood, for instance, may be perceived an illustration of this truth. The red corpuscles, in giving to life the nourishment necessary for the perfection of its operations, are weakened and ultimately destroyed, and their inanimate remains helplessly surrender themselves to certain chemical actions, assume new relations in the system, or through the various emunctories finally find an exit from the body. The moment that digestion fails to replace with new corpuscular elements those which life has used, and in using destroyed, then death, universal death, ensues.

Running up the scale of creation, commencing at the point where the senses almost fail to demonstrate the existence of life, and ending in the sublimest forms of physical and intellectual powers, the same general law obtains, the germs of disease and death are there, they may remain for a time undeveloped, some intercurrent trouble may anticipate the unavoidable casualty; care may retard for a season the evolution of these germs, but sooner or later they pronounce themselves and then the instinct of self-preservation calls aloud for help.

What was true in reference to the blade of grass or the falling leaf, is equally true in reference to man, to whom all sublunary things are subordinate: for whose use and comfort they were indeed created. There is no spot, there is no clime throughout God's universe wherein are found the habitations of man which are not darkened by distemper and desolated by death. The wail that in remote antiquity rent the startled atmosphere, when bloody assassination, done by a brother's hand, spilt the first blood, destroyed for the first time a human life, has been sounding through the centuries ever since, and the dismal melancholy diapason will be hushed only on the consummation of the planet on which we live. Early and late, at midnight and at noon, from the four winds of heaven, from city, hamlet and plain, from the palaces of the rich and great, and from the hovel of the wretched and the poor, comes that never-ceasing cry of agony, moaning over the sick, wailing over the dying, and shrieking over the dead. In the presence, then, of such dreadful truths, whose universality is so perfectly established, and reflecting that medicine is the only power that can cope with nature's infirmities as manifested in the human family, who is mad or impious enough to doubt that benevolence finds in medicine a field for its most comprehensive scope. Working in harmony, medicine and benevolence present a combination whose triumphs are in the strictest sense miraculous, approaching in majesty and splendor the wonders wrought by Him, in whose presence the conscious water saw its God and blushed!

—*Dr. J. Campbell Shorb.*

THE LAW, BENCH AND BAR.

806. The province of the law is as wide and comprehensive as the requirements—natural and artificial—

of human society. Wherever a political organization has existed, its elements have been combined and held together by law. Indeed, without law, such an organization could not exist—it is its vivifying and sustaining spirit. The completeness, justice and efficiency of a nation's laws constitute perhaps the one infallible test of its true advance along the line of civilization; for, as has been shown by Savigny, the progress of legislation is not governed by chance, but is the expression of the very life of a people. The primary, fundamental conceptions which distinguish the jurisprudence of one people, of one age, from another, illustrate most clearly the habits of thought and action, the beliefs and sentiments of the respective times and peoples. They indicate the character of the prevailing industries—the relation of the governors to the governed—of nation to nation. Material progress and mental and moral advance—man's view of his duty to his fellow man and his relation to the unseen world—may be read in the juridicial records of human government, even as the geologist sees in the various strata of the earth the history of its formation. And as the history of man transcends in interest and importance the history of the globe which he inhabits, it would seem that the studies, contemplations and reflections of the juristic explorer must necessarily lead to results surpassing in grandeur and usefulness the minute and laborious observation and profound generalizations of the physical discoverer. The sphere of the latter has fixed limits—that of the former has no boundaries but those beyond which the mental and moral capacities of the race cannot go. These rules, by which the conduct of man as a social being is governed—by many not always consciously felt, and recognized dimly, if at all—are yet as universal and potent in their domain as those natural forces which guide the courses of the planets, and shape the perfect sphere of the dew-drop on the rose.

In the practical application of these rules to the manifold phases of human intercourse—in the enforcement of obligations upon which the protection of life; liberty and property depends—appropriate instrumentalities are demanded. These are what we term the Bench and Bar. In one view, their functions are clearly distinguishable, but practically the one is essential to the other. Whether the old conception of each judicial decision being a direct and special emanation from the Deity, or the other view that judicial duty consists in merely applying a well-known rule to a given state of facts, prevail, the necessity for a class which shall present properly each dispute for determination must be generally recognized. "The advocate," says the great French Chancellor, "is placed for the public good, between the tumult of human passions and the throne of justice, to offer the prayers of the people, and to bear back the response of the law." The responsibility devolving upon the lawyer is, and necessarily must be, of the most weighty, important, and at times awful nature. Life, liberty, property, character are entrusted to his keeping. To his honor, be it said, that weighed in the balance, he has rarely been found wanting. The history of English and American liberty is resplendent with the names of lawyers who have battled as bravely and successfully in the forum for that sacred cause, as any plumed knight or mailed baron in field or fortress. Whether in the humbler walks of the profession or along its mountain tops, the labors of the lawyer are always useful and sometimes indispensable. He, at least, should be "faithful among the faithless." Whether his office be that of priest or acolyte in the sacred temple of Justice, he must be *faithful*—faithful to his client, to society, to himself. To his consciousness should ever be present that most impressive injunction:

> "To thine own self be true,
> And it must follow, as the night the day,
> Thou canst not then be false to any man."

—Henry H. Reid.

307. THE LIVES OF Coke, Plowden, Mansfield, Kenyon, Marshall, Story, and a host of others, honest, sincere, learned and resolute men, have been spent in the examination of laws, in studying them profoundly, with reference to the eternal fitness of things, and the wants of a civilized community. It is no easy thing to frame a system of laws which shall provide for every one of the strangely complicated combinations of society; such a system must be the growth of ages, the fruit of long reflection and still longer experience; and when it is finished and complete, the breath of lawlessness and irreverence can destroy in a single day what centuries of disinterested, intelligent, reverent work have reared. I never go into Court and hear the judge render his decision in a civil case where large property

interests are settled, or speak the sentence by which a human being is adjudged unworthy to live, without a feeling that something more than the utterance of a human being is issuing from his lips. I recognize in the Judge, as he performs his solemn task, a being, clothed for the moment, with the attributes of Divinity itself; the humble court-room swells into the dimensions of a grand temple of justice, where the vice-gerent of God presides.

Whatever view partisans may take of the trial of President Johnson, at Washington, all will be agreed on one point, and that is that the possibility of such a trial, the trial of the Chief Magistrate of the nation, of the Grand Commander of our armies and High Admiral of our navy, before a court of Representatives of the people, that trial taking place at a time when the angry feelings of war had hardly commenced to abate, is the best illustration of the wisdom, and the surest guaranty of the permanence of the institutions of the United States. No such trial could be possible except under a government of the people. Brutus killed his best friend for the love of Rome, and the hope of the Republic rested on the dagger of the assassin. The spirit of English liberty, brutally repressed by the tyranny of Henry the Eighth, stayed in its progress by the genius and womanhood of Elizabeth, fretting and chafing under the pedantic claim of James the First to rule by divine right, at length wields the ax, and as it falls on the neck of Charles the First, the martyred king, the great poet of republics, and of the rights of man—the gentle Milton—stands applauding, proclaiming that a deed, great, good, and essential to England's progress, has been performed. There was no other means by which liberty could assert herself. "Son of Saint Louis, ascend to Heaven!" cries the priest, and the innocent, harmless Louis the Sixteenth mounts the scaffold, a necessary victim, when it is a question of changing a dynasty, which rests on force.

"Andrew Johnson, come into Court!" shouts the crier, and humbly pleading that he is not guilty; that counsel, learned in the law, will prove to his judges that he ought not to vacate his place of monarch; the elected of thirty millions of freemen, submits himself to the law and asks its decision whether he shall reign or not. Has the world ever seen a greater triumph of law?

—*John B. Felton.*

808. SCIENCE IS A COLLECTION OF TRUTHS; an art is a collection of rules for conduct. The end of science is truth; the end of art is work. Since science is conversant about speculative knowledge only, and art is the application of knowledge to practice, jurisprudence, when applied to practice, is an art, whether in enacting laws as in legislation, or in the actual working of the law as in advocacy; but jurisprudence, when confined to the theory of law, is strictly a science. Law as an art aims at the practical object of improving the condition of men in their social conditions; it has reference to conduct; by which we mean all that directly involves the relation of men to one another. When this is done, law, as an art, is satisfied. But then arise further questions. Why is one law better than another? What

is the ultimate nature of law? Whence does law arise? It is the *science* which deals with such questions, and when it has ascertained this, it is satisfied. It is true that the science assists the art, but that is not so much the object of the science. The science arises from human inquisitiveness, proceeding in the same spirit of inquiry which leads men to search the rocks and caves in the bowels of the earth, examine its strata, and thus form the science of geology.

The true aim and object of all human enactments, the real art of legislation, should be to define and establish the relative rights of men; it should not, it cannot interfere with their absolute natural rights. It is in this respect that law has had its chief imperfections, and where it needs most to be guided by science; and the aid of science will enable us, by a study of men in their social relations, to discover principles on which laws may be based, directing and controlling their conduct. By a study of Sociology and Political Economy we have attained to a knowledge of certain principles which we know to be uniform, steady and constant in their operation, wherever there is any social organization; and in so far as positive law is based on a recognition of these principles, it may be claimed to be scientific.
—*John Proffatt, LL. B.*

309. THE CONSTITUTION of the United States guards with jealous care the liberty of the citizen. It provides that he shall be free from arrest, except upon warrant issued upon probable cause, supported by oath or affirmation. But the Constitution was established

not only for times of peace; not only for times when a ready obedience to the laws is yielded by citizens, but also for times of rebellion, of war, and invasion; and it contains within itself all the power requisite for the maintenance of the Government against both foreign and domestic foes. The Government must exist, or the citizen cannot enjoy the liberty which the Constitution intends to secure. And that the Government may exist, the liberty of the individual must sometimes yield to the demands of public safety. The very clause of the Constitution which declares that the privilege of the writ of habeas corpus shall not be suspended, makes the exception, "unless when, in cases of rebellion or invasion, the public safety may require it."—*Judge Stephen J. Field.*

310. A JUDGE is expected to have the feelings and sympathy of a man; yet, in his decisions he should pronounce the law irrespective of circumstances, and let its majesty hush all other considerations. The principle is a plain one, but its practice in some cases is exceedingly difficult. We are liable to be influenced by surrounding circumstances in spite of ourselves, and in many cases unconsciously to ourselves. A consciousness of the difficulty, instead of enabling us to avoid it, frequently unsettles the mind, destroys the judgment, and causes us to rush upon the rock we would fain avoid. A sense of injustice that may be done, presses itself with force upon the mind and jostles it from its propriety. A feeling of this weakness causes it like the pendulum to oscillate perchance

to the other side of truth, in its effort to assert the majesty of the law. Thus, in attempting to sail between Scylla and Charybdis, a Judge is in danger of touching both.—*Judge D. O. Shattuck.*

311. IN TIMES of great public excitement, opinions of men on given subjects of duty, often change from one extreme to another; but, for all that, something is necessarily due in every country to the views of life and duty as they may prevail amongst men. Such opinions are presumed to be based upon what is believed, for the time, to correctly admeasure the duties of men, and to square their conduct with such duties. Often mistaken as public opinion is, time and the various events which supervene in the course of human conduct, furnish a corrective for such errors, and enable wrongs to be redressed not with too great suddenness, but rather with such deliberation and healthy progress as that great harm may not arise from roo rapid changes of public sentiment.—*Judge O. C. Pratt.*

312. THE MOST distinguished lawyers earned their proudest laurels in the battles in which they were obliged, in behalf of the liberties of the people, to war against the oppressions and tyranny of the Courts. The legal profession is also of all others fearless of public opinion. It is of all others candid and sympathetic. It has ever stood up against the tyranny of monarchs, on the one hand, and the tyranny of public opinion, on the other. And if as the humblest among them it becomes me to instance myself, I may say with

a bold heart—and I do say it with a bold heart—that there is not in all this world a wretch so humble, so guilty, so despairing, so torn with avenging furies, so pursued by the vengeance of the law, so hunted to cities of refuge, so fearful of life, so afraid of death—there is no wretch so deeply steeped in all the agonies of vice and misery and crime—that I would not have a heart to listen to his cry, and find a tongue to speak in his defence, though around his head all the fury of public opinion should gather and rage and roar and roll, as the ocean rolls around the rock. And if I ever forget, if I ever deny, that highest duty of my profession, may God palsy this arm and hush this voice forever.—*Gen. E. D. Baker.*

313. THE UNITY OF LAWS must be in some power behind them. All law is will; will, that is law, is one as the sun; law, many as the rays. As every ray is all sun, so every law is all will. If a stone fall to the earth, it falls by the act of some will. If sap rises in the tree, it does so by the act of some will. If heat is transformed into electricity, or electricity into heat, the correlation is the act of some will. Every manifestation in matter is the manifestation of supreme, unresisted will. In conduct, morality is the domination of superhuman will, and immorality the opposition of human to this superhuman will. It is therefore a law only unto itself, and so unto nothing, for by itself nothing is.

We find the same method of evolution in both physical and moral forces. If matter integrates and motion is dissipated, so in morals—ideas unify and agitation ceases. If heat is correlated into electricity, or the reverse, so in morals—the less of virtue, the more of vice. The method of correlation is as exact and inexorable in the one case as in the other. The same way indicates the same will.

Therefore, what we are accustomed to call the laws or facts of nature, are the omnipresent, perpetual lawmaking, the continuous willing, the living law, the unadjourned legislature of some supernal will. Essentially, nothing is fixed. All things exist in will, and will may change its manifestations. Will is eternal, and nothing abides apart from its decisions. In its unity is the unity of law. All opposing will is not law, but lawlessness—*Rev. Wm. H. Platt.*

THE COMMON AND CIVIL LAW CONTRASTED.

314. The Common Law is that system of jurisprudence which, deducing its origin from the traditionary customs and simple laws of the Saxons, becoming blended with many of the customs and laws of the Normans, enriched with the most valuable portions of the Civil Law, modified and enlarged by numerous Acts of the English Parliament, smoothed in its asperities and moulded into shape by a succession of as learned and wise and sagacious intellects as the world ever saw, has grown up, during the lapse of centuries, under

the reformed religion and enlightened philosophy and literature of England, and has come down to us, amended and improved by American Legislation, and adapted to the republican principles and energetic character of the American people. To that system the world is indebted for whatever it enjoys of free government, of political and religious liberty, of untrammeled legislation, and unbought administration of justice. To that system do we now owe the institution of trial by jury, and the privileges of the writ of Habeas Corpus, both equally unknown in the Civil Law. Under that system all the great branches of human industry—agriculture, commerce, and manufactures—enjoy equal protection and equal favor; and under that, less than under any scheme ever devised by the wisdom of man, has personal liberty been subject to the restrictions and assaults of prerogative and arbitrary power.

The Civil Law, on the other hand, is that system which, based upon the crude laws of a rough, fierce people, whose passion was war, and whose lust, conquest—received, in its progress through the various stages of civilization from barbarism to refinement, a variety of additions and alterations, from the Plebiscita of the Roman Plebeians, from the Senatus-consulta of the Roman Senate, from the decrees of Consuls and Tribunes, from the adjudications of praetors, from the responses of men learned in the law, and from the edicts and rescripts of the tyrants of Rome, until, in the early ages of Christianity, the whole chaotic mass was, by the order and under the patronage of the Emperor Justinian, systemized, reduced into form, and promulgated for observance by the Roman people, in the shape of four books called the Institutes, fifty books known as the Pandects, and certain additional edicts, designated as the Novels of Justinian. Thereafter, and until the final downfall of the Eastern Empire of Rome, the Justinian code furnished the guide for legal tribunals throughout the provinces subject to the Imperial sway, in all cases political, civil, and criminal, except so far as particular decisions were commanded, annulled, or modified by the will of despotic power. But, as, century after century, wave upon wave of Northern barbarism poured down on the effeminacy of Southern Europe, sparing in its course neither the intellectual nor the material monuments of civilization, the administration of Roman law was, in city after city, and province after province, gradually obliterated, at the same time, and to the same extent, that Roman power was crushed, and Roman institutions demolished. The whole system of Justinian was at length swept from the face of the earth, or buried in the recesses of cloisters, alike forgotten and unknown. In the twelfth century, however, a copy of it was accidentally discovered at Amalfi, in Italy; and, owing to the arbitrary nature of some of its provisions, as well as to the wisdom and excellence of its general features, it was seized upon with avidity by the clergy, as favorable to their spiritual authority, and by monarchs, as conducive to the support of their despotic power. It was at once taught in the schools, studied in the convents, sanctioned by kings, and commended by the Holy Father himself, who held the keys of heaven. In a few years it became the prevailing system of laws throughout most of that portion of Europe, in which the founder of Christianity was respected, and the saints and martyrs adored. Thus, as in earlier times, the fine arts, literature, philosophy, and graceful superstitions of Greece, had captivated the rude minds and softened the stern natures of the Roman people; so, centuries afterwards, the refined system of Roman jurisprudence overthrew the uncouth customs and ill-digested laws of it conquerors, and led captive kings and nobles, clergy and laity, in the progress of its triumphal procession. With the exception of England alone, the code of Justinian became engrafted upon the local institutions of each separate principality and kingdom, and constituted a general system of European law; but, neither the favor of kings, the denunciations of priests, nor even the fulminations from the Papal See itself, could induce the English barons, or the English Courts, or the English people, to receive it as a substitute for their own favorite and immemorial customs. At this early period, then, when the dawn of a new civilization was just beginning to burst upon the world, the kingdoms of Europe, though united in religious institutions, were divided in reverence for laws. That division has continued to the present day; and has also extended over the islands and continents, not then known, but since discovered and occupied. Wherever the English flag has been unfurled upon a savage or hostile shore, possession has been taken in the name of its sovereign, and in behalf of its laws; and upon whatever coast an English colony has been planted, there also have the colonists established the Common Law, and have ever afterwards clung to it as the birthright of themselves and their children, with a tenacity that no power, no suffering, no fear of danger, no hope of reward, could induce them to relax. In the same way has the Roman or Civil Law gone hand in hand with the extended dominion of the continental nations of Europe. Thus it happens that, at the present time, the whole christianized world is ruled by one system or the other. England, her colonies in all parts of the globe, and the United States, with the exception of Louisiana, adhere to the Common Law; whilst, excepting Russia and Turkey, the nations on the continent of Europe, Mexico, Guatamala, all the republics of South America, together with the Empire of Brazil, maintain the supremacy of the Civil Law, with certain restrictions, limitations and additions, necessary to adapt it to the peculiar organization of each particular State.

It would be a curious, if not an instructive subject of inquiry, were it possible to arrive at a satisfactory conclusion, to ascertain how far the intellectual and moral condition of the people of those countries in which the Civil Law prevails, has been produced by their legal system, and what influence the free principles and exact justice of the Common Law have exercised in developing the sturdy, sagacious, and self-relying spirit of the English and American people. To whatever cause it may be owing, it is nevertheless true, that with a few rare exceptions on either side, there is a strongly marked boundary between the domains of the respective systems. In the one, you perceive the activity, the throng, the tumult of business life—in the other, the stagnation of an inconsiderable and waning trade; in the one, the boldness, the impetuosity, the invention of advancing knowledge and civilization—in the other, feebleness of intellect, timidity of spirit, and the subserviency of slaves; in the one, the strength and freshness of manhood—in the other, the weakness of incipient decay. The one possesses a progressive and reforming nature—the other partakes of quietude and repose; the one is the genius of the present and the future—the other, the spirit of the past; the one is full of energetic and vigorous life—the other, replete with the memories of a by-gone and antiquated order of things.—*Judge Nathaniel Bennett.*

NATURE.

315. Every mountain upholds and supports the herbage on its slopes, and sends down rills to carry off soil to the vales and plains, while they feed herbage there. You cannot find a tree, or plant or flower, that lives for itself. The animal world breathes out gases for the vegetable kingdom, and then the vegetable world exhales or stores up some elements essential to animal health and vigor. The carbonic acid we breathe out here, and which is poison to us, blown eastward by our west winds, may be greedily taken up a few days hence, by vineyards on the slopes of the Sierra, and be returned to us in the sweetness of the grape. The equator sends greeting to the arctic zone by the warm gulf stream that flows near the polar coasts to soften

their winds. The poles return a colder stream, and add an embassy of icebergs, too, to temper the fierce heats. Selfishness is condemned by the still harmonies of the creation. Perfect order issues out of interwoven service.—*Thos. Starr King.*

816. RECOGNIZING the fact that his body is formed and composed of the same elements as the air, the grass, and the insensate stone, and having run its course, shall return to its original elements, man has always struggled in his beliefs, to connect his soul in its origin, nature, office, and end, with the universe it inhabits. Without arts or civilization, men made themselves a part of the universe. The glory of the heavens was theirs, with all their newness. Without knowledge they wandered entranced in peace, and wondered at the new creation. They saw they were subjected to the control of invisible forces, and their emotions became so strongly excited as to demand the deification of all those unseen powers, in forms which their own imaginations and passions suggested. Such was the origin of those forms of religious belief, which coming from the East, the birth place of man, still survive in the creeds of to-day. Nor does the soul manifest less eagerness in communion with nature now than in earlier times. Soiled with sin, we seek the forests and the mountains, and are made better by their influence. Cast to the earth by our enemy, mortified by our weakness and mistakes, we but touch the earth, and like Anteus, the earth-born, we rebound stronger than before. And if tired at last with contests that never

end, with efforts that seem fruitless for good, we retire to country homes, where nature delights us with all her sights and sounds, sweet is the odor of new-mown hay, the breath of cows, fair the broad brows of our oxen that never deceived us. Jocund is the song of birds, pleasant the rustling of leaves, the babble of waters; and if the thought obtrudes that the turf on which we lie is finally to cover us, we are glad to believe that while of the form that is ours there shall not remain one vestige, there shall still survive in grass and tree and flower, in forms of use and of supernal elegance and beauty, all that once was the habitation of an immortal soul.—*J. McM. Shafter.*

317. IT IS the glory of Nature that her laws dip into every part of the universe, making the oscillating planets keep time, the varying temperatures play into zones, and holding man as well as the planet and the pebble, and every state and empire as well as every man, in the coil of her great plan. The prophets long ago saw this, but now science with cooler breath begins to preach it.—*Thos. Starr King.*

318.—

THE PARABLES of Nature run
From the glow-worm to the sun;
There is no land, there is no speech
Nor language, but her voices teach
Therein a truth to every one;
And multitudinous tongues confess
The marvel of her fruitfulness.
—*Chas. Warren Stoddard.*

DEATH.

319. I doubt whether or not we should mourn for any of the dead. I am confident that there should be no mourning for those who render themselves up as sacrifices in any great, just and holy cause. It better becomes us to praise and dignify them.
—*Gen. Jas. A. McDougall.*

320. Do NOT weep for me, I *know* it's right. I wish I could make *you* feel so. I wish I could describe my feelings. They are strange! I feel all the privileges and greatness of the future. I see a great future before me. It already looks grand, beautiful. I am passing away fast. My feelings are strange.—*Dying words of Thos. Starr King.*

321. O, DEATH! How bitter are the memories of thee! How sudden thy coming. How uncertain thy time. How secret thine approaches. Sometimes thou knockest at the door, and sometimes thou comest in unannounced and unbidden. Nor does it grieve thee much to come at the very moment when thou canst most impede the vain designs of mortals. Thou keepest thy watch at the sick man's door, and thou dost flit through chambers lighted by dim tapers. In an hour, yea in a moment, thou dost scatter the labors of years. How dreadful is thy summons! how sharp thy trial! how stern thy judgment! how summary thine execution! And when thou hast levied upon thy victim and stripped him of all that he clung to, thou dost compel Nature to execute to thee a release! How universal is thy dominion. The powerful cannot resist, the wise know not how to evade thee. Thou dost cut off the expectations of heirs, thou dost break up the succession of kings. With thee there is no poverty, neither are there any riches with thee; for gold cannot purchase life. Thou art the sword that is never blunted, the bow before whose arrows all must fall. Thou sendest forth the plague, and whole kingdoms lie half unpeopled by thy ravages. Thou Liberator of prisoners! Thou Emancipator of him that is in bonds! Thou takest forth the precious from the vile, and the vile from the precious; and in this thy mouth is as the call of God. Thou art the inevitable visitor in every home. Thou fillest the world with widows and with orphans. Thou bringest together the beginning and the end of man's career with scarce an inch of time between. Luxury is thy helper, the wine cup is thine ally.

Under the painted face of faded beauty thou dost grin and chuckle; for no counterfeit of youth can deceive thee! and there thou dost make thine approaches confidently and securely.

Flattery courts thee in vain, and thou mockest at the pride of man. Remorseless monster! Thou art deaf alike to the pleading of friendship and the plaintive cry of love. When Art and Learning weep at the early grave of genius, thou standest by with folded arms, and leaning against thy cyprus tree thou dost smile and say, "The prey is mine." Thou dost breathe upon the tender grass and it is blasted. Thou drinkest the winds, thou poisonest the air. All things else have their increase and their decline; but thou O Death! art forever fixed and permanent in thine awful being. The plumed hearse is thy chariot, the coffin thy traveling trunk, Oblivion thine outrider; and far through visionary shades thou dost roam with ghosts, to view thine epitaphs and thy skulls. Reticent monarch! Thou makest us to die; but thou dost not tell us what it is to die; nor dost thou permit any to bring back from thy gloomy portals the mighty secrets that lie beyond. Grim tyrant! Thy carnival is the battle-field; Diseases, Massacres, Poison, Famine, are thy dread ministers. The whole earth is thy cruising ground. All that slumber in the sea belong to thee. All that lie in the innumerable graves are thine. And when they tell thee of a Great Deliverer —one who will sound a mighty trumpet in thy realms, take away thy keys, open thy doors and arouse thy sleepers—one whom thy power could not hold—one who burst thy bars asunder, shook off thy fetters, and rising from the tomb, tauntingly asked thee where was thy sting—one who will gather together all thy victims —yea every atom of dust which thou hast embezzled and hidden away, of all the souls which thou hast robbed of their tenements and scattered far and wide over the universe, making up for them bodies clothed with immortality—when they tell thee all this, thou dost laugh; and taking thy downward flight through space, thou standest at the gates of Hell and shakest thy keys!—*Geo. Barstow.*

322. ON MY RETURN to the island of Nantucket, after an eleven years' sojourn in California, as I was rambling among the familiar scenes, I strolled out upon the Mill Hills, and soon found myself treading among

the grassy mounds of the neighboring cemetery. There I came upon a simple shaft bearing this inscription upon one of its sides: "A teacher of youth." The literature of the tombstone deserves far more of the critic's analysis and of philosophic reflection than it has ever received. Each age, each nation, writes above its dead, not only its sorrows, but its religion, and the standard whether physical, intellectual or moral, by which it appreciates greatness. The tomb-stone is a wondrous tell-tale. What it tells of the dead, indeed is almost valueless, save to personal friends who need not its record. But what it tells of the living is invaluable to after times. Even the pompous, ill-merited epitaph, and the quaint, rude couplet, each bears a secret in its core concerning the living, and tells it to those who come after. The language of the tomb-stone is perhaps the tersest and most remarkable of all literature. In it is a world of meaning. In the catacombs of Rome, you shall read the inscription: "Atrox, O Fortuna, truci quæ funere caudes, quid mihi tam subito Maximus eripitur."

In that cry of the bereaved mother: "O, relentless fate, who delightest in cruel death, why so early is my Maximus torn from me?" you read all Roman Heathenism, hopeless and despairing. Turn to the other side of the gallery and there your eye shall rest upon the words, "Domiti in pace. Lea fecit." But, although the latinity of such may shock the cultivated eye in that straggling, misspelt scrawl, "My Domitius in peace, Lea erected this," you shall yet read all christianity with its hopes and consolations. Between those two epitaphs, which almost jostle each other in the catacombs, is the wide religious gulf which separates Cæsar and Nero from St. John and St. Chrysostom. To the eye of the modern wayfarer, perchance, as he leans against some cemetery fence, a stone will present itself bearing only the words, "Our little Kate." How short in phrase, but how multiplex in suggestion. Whose little Kate? No matter. It is enough that *they* know. But bound up in those three sweet words is the record of all her prattling childhood, with its merry romps and ringing laugh; they tell the pondering wayfarer of the staircase where she trod, of the chamber where she slept, of the days and nights of her sickness, of the alternating fears and hopes, of the funeral, and then afterwards of the playthings and the little folded dresses and the desolate room that break the very heart—all the sweet memories written out in those three short words, "Our little Kate." Ah! the white leaves with which the hand of affliction has strewn our cemeteries contain a marvel of thought and suggestion.—*Rev. F. C. Ewer.*

323.—

O, DEATH! Mysterious power!
Thou stern apostle in whose presence dread
My soul hath cowered like a frightened child—
Do I behold thee now, at last, aright?
Lo, on thy brow the stamp of majesty
Now seems impressed; and from thy sunken eye
There gleams perennial promise for our race,
While inspiration burns thy hollow cheek!

Thou art God's minister,
And dost but execute His sovereign will.
Thou canst not then be evil; and thou dost
Deserve, as little as thou heedest, human hate.
Thy mission is, to sap colossal pride,
To turn us from our butterfly pursuits,
To teach us what we are, and how to live
Both here and in a world where thou art not.

Sweet thought that strengthens Faith!—
That harbinger of immortality,
Of tireless and illimitable flight!
Soaring with golden plumes and speaking eye
Above the weeping willows of the heart—
'Tis thine to point the jaded soul to God,
And lift it up on thy triumphant wings
Into the radiant realm of perfect Day!
—*Oscar T. Shuck.*

324.—On a pressed flower.

A simple, little flower,
Born of the sun and shower,
Unfolded slowly;

Poor blossom! but to lie
So colorless and dry—
Forgotten wholly.
—*G. C. Hurlbut.*

A FAREWELL TO SYRIA.

325. It was upon a bright and sunny afternoon that we loaded our trunks and carpet-bags upon the

backs of a dozen lusty Beirutan porters and followed them down to the custom-house of that city. The *Archduchess Carlotta*, the same steamer in which, a month before, we had left Alexandria for Syria, lay rolling gently in the waves of St. George's Bay, only waiting for our little party to sail away from Cyprus. In half an hour we had got through with the last of Syrian officials, public and private, and were standing upon the quarter-deck of the little Austrian steamer, stancher and sounder, we hoped, than her unfortunate patron at Miramar. Beyrout had never seemed so lovely; her harbor so graceful, her shores so inviting, as at this, the moment we were to take leave of them forever. It seemed as if old Lebanon himself leaned over toward the pure waters of the bay, almost nodding his snow-crested head in final adieu, while the mulberry groves upon his venerable sides gently waved their dark green foliage, as if in solemn warning to us that we should look upon their beauties no more. It is a sad thing to feel that you are looking for the last time upon any material object. The dying man bids his attendant raise him up and to open the window. "Let me look out once more at the glorious sun, the green fields, and the running brook, for I shall see them no more. Now, lay me down and shut the window." It is done, and he sails away. We are all either dying men or dying women, or are children who have come into this beautiful world with the seed of disease which carries us away from the bright landscape, the beautiful bay, or the lofty mountain, and which is sure to shut the window upon us, in a few brief days or years at the most.

Farewell, Syria! Thy mountains and streams, thy beautiful cities and pleasant groves; the land of Abraham, of Isaac and of Jacob—the birthplace of the worship of the living God, where Christ lived and died for man-kind—a long farewell!

A tremor passes through the bones of the *Archduchess*, a splashing is heard over the side, the pure waters are cloven asunder at the prow, and pass away in foam at the stern. The huge mountain straightens up in his seat and sinks back into the fading horizon; the groves of mulberry cease waving their adieus, and retire. They are shutting the window.—*John F. Swift.*

326.—ON RECROSSING THE ROCKY MOUNTAINS AFTER MANY YEARS.

Long years ago I wandered here
In the mid-Summer of the year—
   Life's Summer too;
A score of horsemen here we rode,
The mountain world its glories showed,
   All fair to view.

These scenes in glowing colors drest,
Mirrored the life within my breast,
   Its world of hope;
The whispering woods and fragrant breeze
That stirred the grass in verdant seas
   On billowy slope;

And glistening crag in sunlit sky,
Mid snowy clouds piled mountain high,
   Were joys to me;

My path was o'er the praries wide,
Or here on grander mountain-side,
    To choose, all free.

The rose that waved in morning air,
And spread its dewy fragrance there
    In careless bloom,
Gave to my heart its ruddiest hue,
O'er my glad life its colors threw
    And sweet perfume.

Now changed the scene and changed the eyes
That here once looked on glowing skies,
    Where Summer smiled;
These riven trees and wind-swept plain
Now show the Winter's dread domain,
    Its fury wild.

The rocks rise black from storm-packed snow,
All checked the river's pleasant flow,
    Vanished the bloom;
These dreary wastes of frozen plain
Reflect my bosom's life again,
    Now lonesome gloom.

The buoyant hopes and busy life
Have ended all in hateful strife,
    And thwarted aim.
The world's rude contact killed the rose,
No more its radiant color shows
    False roads to fame.

Backward, amidst the twilight glow
Some lingering spots yet brightly show.

On hard roads won,
Where still some grand peaks mark the way
Touched by the light of parting day
And memory's sun.

But here thick clouds the mountains hide,
The dim horizon bleak and wide
No pathway shows,
And rising gusts and darkening sky
Tell of "the night that cometh" nigh,
The brief day's close.
—*Gen. John C. Fremont.*

THE COMET OF 1858.

327. If to-night, you will look out from the glare of your illuminated city into the northwestern heavens, you will perceive, low down on the edge of the horizon, a bright stranger pursuing its path across the sky. [Atlantic Cable Oration, San Francisco, September 27, 1858.—EDITOR.] Amid the starry hosts that keep their watch, it shines, attended by a brighter pomp and followed by a broader train. No living man has gazed upon its splendors before. No watchful votary of science has traced its course for nearly ten generations. It is more than three hundred years since its approach was visible from our planet. When last it came it startled an Emperor on his throne; and while the superstition of his age taught him to perceive in its presence a herald and a doom, his pride saw in its flaming course and fiery train, the announcement that his own light was about to be extinguished. In common with the lowest of his subjects, he read omens of destruction in the baleful heavens, and prepared himself for a fate which alike awaits the mightiest and the meanest. Thanks to the present condition of scientific knowledge we read the heavens with a far clearer perception. We see in the predicted return of the rushing, blazing comet through the sky, the march of a heavenly messenger along its appointed way and around its predestined orbit. For three hundred years he has traveled amid the regions of infinite space. "Lone, wandering, but not lost," he has left behind him shining suns, blazing stars, and gleaming constellations, now nearer the eternal throne, and again on the confines of the universe. He returns with visage radiant and benign; he returns with unimpeded march and unobstructed way; he returns, the majestic, swift, electric telegraph of the Almighty, bearing upon his flaming front the tidings that throughout the universe there is still peace and order; that, amid the immeasurable dominions of the Great King, His rule is still perfect; that suns and stars and systems tread their endless circle and obey the eternal law.—*Gen. E. D. Baker.*

THE MIST.

328.—

I watched the folding of a soft, white-wing
    Above the city's heart—
I saw the mist its silent shadow fling

O'er thronged and busy mart—
Softly it glided through the Golden Gate,
    And up the shining Bay—
Calmly it lingered on the hills to wait
    The dying of the day.
Like the white ashes of the sunset fire
    It lay within the West,
Then onward crept, above the lofty spire
    In nimbus-wreaths to rest.
It spread anon—its fleecy clouds unrolled
    And floated gently down.
And thus I saw that silent wing enfold
    The Babel-throated town.
A spell was laid on restless strife and din,
    That bade its tumult cease—
A veil was flung o'er squalor, woe, and sin,
    Of purity and peace;
And dreaming hearts, so hallowed by the mist,
    So freed from grosser leaven,
In the soft chime of vesper-bells could list
    Sweet, echoed tones of Heaven;
Could see, enraptured, when the starlight came,
    With lustre soft and pale,
A sacred city, crowned with "ring of flame,"
    Beneath her misty veil.
                —*Miss H. M. Skidmore.*

THE NORTH WIND.

329.—
All night, beneath the flashing hosts of stars,
The North poured forth the passion of its soul

In mighty longings for the tawny South,
Sleeping afar among her orange-blossoms.
All night, through the deep canyon's organ-pipes,
Swept down the grand orchestral harmonies
Tumultuous, till the hills's rock buttresses
Trembled in unison.

     The sun has risen,
But still the storming sea of air beats on,
And o'er the broad green slopes a flood of light
Comes streaming through the heavens like wind,
Till every leaf and twig becomes a lyre,
And thrills with vibrant splendor.

       Down the bay
The furrowed blue, save that 'tis starred with foam,
Is bare and empty as the sky of clouds;
For all the little sails, that yesterday
Flocked past the islands, now have furled their wings,
And huddle frightened at the wharves—just as,
A moment since, a flock of twittering birds
Whirled through the almond trees like scattered leaves,
And hid beyond the hedge.

     How the old oaks
Stand stiffly to it, and wrestle with the storm!
While the tall eucalyptus' plumy tops
Tumble and toss and stream with quivering light.
Hark! when it lulls a moment on the ear.
The fir-trees sing their sea-song—now again
The roar is all about us like a flood;
And like a flood the fierce light shines, and burns
Away all distance, till the far blue ridge,

That rims the ocean, rises close at hand,
And high, Prometheus-like, great Tamalpais
Lifts proudly his grand front, and bears his scar,
Heaven's scathe of wrath, defiant like a god.

I thank thee, glorious wind! Thou bringest me
Something that breathes of mountain crags and pines;
Yea, more—from the unsullied, farthest North,
Where crashing icebergs jar like thunder-shocks,
And midnight splendors wave and fade and flame,
Thou bring'st a keen, fierce joy. So wilt thou help
The soul to rise in strength, as some great wave
Leaps forth, and shouts, and lifts the ocean-foam,
And rides exultant round the shining world.
—*E. R. Sill.*

WOMAN.

330. William H. Seward, upon his return from his journey round the world, said, "There are, in all the East, no homes." What a commentary upon the state of society in the oldest lands! No homes! Because woman is degraded and enslaved. No homes! Because both religions and governments studiously and systematically keep mothers and daughters in the darkness of ignorance.—*Rev. W. E. Ijams.*

331. MANY A WOMAN who, as a belle, was a triumphant success, as a wife and mother is a pitiable failure. Her nominal value is what she passes for on the promenade; but her intrinsic worth is measured by the beauty

and excellence of her home-life—by what she adds to
the wealth and glory of humanity. The mere act of
accepting wifehood should be equivalent to the most
solemn vows; and no wife can hope to preserve full
empire over the heart of a true husband whose desires
and longings are forever reaching outside the blessed
atmosphere of home; who does not possess, in some
measure, a character the keystone of which is that
whereon motherhood has its foundation—self-sacrifice.
Happy the man, whatever his ungracious fortune, who,
amid the fretting and distracting din of the wearisome
day, is forever catching the echoes of home-harmonies,
awaiting him just a little ahead, in the twilight. Such
melodies are never voiced by women who forsake the
pole-star of duty that they may chase the *ignis-fatuus*
of Pleasure.—*Sarah B. Cooper.*

332. THE HISTORY of civilization, nay of Christianity, has been marked by the removing, one after
another, of the shackles which an early and dark, not
to say a savage period of our race, heaped upon woman.
And if there be a fact as certain as that when the faint
streaks of dawn mark the East the day is about to
break, it is the fact that this great nation will sooner or
later rise and lift woman to the double throne (not, indeed of art and literature, for she sits there now) but
of science, of philosophy, of oratory, of religion, and of
politics. The subjects presented by Providence for
man's investigation and knowledge are many-sided.
The angle at which woman looks upon subjects is different from the angle at which they appear to the vision

of man. For a complete knowledge, therefore, in the realms of science, philosophy, religion, politics, which man alone cannot attain to, fixed as he is by heaven at the masculine angle of vision, man needs, and will eventually demand and have the indispensable and unshackled aid of woman. Woman is the purifying element of our social life.—*Rev. F. C. Ewer.*

333. MORE THAN railroads and telegraphs, more than the subtile connections of commerce and literature, woman is spinning the delicate threads that are to bind the English-speaking people together and blend their hearts in sympathy and love. *Duty*, not *glory*, is the corner-stone of the Anglo-Saxon creed, and from the homes in three continents which rest on this foundation, rises the arch of promise which spans alike the stormy and the peaceful sea, and braids into bright and uplifted characters the noblest hopes of mankind. And if, amidst the teeming civilization of the present day, when in a thousand organized forms, the strength of low ambition and unscrupulous wealth is felt, liberty and virtue are not to be parted; if statesmen are to rise above the mists and obscurities of a narrow patriotism or a passionate revenge to the serene hights of wisdom and honor; if peace is to shed over all distracted lands its mild light and its perfumed warmth; if religion is to cleanse its garments of dogmatism and intolerance, and walk among men in the "beauty of holiness;" to the moulding influence of woman, more than to all other earthly causes, will these mighty results be due. In woman, in the perfection of her attributes and of her

power, imagination and fact are but the faithful reflections of each other. The earnest Ruth, gleaning in the fields of Boaz; Mary, dropping repentant tears upon the Master's feet; Priscilla, exhibiting to the red Savages the stern beauty of a Puritan enthusiast; the lovelorn Evangeline, listening to the mysterious undertone of the trackless ocean; the twin sisters of mercy in England and America, soothing pain and anguish in prisons and hospitals and asylums, and even on the tented field, awakening contrition in the heart of guilt, and lifting the black curtain between despair and peace —all these are types and illustrations of character which shall form the loftiest themes of poetry and song, till the records of time shall close. No marvel that to man—furrowed and hardened by the toil and the pain of life—down through the weary years, floats the sweet music of a woman's voice, returns the dewy brightness of her glance, and charms away selfishness and vice. No marvel that the dying soldier kisses a woman's shadow on his pillow. No marvel that our holiest feelings stir as, with one mind and one heart, we give our highest honors to the name of woman.—*Henry E. Highton.*

334. THERE IS a great amount of genuine satisfaction in freely acknowledging the real empire which woman holds over our hearts and minds, our thoughts and actions, our motives, hopes and ambitions, and (I may add, I trust, without offense) our pockets. None of us, I think, will deny her right to love us and be loved in return, (indeed we take no small delight in

having her exercise that prerogative in our individual cases)—or her right to wheedle and caress us, and to draw as well upon our affections as upon our bank accounts; to be sheltered and protected by us, and yet, in her own insidious, charming way, to rule and govern us just as autocratically as she pleases, as long as she sways the scepter of a true woman, and does not so far forget herself as to become transformed into a sort of moral hybrid, with a perverted ambition to enter upon the hard, and to her, degrading duties of man's sphere (for which her tender and susceptible nature so entirely unfits her,) impatient of wearing the modest but captivating drapery, both of mind and person, that are native to her; for she is as misplaced in the more masculine habits and attire as would be the Capitoline Venus in the heavy armor of Achilles. There are servitudes more delightful than the wielding of power; and the homage we pay to the soft sway of woman, which finds its strength in her very weakness, is one of these. It is a delight to serve, when that service is, as we flatter ourselves, a protection.

The great mastiff is gentle and obedient to the control of a child, and the strongest man is easily conquered and taken captive by the charming little ways of the weakest woman. But she must be a woman. Herein lies the singular power and sway of that great and noble sovereign, the anniversary of whose natal day we celebrate. [Queen Victoria—EDITOR.] We delight to honor her. We yield her spontaneous respect through the compelling power of her womanly virtues. We yield the same obedience, the same love, the same respect to every true woman. Our hearts turn toward them for sympathy and encouragement in our griefs and trials, for a shared, and thereby increased joy in our success, for those high impulses and truer aspirations, which her purer and more delicately organized nature can alone afford us, and which have power to save us, from utter submersion in the sordid cares and bitter struggles of every-day life.

> "O, woman! lovely woman! nature made you
> To temper man; we had been brutes without you.
> Angels are painted fair to look like you.
> There's in you all that we believe of heaven—
> Amazing brightness, purity and truth,
> Eternal joy, and everlasting love."

—William Hayes.

335. DELILAH.—

[On seeing Mr. Story's beautiful Statue, the property of Mrs. Shillaber, of San Francisco.]

I see thy traitor face, thy dimpled arms,
Thy downcast head and snowy bosom's charms,
  Fair false Philistine maid.
And the cold marble seems to throb and glow
With life's hot blood, the pulse to come and go
  Along each chisel'd vein.

I hear thee say, "Come sleep upon my knees,
My lion-hearted Nazarite—take thine ease;
  My love shall guard thee well.
I fain would sing to thee a Sorek air,
And comb the tangles of thy tawny hair—
  My Samson, rest thee here."

"Thy strength a thousand men could not withstand,
Nor Gaza's brazen gates thy God-like hand;
   Whence cometh it, my love?"
I see thee stoop to kiss his drowsy brow
And bend thee low to catch his secret, now
   I see thy false, false smile.

Call in thy people, let them shout for joy,
For at thy feet lies all his Strength: a boy—
   A child may bind him now.
Aye draw thy mantle—hang thy head for Shame,
Clutch tight thy gold and bear a wanton's name,
   Fair, frail Philistine girl.
      —*Charles F. Craddock.*

THE IRISH RACE.

336. History tells us that nations are subject to the universal law of decay. The shores of time are strewed with the wrecks of empires. Not only does the outward structure of government disappear, but the living pillars of the edifice—the people—fall, never to rise again. Some kingdoms perish through inherent weakness, others from conflict with a stronger power. When an exception to this apparently unrelenting law is found; when an ancient nation presents itself which has never felt the breath of decay, but exhibits the same vitality, energy, and power that it displayed centuries ago, it is a cause of astonishment to the historian and of delight to him who can call such a nation his own. It has been said that the greatness of a country may be traced in the monuments of past ages. Is it not wonderful to behold a race which refuses to be judged by its architectural wonders alone, but raising aloft its voice, exclaims: "Study not the inscription on my ruins. Behold me in the bloom of youth; the glow of health is on my cheek, the sparkle in my eye. I am not aged though my name is found among the oldest nations of the earth. In years gone by I ranked with the first; but fate robbed me of my high position, and abandoned me to my conquerors. Crushed under the heel of oppression my body was apparently dead, but my spirit, the spirit of nationality lived, and now lives, to cheer, to animate, to enrapture my children's hearts."

What must constitute a nation? There must be something that lies deeper than the mere form of government. This alone cannot suffice. God forbid that it should. No! a national soul must exist. The race must have a history, genius, character.

Have the Irish genius?—that wondrous power which, disdaining the limit of cold words, seeks the magnetism of hearts—which, led by science, has swept along the silvery stars and outshone the fiery meteor in brilliancy —which has filled nations with an ardent desire to gaze on Freedom's face and receive from her divine hands the charters of their liberties—which gives to art its inspiration, to poetry its feeling, to eloquence its fire, to war its dazzling radiance—which, springing from the head of the Omnipotent, partaking of His glory, gilds with its golden beams the universe and knows no limit but eternity. Yes! the Irish have been blessed with this wondrous gift.

Whether it sparkles forth in the bright wit that all the people of that race possess; or it be shown in the achievements of the great and glorious past by its bards, its brehons, its warriors, or its saints; or in modern times by a Burke, leading the van in statesmanship, or by a Sheridan, pleading the cause of an oppressed nation with sublime eloquence, and astonishing the world by his varied powers, or by a Grattan in the Senate, or by a Curran at the bar, pouring forth in burning words Erin's protest against tyranny; or by a Goldsmith, a Moore, a Davis, a McCarthy, touching the heart by their poetry and crowning their own Green Isle with the laurels of song; or by a Barry, a Maclise, a Hogan, a Foley, drawing down the fire of Heaven, and imparting the breath of life to the canvas, marble, or bronze; or by a Balfe, a Wallace, bringing back the clustering memories of the bards of old by their musical skill—the verdict of the admiring world is and will be that wherever, and in whatever capacity they are found, the children of Erin are the children of Genius.

The three great features of Irish character are religious enthusiasm, love of country, and lightness of heart. In the gloom of the past this trinity of qualities supported the heroic people through the most blood-curdling tyranny that the pen of history has ever recorded. Confiscation robbed them of their land in the name of justice, penal statutes struck at their conscience and their liberty in the name of law; gaunt famine preyed upon their hearts in the guise of political econ-

omy. All these horrors were born of British hate and British rule. But suffering could not deprive the Irish people of their noble attributes. Three hundred years of continued persecution have failed to shake their faith in the creed that Patrick gave them. That religion still remains as the record of their endurance, and the adamant of their hopes. It is more august, more inspiring, loftier, and more thrilling in its memories than any monument of antiquity, for its foundation is divine and its superstructure is cemented by a people's blood.
—*Francis J. Sullivan.*

337. CHRISTMAS—
O, winds that blow
From palmy isles, or realms of snow,
  Be still!
O, waves that roll,
In majesty from pole to pole,
  Be still!
O sea, no more
With vain complaining vex the shore;
  Be still!
Peace, peace to winds, and waves and sea,
God's peace for all eternity!

Lo! wise men bring
From the rich East their offering
  To Judah's king!
And at his feet,
With precious gifts and odors sweet,
  Fall worshipping.

O, stars that gleam
From bending skies, on Jordan's stream,
   Together sing—
Peace, peace, God's peace on land and sea,
Good will to men eternally!

Chas. F. Craddock.

GENIUS.

338. How often do we find all the conditions of good writing fulfilled, yet the net result, weakness. The beam of sunlight has, besides the seven rays into which the prism untwists it, another, the actinic ray, the very soul of the beam, which glides unbent through the prism. Something more than the bare truth is needed to make words impressive; there must be the vivifying vigor shed into them from the man behind. It is not enough to have truth stored in the reservoirs of memory, where it can be pumped out for occasion. It must come first-hand from the soul, or it is powerless. Substances, when burned, develop just so much heat as is latent in them—just so much as they sucked from the sun at their creation. So the opinions and sentiments of different men exert force according to the degree in which they have been organized into their natures. Is there anything more dreary than to hear truth chattered to us, spirted out from behind the teeth of persons who do not possess it? In many, truth lies like the candle in the boy's pumpkin-lantern on autumn evenings. When an idea gets into their head, they pumpkin-lanternize it, and make the truth, like themselves, a bore. The secret of eloquence is to be found in this vitalizing power, and the same language uttered by men who believe and feel what they are saying, and by men who do not feel it, differs as a tree pictured in mosaic does from a tree that has grown. It was not so much the clearness of Webster's thoughts as the ponderous substance and swing of his whole constitution that made his words come down like trip-hammers. When he said, "There is Lexington, there is Concord, there is Bunker Hill," it was not the simple words that made them memorable, but that his hearers felt there was a storm of feeling entangled and swept down with them. The great thing is, not to get strong things said, but to get the man big enough to say them. The same sentence uttered by one man is a mere wreath of breath—by another, a hurricane. Notes of hand are as easily and as prettily written by a pauper as by a Crœsus, but their power to draw the bullion depends very much on the name you get subscribed.

—*Thos. Starr King.*

389. THE SUPPLY of genius is all ordered by an immutable law. What have all our Presidents since Washington done, compared with the man who first organized the possibility of a telegraph?—with him who devised the cotton-gin?—with him who saw in imagination the steamships wrestling with the Atlantic, and who demonstrated that his vision could be copied into actual steam and steel? What a land ours would be if our will and our votes could as wisely and as

surely move the right men into the right places, as nature provides for the succession in the hierarchy of science—as she orders the great thinkers to go to their own places, though so widely apart in the crowds of common men—Moses to his post when the Prince of legislators was wanted, Washington to his when so much patriotism and prudence and commanding ability were in demand! The rule is inflexible that every century will produce its two or three great thinkers. Society is cared for by a power that will not leave civilization to be wasted, nor the rivers of our better life to stagnate.—*Thos. Starr King.*

OVER THE HILL.

840.—

I.

MARGUERITE (musing.)

Three times over, four-leafed clover
Promised me a noble lover;
Daisy-leaf and apple-seed
With the oracle agreed;
And the omen did not alter,
Tested by the holy psalter.
Will he come from East or West?
Will he know and love me best,
Though I wear a homespun gown,
And my hands be rough and brown?
Will he see that I am not

Suited to this humble lot,
But have loveliness to grace
Anywhere a lady's place?

Golden bees and butterflies
Ranging under other skies,
Have you seen my lover there—
Did you know him, brave and fair?
Said he when he came this way—
In a year, or in a day?
When again you sip the flowers
Round that future home of ours,
Tell him he will find me leal,
Sitting by my spinning wheel,
Watching o'er the mountain rim,
Keeping all my love for him,
Holding being in suspense
Till he come to take me hence.

II.

MOTHER.

Fie, child! here you are again, idle and sighing,
And gazing away with a lackaday stare;
Go call back your fancies and set your wheel flying,
For while you go dreaming, the children go bare.

MARGUERITE.

O, mother! if you could have done with your fretting,
And close down your eyelids, or look far away,
And see,—as I see myself,—stitching and netting
With fair dames—yet somehow I fairer than they;

Embroidering and tambouring, braiding, and quilting,
While soft sounds and odors steal into the hall,
And out through the lattice we see the knights tilting
For favor of beauty—my favor of all;

You would know how it is my spindle stops turning,
That my purpose fades out and my fingers grow still,
While my eyes steal away with unspeakable yearning
To welcome the visions from over the hill.

MOTHER.

From over the hill! ay, from over and over
The hills, since the world had a hill and a girl!
To all of our spinning there comes a high lover,
To most of our choosing there comes but a churl.

MARGUERITE.

Ah! no churl for me, mother, though I die lonely;
For I was not formed for a fate like the rest;
The omens have told me my knight, and him only,
Shall ever be crowned as the lord of this breast.

And why, if he never will come, should he seem to be
Always about to come over the hill?
Or why, if he never will come, should I dream to be
Always so fain and so certain he will?

MOTHER.

Poor child! you are blowing a dangerous bubble;
Your mother and wheel are your truest friends still;

If they bring you less joy, they will leave you less
    trouble,
But your Knight will fetch sorrow from over the hill.

III.

MARGUERITE (singing to her babe.)

Have the elves disturbed your sleep?
Come, my baby, laugh and leap;
Let me by the armful measure
All the vastness of my treasure.
If you knew your story, Pet,
Would you clasp and love me yet?
If I always o'er you stood,
Bountiful of motherhood,
Would it matter anything
That I lacked a wedding-ring?
O, my beautiful—my jewel!
I was feeble, he was cruel;
His the baseness, mine the blame,
Baby, baby, yours the shame!

Clasp me, beauty, hug and press;
Will you ever love me less?
Better, howsoe'er it grieve us,
Bury love than see it leave us.
I could lay you low, Mignon,
Knowing you were all my own,
With a less reluctant heart
Than to watch your love depart,
Following from out my day

Footsteps that have died away.
O, my beautiful—my jewel!
I was feeble, he was cruel;
His the baseness, mine the blame,
Baby, baby, yours the shame!

Kiss me darling, clasp me tight,
Strain with all your baby might;
Something fond my nature misses,
Yearns for love and gentle kisses.
There! and there! and there, Petite!
But your lips are pure and sweet!
Grant that mine be dead and gone
Ere yours lisp a baby tone;
They would surely "Papa" call;
I must say—if say at all—
O, my beautiful—my jewel!
I was feeble, he was cruel;
His the baseness, mine the blame,
Baby, baby, yours the shame!

—*Joseph T. Goodman.*

341. THOUGHT.—It is true that cities and kingdoms die, but the eternal thought lives on. Great thought, incorporate with great action, does not die, but lives a universal life, and its power is felt vibrating through all spirit and throughout all ages.—*Gen. Jas. A. McDougall.*

342. THE HIGHEST GIFT OF MIND.—The gift of expression, though not the highest, is next to the high-

est gift. I conceive that the very highest gift of mind, and that which most contributes to the progress of mankind, is the gift of invention. Next comes the gift of expression, which can take the new thought and introduce it to the world, notwithstanding the prepossessions and hostility of conservatism. Here is the magic influence of eloquence. The man of commanding and universal influence is a man of a very high order of mind. He is born king among men.—*Rev. W. E. Ijams.*

343. Personal Power.—In the absence of a quality, material or acquired, there is always compensation, if not complete, at least partial. Public speaking is an art which I have often coveted. To hold in rapt attention a thousand listeners whose presence and sympathy should feed fires radiating in dazzling conceits, is a fascination often arising before the student of ardent longings, and most vividly of all in the mind of him in whom such talents are lamentably absent. Yet the rule is, to which I know there are exceptions, that the brilliant speaker is seldom the best scholar or the most profound thinker.

It is told of the vocalist, Lablache, that by facial expression he could represent a thunder-storm, in a most remarkable manner. The gloom which overshadowed the face, as clouds the sky, deepened into darkness, then lowered as an angry tempest. Lightning flashed from the winking eye, twitching the muscles of the face and mouth, and thunder shook the head. Finally the storm died away and the returning sun illumined the features, and wreathed the face in smiles.

Sensitive as is the actor to the sympathy or indifference of his audience, the author is but little behind him. To talk or to write without being able to command the attention of the listener or reader, would stop the mouth and dry the pen about as quickly as anything.

There is something irresistible in the tone and manner of an eloquent speaker; likewise in the glowing thoughts of a graceful writer—as in meeting a stranger, we are at first attracted by the dress and polish which conceal character, rather than by qualities of the head and heart of which we know nothing. But since science now so often strips from the shell of things their soft and comely covering, history is no longer willing to sacrifice life for meat, or the body for raiment.
—*Hubert H. Bancroft.*

344. Epigrams.

If every Jack should mate his Jill,
What gills of Jacks this world would fill.

A dangerous rock is intellect,
On which the wisest oft are wrecked.

Nature from many a rough-hewn log
Has made a rougher pedagogue.

A man who's leaner than a hawk
Often contains a ton of talk.

Nothing in nature is so dense
As what is known as common sense.

Times are so hard—so Stubbs confesses—
He cannot now pay his addresses.

Of Jockeys Adam was the first—
This fact is vouched by pundits, versed
In lore historic—him they place
As Father of the Human Race!

Love, like a sausage, always needs
From him or her who on it feeds—
What is of utmost consequence
To its enjoyment—confidence.

Though Wisdom mankind lightly prize
They rarely fail to idolize
A downright fool, when, richly rolled
Like Israel's calf, he shines in gold.

Beware of what is called a prude;
Peaches are bad when over-good.

Position does not merit show;
The largest birds oft nestle low;
While tiny insects rest so high
They're unseen by the keenest eye.

—*Hector A. Stuart.*

348. ORGANIZATION.—An organization is far greater than an idea, for a principle is always connected with it; but it is a corporeal idea—a principle in action. And what is grander in the domain of awful effects? Until thus clothed, an idea is powerless, and bears about the same analogy to its active operations as does a shadowy ghost to a sturdy man.

A crystalized gem is the most attractive form of solid matter, because more thought and skill are expended in its structure than in any other stony combination of atoms. A flower is of a higher order of charm, for more various and more subtle elements are wrought into its composite loveliness; and then the provisions for the growth and support of the flower affect us more profoundly still—the mixture of the air, the various powers hidden in the sun ray, the alternation of day-light and gloom, the laws of evaporation and of clouds, and the currents in the air that carry moisture from zone to zone for the nutriment of vegetation. We soon find in nature that no element or force exists unrelated. It is in harness with other elements, for a common labor, and an interchange of service for a common end. Organization is the idea which science impresses upon us as the secret of life, health, power, and beauty in her realm. But the great glory of organization is when it is revealed in human life. The highest structure of the creative art is the body of man, representing in its complexity and the friendly partnership of its powers, the system and co-ordination which society should attain; and it is a marked epoch in history when a new movement is made which succeeds in organizing men, widely and permanently, for noble and beneficent ends.

Thos. Starr King.

346. HISTORY.—History is a magician's bottle out of which we can pour any kind of wine the human appetite craves. Sophocles pictured humanity as it ought to be. Euripides as it was. Thucydides wrote down democracy; Tacitus, imperialism. Was either of them true to the interests of the opposite side? Would they not have been accounted by their respective parties traitor-

ous fools had they been wholly impartial, and would not their names and works have soon perished in consequence? Macaulay looks upon the ills of the English poor two centuries back; Cobbett and Hallam dwell more upon their comforts. Read one and you would imagine them the most unhappy of mortals; read the others and you would think how much happier they were then than now. To the character of Philip II, Prescott applies the words, bigoted, perfidious, suspicious, cruel, which were enough even for so powerful a prince; but when Motley adds to these the terms, pedant, and idiot, one begins to wonder how such a driveller was able to manage his estate of half a world so long and so well.—*Hubert H. Bancroft.*

THE STUDY OF MANKIND.

347. The tendency of philosophic inquiry is more and more toward the origin of things. In the earlier stages of intellectual impulse the mind is almost wholly absorbed in ministering to the necessities of the present; next, the mysterious uncertainty of the after life provokes inquiry, and contemplations of an eternity of the future command attention; but not until knowledge is well advanced does it appear that there is likewise an eternity of the past worthy of careful scrutiny—without which scrutiny, indeed, the eternity of the future must forever remain a sealed book. Standing, as we do, between these two eternities, our view limited to a narrow though gradually widening horizon, as nature unveils her mysteries to our inquiries, an infinity spreads out in either direction, an infinity of minuteness no less than an infinity of immensity; for hitherto attempts to reach the ultimate of molecules have proved as futile as attempts to reach the ultimate of masses. Now man, the noblest work of creation, the only reasoning creature, standing alone in the midst of this vast sea of undiscovered truth—ultimate knowledge ever receding from his grasp, primal causes only thrown farther back as proximate problems are solved—man, in the study of mankind, must follow his researches in both of these directions, backward as well as forward, must indeed derive his whole knowledge of what man is and will be, from what he has been. Thus it is that the study of mankind, in its minuteness, assumes the grandest proportions. Viewed in this light there is not a feature of primitive humanity without significance; there is not a custom or characteristic of savage nations, however mean or revolting to us, from which important lessons may not be drawn. It is only from the study of barbarous and partially cultivated nations that we are able to comprehend man as a progressive being, and to recognize the successive stages through which our savage ancestors have passed on their way to civilization. With the natural philosopher there is little thought as to the relative importance of the manifold works of creation. The tiny insect is no less an object of his patient scrutiny than the wonderful and complex machinery of the cosmos. The lower races of men, in the study of humanity, he deems of as essential importance as the higher; our present higher races being but the lower types of generations yet to come.—*Hubert H. Bancroft.*

THE PIONEER.

348. The gallant Pioneer! He is the noblest type of American manhood, for he has

> "Honor and courage;
> Qualities that eagle-plume men's souls
> And fit them for the sun."

He climbs like a huge fly upon the bald skull of some lofty mountain, and the primeval hills welcome his daring footsteps. He taps with the prospector's pick at the adamantine doors of the earth's treasure chambers, and at his demand they reveal their shining secrets. His glittering ax lays low the green-plumed forest monarch, and on the surface of the emerald-hued prairies he marks the sites of cities yet to be. Not for him the science of the school, not for him the graces of culture, not for him the joys of home, not for him the sweet solaces of life. But he reads the story of the ages written on the rocks, and hears the tale of mysterious forces whispered by the mid-night stars, and the priest-robed mountains, and the smiling lakes, and white-lipped sunset seas are his palaces and his kindred. Southward you shall behold him, undaunted by the roar of the Colorado, or the stealthy step of the Apache, pressing onward and still onward to listen to the wash of tropic waters. Northward his resolute face is turned toward the wooing mountains of crystal, until the North Star gleams like a mighty diamond in its gold and crimson setting of northern lights, and the sullen sun but for an hour hangs upon the verge of the polar night, a faint reminder of the lost southern clime while the booming artillery of the Ice King hails the Pioneer of polar seas. Westward—ah! there is no longer a west. The iron lace with which progress fringes her garments reaches now to where the Golden Gate swings back upon her hinges. Asia and the farther Indies are just beyond, and the Orient of Europe is the Occident of America.

And still from the silver and the orange blossom of cactus-fringed and snow-crowned Mexico, northward to where the icebergs glitter against an Arctic sky, our Pioneers are marching and toiling. In the track which their fierce feet are breaking, our country is marching onward to her greatness. The army of civilization swells upon their pathway. Art, Science, Progress, the Wealth of Nations, the Power and Glory of the Republic, follow. All honor and all hail to those brave hearts who lead the vanguard.—*Thomas Fitch.*

TRANSITION.

349.—

When leaves grow sere, all things take sombre hue,
The wild winds waltz no more the woodsides through,
All day the faded grass is wet with dew.

A gauzy nebula films the pensive sky,
The golden bee buzzes supinely by,
In silent flocks the bluebirds southward fly.

The cynic frost is riotous of blame,
The forests' cheeks are crimsoned o'er with shame,
The ground with scarlet blushes is aflame!

The one we love grows lustrous-eyed and sad,
With sympathy too thoughtful to be glad,
While all the colors round are running mad.

The sunbeams kiss askant the tawny hill,
The naked woodbine climbs the window sill,
The air the noons exhale is faint and chill.

The ripened nuts drop downward day by day,
Sounding the hollow tocsin of decay,
And bandit squirrels smuggle them away.

Vague sighs and scents pervade the atmosphere,
Sounds of invisible stirrings hum the ear,
The morning's lash reveals a frozen tear.

The hermit mountains gird themselves with mail,
Mocking the threshers with an echo flail,
The while the afternoons grow cold and pale.

Inconstant Summer to the tropics flees,
And, as her rose-sails catch the amorous breeze,
Lo! bare, brown Autumn trembles to her knees.

The stealthy nights encroach upon the days,
The earth with sudden whiteness is ablaze,
And all her paths are lost in crystal maze!

Tread lightly where the tender violets blew—
Where, to Spring winds their soft eyes open flew;
Safely they'll sleep the churlish Winter through.

Though all Life's portals are indiced with woe,
And frozen pearls are all the world can show,
Feel! Nature's breast is warm beneath the snow!

With blooms full-lapped again will smile the land,
The pall is but the folding of His hand,
Anon with fuller glories to expand!

The dumb heart hid beneath the wintry tree
Will throb again; so shall the torpid bee
Drone on the listening ear his drowsy glee.

So shall the truant bluebirds backward fly,
And all loved things that vanish or that die
Return to us in some sweet by-and-by.
—*W. A. Kendall.*

THE HUMAN MIND.

350. The resources of the human mind and the energies of the human will are illimitable. From the time when the new philosophy, of which Francis Bacon was the great exponent, became firmly written in a few minds, the course of human progress has been unfettered—each established fact, each new discovery, each complete induction, is a new weapon from the armory of truth; the march cannot retrograde; the human mind will never go back; the question as to a return to barbarism is forever at rest. If England were to sink beneath the ocean, she has planted the germ of her thought in many a fair land beside, and the tree will shadow the whole earth. If the whole

population of America were to die in a day, a new migration would re-people it, not with living forms alone, but with living thought, bright streams from the fountains of all nations.

We turn with wonder and delight to behold on every hand the results of scientific method everywhere visible and everywhere increasing; but amid that wonder and delight, we turn to a still greater wonder—the human mind itself. Who shall now stay its progress? What shall impede its career? No longer trammeled by theories or oppressed by the despotism of authority, grasping, at the very vestibule, the key to knowledge, its advance, though gradual, is but the more sure. It is engaged in a perpetual warfare, but its empire is perpetually enlarging. No fact is forgotten, no truth is lost, no induction falls to the ground. It is as industrious as the sun—it is as restless as the sea—it is as universal as the race itself—it is boundless in its ambition, and irrepressible in its hope!

And yet, in the very midst of the great works that mark its progress, while we behold on every hand the barriers of darkness and ignorance overthrown, and perceive the circle of knowledge continually widening, we must forever remember that man, in all his pride of scientific research, and all his power of elemental conquest, can but follow at an infinite distance, the methods of the Great Designer of the Universe. His research is but the attempt to learn what nature has done or may do; his plans are but an imperfect copy of a half-seen original. He strives, and sometimes with success, to penetrate into the workshop of nature; but whether he use the sunbeam, or steam, or electricity—whether he discover a continent or a star—whether he decompose light or water—whether he fathom the depths of the ocean or the depths of the human heart—in each and all he is but the imitator of the Great Architect and Creator of all things.—*Gen. E. D. Baker.*

OF CALIFORNIANS.

...of Saints... and Patriotic Songs.

Editor Inquirer: I am sure it will accord with the genius of your patriotic and high toned paper to present to the Endeavorers and their hosts of friends, in a convenient way for preservation, four patriotic and purposeful California hymns. The last one has been specially written for the present crusade against the rum power.

Yours faithfully,
EDWIN SIDNEY WILLIAMS.

No. 1, by A. L. Stone, D. D., born in Oxford, Conn., November 25, 1815; died in San Francisco January 17, 1892. He was famous as pastor of Park street Church, Boston — "Brimstone Corner," so-called, and served the First Congregational Church of San Francisco many years:

Tune, Duke Street.

We call our home "The Golden State,"
And count its treasures o'er with pride,
Its mines of wealth, its "Golden Gate,"
Key to the vast Pacific tide.

This heritage is thine, O Lord,
For Thou hast paid the costly price,
Great beyond all descriptive word,
The Lamb's atoning sacrifice.

We yield to Thee "The Golden State."
Be Thou its sovereign Ruler blest;
The whole to Thee we consecrate,
The Christian Empire of the West.

Let Shasta, in his robe of snow,
And Sacramento's lordly stream,
And hill and valley high and low,
In lustrous, living beauty gleam.

The beauty of the loving heart,
The beauty of the subject will,
A glory never to depart,
But down the ages shining still!

No. 2, composed by Rev. J. A. Benton, D. D. He was a famous '49er and besides serving the Sacramento church was the spiritual father of the Pacific Theological Seminary of which he was many years professor:

Tune, Autumn.

California, golden sandaled,
Decked in robes of living green,
Flashing gems are in her girdle,
On her brow a snowy sheen.
Throned upon her hills of beauty,
Flowers and fields before her strown.
Waves her hand in wide dominion,
Isles and oceans are her own.

Speed the day of her redemption,
Haste, brave heralds of the truth,
Tell ye out Life's gracious story,
Hallow now her radiant youth.
Hail the joy of her salvation,
Reapers, bring ye in your sheaves
Sing of faith in love, triumphant,
O'er a realm that Christ receives.

No. 3, Mrs. L. M. H...
two succeeding hymn
with a heart warm
She is a sister of Rev.
whose fame as poet, o
delightfully among th

Tune, Be...

Lord, bless our land,
With summer sun and
And flowers, that fres
Look up to skies of d

Chorus—
This golden land,
By fair Pacific's be
From Shasta's sno
From eastern slop
This land beside t
We want it all de

Its mountains stand w
And like huge watche
They guard the fertile
That lie in beauty at t

'Tis rich in flocks upo
In waving grain, in g
'Tis rich in corn and f
Lord, may its riches a

O may thy servants tr
Work on in faith this
Till o'er it bright sha
Thy Light, Thou bles

Chorus for fourth v
Then this dear la
By fair Pacific's b
From Shasta's and
From eastern slop
This land beside t
The glory of all la

No. 4. Endeavorer
fore published.

Tune, "I Will Sin...

Are you ready f
Are you loyal
Dare you fight
Dare you strik

Chorus—
"No surrender"
For we fight f
Home and coun
And we'll sou

For to-day a wa
'Gainst a migh
That it shadow
Dims the glor

With its baleful
All our holy f
In its grasp so
Holds our nob

But at last we'
Sure to crush
And the land w
As we our vic

...the Vote...

INDEX.

[THE FIGURES REFER TO THE PARAGRAPH NUMBERS.]

"Affection, Forgiveness, Faith,"
  Gen. E. D. Baker............137
"Agassiz, Louis,"
  W. H. Dall..................247
"Agriculture,"
  Samuel B. Bell......147, 160, 162
  James G. Howard............156
  Thos. Starr King...148, 150, 152, 158, 163.
  Zachary Montgomery.........154
  W. H. Rhodes...............153
  Tod Robinson...............155
  Leland Stanford............161
  Joseph W. Winans...........151
"All Does Not Fade,"
  Rev. Wm. Speer............. 82
"American Legion of Honor,"
  See "Fraternal Societies,"....245
"Ancient Order of United Workmen,"
  Philip M. Fisher...........244
  See "Fraternal Societies,"....245
Anderson, Rev. T. H. B.
  "Books,"................... 47
  "Children,"................ 92
  "Labor,"...................109
"Architecture,"
  Frank Tilford.............. 27
"Art,"
  W. C. Bartlett............. 25
  John W. Dwinelle........... 26
  Prof. Joseph LeConte....... 22
  Dr. A. B. Stout............ 23
  Frank Tilford.............. 27
  E. G. Waite................ 24
"Asceticism,"
  W. C. Bartlett............. 93
"Atheism,"
  Thos. Starr King...........138
"Atlantic Cable, The,"
  Gen. E. D. Baker...........302
  Judge E. D. Wheeler........303
"Authorship in California,"
  W. C. Bartlett.............301
"A Pressed Flower,"
  G. C. Hurlbut..............324

Baker, Gen. E. D.,
  "Affection, Forgiveness, Faith." 137
  "The Atlantic Cable,".........302
  "The Comet of 1858,".........327
  "The Human Mind,"...........350
  "The Law, Bench and Bar,"...312
  "The Press,"................ 42
  "Dueling,"..................165
  "Freedom,"..............195, 199
  "Politics,".................180
  "Our Country,"..............220
  "Science,"................... 1
  "War,".....................202
  "Etc,"..................... 57
"Baker, Gen. E. D.,"
  Samuel B. Bell.............251
  Newton Booth...............248
  Gen. J. A. McDougall.......250
  Mrs. James Neale...........249
Baldwin, Judge Joseph G.,
  "Stephen J. Field,".........261
  "Aaron Burr,"..............256
"Baldwin, Joseph G.,"
  Judge Stephen J. Field.....252
Bancroft, Hubert H.,
  "The Brave Days of Old,".... 77
  "California,"...............292
  "Catholicity of Spirit,".....168
  "Home,".................... 87
  "History,"..................340
  "Labor,".........107, 108, 112, 113
  "Personal Power,"...........343
  "Popular Corruption,".......166
  "Riches,".................97, 99
  "Social Advance,"...........171
  "The Study of Mankind,".....347
  "Etc,"................... 35, 59
Barnes, Gen. W. H. L.
  "Recuperative Power of our Nation,"....................215
Barstow, George,
  "Death."....................321
  "Freedom,".................194
  "Home,".................... 88
  "War,"......................200

Field, Stephen J.
  "Jos. G. Baldwin,"............232
  "Edward Norton,"............275
  "Law, Bench and Bar,".........309
Finney, Selden J.
  "The Spiritual Feeling,".......144
Fisher, Philip M.
  "The United Workmen,".......244
Fitch, Thomas,
  "Our Country,"...............204
  "The Order of Red Men."......243
  "The Pioneers,"...............348
  "The Press,"................... 43
  "William C. Ralston,"..........277
Foote, Gen. L. H.
  "El Rio Sacramento,".........296
"Fraternal Societies,".....223 to 245
"Freedom,"
  Gen. E. D. Baker......195, 199
  Geo. Barstow 194
  Henry George...............197
  Dr. J. C. Shorb 193
  Joseph W. Winans 196
  E. C. Winchell..............198
Freelon, Judge T. W.,
  "Faith," 136
  "Our Country,"...............209
  "Our Duty and Destiny,"......294
"Freemasonry,"
  N. Greene Curtis.............231
  John B. Felton...............232
  Dr. H. M. Gray..............228
  Henry E. Highton............233
  Thos. Starr King...223, 224, 225, 226, 227.
  Milton S. Latham 230
  Frank Tilford..........234, 235
  Samuel M. Wilson...........229
Fremont, Gen. John C.,
  "Recrossing the Rocky Mountains."....................326
"Free Trade,"
  Henry E. Highton............181
"Friendship,"
  Sarah B. Cooper 94
"Gardening."
  W. C. Bartlett...............149
  Chas. H. Shinn..............159
"Gardens of Peterskoi,"
  J. Ross Browne..............164
"Garibaldi and Washington,"
  Dr. Franklin Tuthill..........288
"Genius,"
  Thos. Starr King........338, 339
George, Henry,
  "Capital and Labor,"..........183
  "Children," 91
  "Freedom,"...................197
  "Immortality,"...............131
  "Influence of Example,"....... 81
  "One-sided Progress,".........176
  "Our Land Policy,"............221
  "The Cause Calls the Man,"....175
  "The Future Life," 146
"Ghosts,"
  Thos. Starr King............ 66
"God,"
  John B. Felton..............121
  Thos. Starr King............116
  Prof. Jos. LeConte...........125
Goodman, Jos. T.,
  "Over the Hill,".............340
Gordon, George,
  "Robert Burns,"..............255
Gray, Dr. H. M.,
  "Freemasonry," 228
"Greatness,"
  Thos. Starr King.........78, 246
Guard, Rev. Thos.,.....(See Etc., 120)
"Henry H. Haight,"
  John W. Dwinelle...........262
Hallidie, A. S.
  "Labor,"....................106
Hamilton, Rev. L.
  "Oscar L. Shafter,"............278
Harmon, John B.
  "Odd Fellowship,"............241
Harte, F. Bret,
  "Dickens in Camp,"..........258
  "Thos. Starr King,"......265, 267
"Harte, F. Bret,"
  W. C. Bartlett..............300
Hayes, William,
  "Woman,"...................334
Highton, Henry E.
  "Freemasonry,"..............233
  "Free Trade,"................181
  "Woman,"...................333
"History,"
  Hubert H. Bancroft..........346
"Holiness,"
  Prof. Jos. LeConte...........124
"Holmes, Oliver Wendell,"
  Henry H. Reid..............263
"Home,"
  Hubert H. Bancroft.......... 87
  Geo. Barstow............... 88
  Thos. Starr King........... 89
  Chas. H. Shinn.............159
"Horticulture," (See "Gardening.")
Howard, James G.
  "Farming,"..................156

INDEX. 467

"Labor,".....................110
"Marriage,"................... 70
"Human Temple, The,"
   Thos. Starr King............ 79
"Humorists of California,"
   W. C. Bartlett..............300
Hurlbut, G. C.
   "A Pressed Flower,"..........324
Ijams, Rev. W. E.,
   "Christianity,".......117, 118, 141
   "Decline of Orthodoxy,".......123
   "Emotional Religion,".........122
   "Religion,".....................143
   "Woman,".......................330
   "The Highest Gift of Mind,"...342
   (See also "Etc.,").........61, 75
"Immortality,"
   Henry George...............131
   W. A. Kendall..............133
   Thos. Starr King........129, 130
   Prof. Jos. LeConte...........132
"Infinity,"
   Prof. Jos. LeConte...........134
"Intellectual Honesty,"
   Rev. H. Stebbins............ 34
"Intemperance,"
   Gen. John A. Collins.........102
   Daniel O'Connell..........104
   Thos. Starr King............103
   Dr. A. B. Stout..............101
"Irish Race, The,"
   Francis J. Sullivan 336
"Jenner, Edward,"
   Dr. J. C. Shorb 264
"Justice,"
   Frank Tilford............... 63
Kellogg, Prof. Martin,
   "Henry Durant,".............260
Kendall, W. A.,
   "Immortality,"...............132
   "Transition,"................349
Kewen, Col. E. J. C.,
   "John A. Sutter,".............284
King, Thomas Starr,
   "Agriculture,"...... 148, 150, 152, 158, 163.
   "Atheism,"...................138
   "Books,"............44, 45, 49, 50
   "Conservatives and Radicals,"..174
   Dying Words of............320
   "Decay of Empires,"..........177
   "Duty," 54
   "Freemasonry,".....223, 224, 225, 226, 227.
   "Genius,".................338, 339
   "Ghosts,".................... 66

"God,".........................116
"Great Men,".................246
"Greatness,"................... 78
"Home,"....................... 89
"Immortality,"..........129, 130
"Intemperance,"..............103
"Life,"........................ 96
"Love,"....................... 65
"National Character,"..........182
"Nature,"................315, 317
"Noble Lives,"................ 68
"Novels,"..................... 52
"Organization,"...............345
"Originality,"................. 74
"Our Moral Inheritance,"......172
"Prescott and Macaulay,".....274
"Revivals,"...................145
"Riches,"..................... 98
"Socrates,"..............281, 282
"Style,"...................... 40
"The Human Temple,"........ 79
"The Inner Life,".............126
"The Words of Christ,".......127
"Washington,"................287
(See also "Etc.,"..58, 62, 64, 67)
"King, Thos. Starr,
   Chas. Russell Clarke.........266
   F. Bret Harte...........265, 267
"Labor,"
   Rev. T. H. B. Anderson......109
   Hubert H. Bancroft.....107, 108, 112, 113.
   A. S. Hallidie................106
   James G. Howard 110
   Jos. W. Winans.............111
"Lafayette,"
   Milton S. Latham 268
"Land and Land Policy, Our,"
   Henry George..............221
"Law, Bench and Bar,"....206 to 314
Latham, Milton S.,
   "Freemasonry," 230
   "Our Country," 267
   "Lafayette,"..................268
   "Science,"...................3, 9
LeConte, Prof. John,
   "The Rearing of Children,"....188
LeConte, Prof. Joseph,
   "Art,"........................ 22
   "Evolution,"................12, 13
   "Evolution and Materialism,".. 11
   "Foreknowledge of God,".....125
   "Holiness,"...................124
   "Immortality,"................133
   "Infinity,"....................134
   "Science,".... 2, 4, 5, 6, 10, 11, 15

"Lessons of the Hour,"
  Chas. H. Shinn.............115
"Life, The Conduct of,"....54 to 115
"Life, What it May Be,"
  Thos. Starr King........... 96
"Life, The Inner,"
  Thos. Starr King...........126
"Life, This Leads to Another,"
  Henry George..............146
"Literature and Education," 28 to 53
"Love,"
  Sarah B. Cooper............ 71
  Thos. Starr King........... 65
"Macaulay and Prescott,"
  Thos. Starr King...........274
"Mankind, The Study of,"
  Hubert H. Bancroft.........347
"Man's Mission,"
  Gen. John A. Collins.......140
"Marriage,"
  Jas. G. Howard............. 70
Marshall, E. C.
  "California Pioneers,".....291
  "Our Country,"............205
"Masonry," (See "Freemasonry.")
"Materialism,"
  Dr. A. B. Stout...........304
McDonald, Dr. R. H.
  "Smoking,"...............105
McDougall, Gen. James A.,
  "Gen. E. D. Baker,".......250
  "Death,".................319
  "Thought,"...............341
McKinstry, Judge E. W.,
  "Our Duty and Destiny,"...295
"Medicine, the Science of,"
  Dr. J. Campbell Shorb.....305
"Men of Thought and Men of Action,"
  Rev. J. H. C. Bonte........ 85
"Mind, The Human,"
  Gen. E. D. Baker..........350
"Mind, The Evolution of,"
  Dr. A. B. Stout........... 36
"Mind, The Highest Gift of,"
  Rev. W. E. Ijams..........342
Montgomery, Zachary,
  "Children,"............... 90
  "The Farmer,"............154
"Moore, Thomas,"
  Francis J. Sullivan 270
  Oscar T. Shuck............271
"Morality Essential to success,"
  Dr. C. A. Shurtleff........ 80
"Mulford, Prentice,"
  W. C. Bartlett............300

"Napoleon Bonaparte,"
  John B. Felton.............272
"National Character,"
  Thos. Starr King...........182
"Nature,"
  Thos. Starr King 315, 317
  Jas. McM. Shafter..........316
  Chas. Warren Stoddard......318
Neale, Mrs. James,
  "Gen. E. D. Baker,".......249
"Noble Lives,"
  Tho . Starr King........... 68
"Norton, Edward,"
  Judge Stephen J. Field.....275
"Novels,"
  F. P. Deering.............. 51
  Thos. Starr King........... 52
"Odd Fellowship,"
  Newton Booth..............238
  Gen. John A. Collins.......240
  John B. Harmon............241
  Geo. R. Moore 237
  L. E. Pratt...............242
  A. A. Sargent.............239
  Chas. A. Sumner...........236
"One-sided Progress,"
  Henry George..............176
"Organization,"
  Thos. Starr King..........345
"Originality,"
  Thos. Starr King........... 74
"Orthodoxy, Decline of,"
  Rev. W. E. Ijams..........123
"Our Country,"
  Gen. E. D. Baker..........220
  Gen. W. H. L. Barnes......215
  Newton Booth..............206
  Eugene Casserly...........214
  R. D. Crittenden..........211
  Thomas Fitch..............204
  T. W. Freelon.............209
  Milton S. Latham 207
  E. C. Marshall............205
  F. M. Pixley..............216
  Rev. Dr. A. L. Stone......212
  J. H. Warwick.............213
  Jos. W. Winans.208, 210, 217, 219
  E. C. Winchell............218
"Our Moral Inheritance,"
  Thos. Starr King..........172
O'Connell, Daniel,
  "Drunk in the Street,"....104
"Over the Hill,"
  Jos. T. Goodman...........340

"Parker, Samuel,"
    Chas. A. Sumner............236
"Patriotism,"
    Hubert H. Bancroft..........178
    Newton Booth...............179
"Pen, The,"
    William Bausman............ 37
"Personal Power,"
    Hubert H. Bancroft..........343
"Pioneers of California,"
    E. C. Marshall..............291
Pixley, Frank M.,
    "Our Country,"..............216
"Plato,"
    Dr. J. Campbell Shorb 273
Platt, Rev. Wm. H.,
    "The Unity of Laws," 313
"Pleasures, Physical and Mental,"
    John B. Felton............. 38
POETRY.—
"Louis Agassiz,"
    W. H. Dall.................247
"Gen. E. D. Baker,"
    Mrs. Jas. Neale 249
"Christmas,"
    Chas. F. Craddock..........335
"Death,"
    Oscar T. Shuck..............323
"Delilah,"
    Chas. F. Craddock..........337
"Dickens in Camp,"
    F. Bret Harte...............258
"Discipline,"
    Ina D. Coolbrith............. 76
"Drunk in the Street,"
    Daniel O'Connell...........104
"El Rio Sacramento,"
    Gen. L. H. Foote............296
"Immortality,"
    W. A. Kendall...............133
"On a Pressed Flower,"
    G. C. Hurlbut...............324
"Over the Hill,"
    Jos. T. Goodman............340
"Recrossing the Rocky Mountains,"
    Gen. J. C. Fremont..........326
"Thos. Starr King,"
    Chas. Russell Clarke........266
    F. Bret Harte...........265, 267
"Lessons of the Hour,"
    Chas. H. Shinn..............115
"Thomas Moore,"
    Oscar T. Shuck..............271
"The Mist,"
    Miss H. M. Skidmore........328

"The North Wind,"
    Prof. E. R. Sill..............329
"Nature,"
    Chas. Warren Stoddard......318
"Science,"
    A. G. Bierce 19
"Sunrise from the Sierras,"
    Chas. A. Sumner............293
"Transition,"
    W. A. Kendall..............349

"Politics, The Pursuit of,"
    Gen. E. D. Baker............180
"Popular Corruption,"
    Hubert H. Bancroft..........166
"Popular Justice,"
    Gen. John A. Collins.........167
Pratt, L. E.,
    "Odd Fellowship"...........242
Pratt, O. C., (See Law, Bench and
    Bar.)......................311
"Prescott and Macaulay,
    Thos. Starr King...........274
"Press, The,"
    Gen. E. D. Baker............ 42
    W. C. Bartlett.............. 41
    Thos. Fitch................. 43
Proffatt, John,
    "The Law, Bench and Bar,"....308
"Punctuality,"
    Dr. G. A. Shurtleff......... 56
"Radicals and Conservatives,"
    Thos. Starr King............174
"Ralston, William C.,"
    Thos. Fitch.................277
    Dr. J. Campbell Shorb.......276
Randolph, Edmund,
    "The Acquisition of California,".289
    "The California Pioneers,".....290
"Recuperative Power of the Nation,"
    Gen. W. H. L. Barnes........215
Redding, B. B.,
    "Sanitary Influence of Trees,"..157
    "Teaching,"................... 31
"Red Men, Order of,"
    Thos. Fitch 243
Reid, Henry H.,
    "Law, Bench and Bar,"........306
    "Oliver Wendell Holmes,".....263
"Republic of Letters, The,"
    Newton Booth............... 30
"Revivals, The Corrupting Influence of"
    Thos. Starr King 145

"Religion and The Future Life,"
116 to 146.
"Religion and Science,"
  Rev. Dr. W. A. Scott....... 20
  Rev. Horatio Stebbins........ 21
Rhodes, Wm. H.,
  "Apostrophe to Chemistry,".... 17
  "The Farmer,"................153
"Riches,"
  Hubert H. Bancroft........97, 99
  J. Ross Browne..............100
  Thos. Starr King............. 98
Robinson, Tod,
  "The Farmer,"............ 155
"Rocky Mountains, Recrossing,"
  Gen. J. C. Fremont...... 326
Royce, Josiah,
  "Percy Bysshe Shelley,".......280
"Rural Homes,"
  Chas. H. Shinn..............159
"San Francisco,"
  John W. Dwinelle...........297
Sargent, A. A.
  "Odd Fellowship,"............239
"Sceptic, The,"
  Dr. J. Campbell Shorb........142
"Science,"
  Gen. E. D. Baker............ 1
  A. G. Bierce................ 19
  Prof. Geo. Davidson... 7
  John B. Felton.............. 18
  Milton S. Latham..........3, 9
  Prof. Jos. LeConte, 2, 4, 5, 6, 10, 11, 15.
  W. H. Rhodes............... 17
  Oscar T. Shuck.............. 16
  Rev. Horatio Stebbins........ 8
"Science and Art,"
  John V. Wattson............. 14
"Science and Religion,"
  Rev. Dr. W. A. Scott........ 20
  Rev. Horatio Stebbins....... 21
Scott, Rev. Dr. W. A.
  "Science and Religion,"........ 20
"Sculpture,"
  John W. Dwinelle........... 26
Shafter, Jas. McM.
  "Capital and Labor," 185
  "Communion with Nature,"....316
"Shafter, Oscar L."
  Rev. L. Hamilton............278
"Shakespeare,"
  Frank Tilford...............279
Shattuck, Judge D. O.,
  (See "Law, Bench and Bar,").310

"Shelley, Percy Bysshe,"
  Josiah Royce................280
Shinn, Chas. H.,
  "Lessons of the Hour,"........115
  "Rural Homes,"..............159
  "Rearing of Children,"........192
Shorb, Dr. J. Campbell,
  "Freedom,"..................193
  "Edward Jenner,"............264
  "Plato,".....................273
  "William C. Ralston,".........276
  "The Sceptic,"...............142
  "The Science of Medicine,"....305
Shuck, Oscar T.,
  "Thomas Moore,"............271
  "Death,"....................323
  "Fraternal Insurance Societies,".245
  "Science,".................. 16
Shurtleff, Dr. G. A.,
  "Morality Essential to Success," 80
  "Punctuality,"............... 56
Sill, Prof. E. R.,
  "The North Wind,"..........329
Skidmore, Miss H. M.,
  "The Mist,"..................328
"Smoking,"
  Dr. R. H. McDonald.........105
"Social Advance,"
  Hubert H. Bancroft..........171
"Social Artifices,"
  Sarah B. Cooper.............169
"Socrates,"
  Thos. Starr King........281, 282
Soule, Frank,
  "David C. Broderick,".... 254
Speer, Rev. Wm.,
  "All Does Not Fade,".......... 82
"Spiritual Feeling, The,"
  Selden J. Finney 140
Stanford, Leland,
  "Agriculture,"................161
Stanly, Edward,
  "Washington,"...............285
Stebbins, Rev. Horatio,
  "Capital and Labor,"..........187
  "Centennial Oration, 1876,"....222
  "Education,"................. 28
  "Intellectual Honesty,"........ 34
  "Science,"................... 8
  "Science and Religion,"........ 21
Stoddard, Chas. Warren,
  "Nature,".................... 318
Stone, Rev. Dr. A. L.,
  "Our Country,"..............212
Stout, Dr. A. B.,

INDEX. 471

"Drawing,"................... 23
"Evolution of Mind,"......... 36
"Intemperance,".............101
"Materialism,"...............304
Stuart, Hector A.,
 "Epigrams,"..................344
"Style,"
 Thomas Starr King.......... 40
Sullivan, Francis J.,
 "Charity,"................... 72
 "Thomas Moore,"............270
 "The Irish Race,"............336
Sumner, Chas. A.,
 "Odd Fellowship,"...........236
 "Sunrise from the Sierras,"....293
"Sunrise from the Sierras,"
 Chas. A. Sumner...........293
"Suspicious Man, The,"
 John B. Felton............. 84
"Sutter, John A,"
 Col. E. J. C. Kewen........284
 Joseph W. Winans..........283
Swift, John F.,
 "A Farewell to Syria,".......325
"Sympathy,"
 John B. Felton............. 95
"Teaching,"
 Rev. F. C. Ewer............. 32
 B. B. Redding.............. 31
"The Mist,"
 Miss H. M. Skidmore........328
"The North Wind,"
 E. R. Sill...................329
"Thought,"
 Gen. J. A. McDougall.......341
"Thoughts, Let them Grow,".....
 M. J. Upham 69
Tilford, Frank,
 "Architecture,"............. 27
 "Freemasonry,"..........234, 235
 "Justice,".................... 63
 "Shakespeare,"...............279
Tompkins, Edward,
 "Christ,"....................119
"Transition,"
 W. A. Kendall...............349
"Trees, Sanitary Influence of,"
 B. B. Redding...............157
"Truth,"
 John B. Felton............. 86
Tuthill, Dr. Franklin,
 "Washington and Garibaldi,"..288

"Twain, Mark,"
 W. C. Bartlett..............300
Upham, M. J.,
 "Let Your Thoughts Grow,"... 69
Waite, E. G.,
 "Art,"....................... 24
"War,"
 Gen. E. D. Baker 202
 George Barstow 200
 Newton Booth...............203
 Samuel Williams............201
Warwick, J. H.,
 "Our Country,"..............213
"Washington,"
 Eugene Casserly............286
 Thos. Starr King...........287
 Edward Stanly..............285
"Washington and Garibaldi,"
 Dr. Franklin Tuthill........288
Wattson, John V.,
 "Science and Art,"........... 14
Wheeler, Judge E. D.,
 "The Atlantic Cable,".........303
"Wildey, Thomas,"
 Charles A. Sumner..........236
Williams, Samuel,
 "Conflict and Progress,".......114
 "Conflict Eternal,"........... 83
 "War,"......................201
Wilson, Samuel M.,
 "Freemasonry,"..............229
Winans, Joseph W.,
 "Agriculture,"...............151
 "Clay, Webster and Calhoun,".257
 "Education,"..........29, 33, 35
 "Freedom,"..................196
 "Labor,"....................111
 "Our Country,"..208, 210, 217, 219
 "Religion,"..................139
 "Gen. John A. Sutter,".......283
"Wine,"
 W. C. Bartlett..............173
Winchell, E. C.,
 "Freedom,"..................198
 "Our Country,"..............218
"Woman,"
 Sarah B. Cooper.............331
 Rev. F. C. Ewer 332
 William Hayes.. 334
 Henry E. Highton...........333
 Rev. W. E. Ijams............330

www.ingramcontent.com/pod-product-compliance
Lightning Source LLC
Chambersburg PA
CBHW051237300426
44114CB00011B/772